See Jane Fly

Feminism in Aviation

PETER PIGOTT

SunRise

SunRise

First published in Great Britain in 2022 by SunRise

SunRise Publishing Ltd
Kemp House
152–160 City Road
London EC1V 2NX

ISBN 978-1-9144890-6-8

A CIP catalogue record for this book is available from the British Library.

Typeset in Minion Pro and Impact.

This one's for the girls who dream without holding back. For my granddaughter, Aria: Never do anything by halves if you want to get away with it. Be outrageous. Go the whole hog. Make sure everything you do is so completely crazy, it's unbelievable.

Contents

O tiger's heart wrapp'd in a woman's hide!

William Shakespeare, Henry VI — Part 3

ACKNOWLEDGEMENTS

In another life, writing for *Frontline* magazine, I covered some of the war in Afghanistan. The last time there, I was to do an article on the Afghan Air Force, which was about to receive refurbished G222s, its first fixed wing aircraft. A public relations officer took me around the sprawling air base in Kabul, his smooth patter in character with the profession everywhere. He ended the tour by trotting out the showpiece for foreign media — the air force's only female pilot. She was finishing her lunch on the mess hall steps and seemed resigned to her fate. But when we were alone, she was guarded and reluctant to be interviewed: it led to resentment from her male colleagues, and death threats to her family. But she wanted to know if on my tour, I had seen a toilet for women. I couldn't recall if I had. Oh, there is one, she said, with a heart wrenching smile — and pointed to a tree. Although I wasn't aware of it then, this book began that day.

Writing during the pandemic lockdowns, I relied on family and friends to keep me on track. To my wife Donna Hudson whose conversations at the dinner table began with, "Can we talk about something else now?" my apologies. Beginning some twenty years ago, Edie and Dennis Mockford, Allison and Chris Stewart, Jen Gravel and Randy Vanasse were early supporters of my work. Their wry humor hides warm hearts. To my family in Ottawa and Toronto, (and now Bideford and Saltdean) who have endured a lifetime of my writing, thank you.

I submitted the concept of *See Jane Fly* to several publishers, brashly overconfident of its acceptance. The rejection emails were blunt: "Only men buy books on aviation and they would not be interested in women's 'problems'." Or "Because of the #MeToo movement, we have received too many stories on sexism to publish more." Or "We see no market for a book about women in planes, unless it is of the *Coffee, Tea or Me* variety". I am thus incredibly grateful to my publisher, Malcolm Turner, who took a chance on this.

With the pandemic, I was unable to get to or communicate with the museums and universities that are the repositories of women's aviation history. Thus, a very heartfelt thank you to all who answered my plea for help. My gratitude to Murray Balzer, Greg Principato, Ariane Morin, Amy Spowart, Patty Wagstaff, Amanda Hauck, Noreen Newton, Zara Rutherford and Helen Murdoch. To those who took offense to the book's cover and subtitle, I am saddened. Nothing is more expensive than a missed opportunity. The word "feminism" I have since been informed, has become "weaponized", no longer meaning, as used in the book, the advocacy for equality of the sexes. To those women's empowerment groups who assumed the worst intentions and replied that they already had "enough charity work on their plate" or expected to be paid for their input, you confused my bank account with another author's — J K Rowling's.

Tracing women's acceptance in aviation, from the distant past to the vibrant present, *See Jane Fly* is about tenacity and adventure, femininity and friendship, lives and deaths, sexism and patriotism — and just sheer courage. Their flying skills considered insufficient, without control over their actions, ambitions or bodies, the women in this book used the only powers afforded their gender: that of survival, and the hope one day for equality. Feminism, Gloria Steinem famously said, is not about wanting a piece of the pie, but "baking a whole new pie."

INTRODUCTION

The story of women in aviation, of femininity and feminism began in my childhood. I was born into an aviation family of the 1950s — I cannot think of my parents without hearing the Patti Page song *You Belong to Me*, especially the line "Fly the ocean in a silver plane." My father, who had served in the Royal Air Force during the war, was the station superintendent for Trans World Airlines at Santa Cruz Airport, Bombay (now Mumbai), India. My mother had been an officer in the Women's Royal Naval Service (WRNS) and survived a crashlanding at Castel Benito, Libya. All she would tell me about this was on arrival at an airfield in England, she stepped out of the plane and said, "Look at all the pansies!" at which the airmen around her collapsed in laughter.

We lived across from the main runway and as I played in the front garden, I was daily treated to the spectacle of smoky, shiny airliners clawing their way into the sky. In those shockingly innocent times, as a ten-year-old, I could hop onboard a TWA Constellation and — without passport or money — traverse the airline's routes: Bombay-Cairo-Athens-Rome-Frankfurt and onwards to London where my dad had already telexed his colleagues to put me on the return flight. I was a "non-rev" (non-revenue passenger) and as long as I remained on board or in the airport transit lounge (so I could tell my classmates that I had physically "set foot" in Greece, Italy, and England) I was safe. I even brought my own "Occupied" card with me — the laminated sign that had to be left on your seat when you exited the plane to stretch your legs. In flight, I was spoiled by the crew, all of whom knew my Dad. In my memory, the pilots' identifying pins proclaimed them as "Captain Jake Armstrong" or "Commander Max Rodding". Years later, I realized that just over a decade before, they had been dodging flak over Germany or threading their way over "The Hump" to China.

Invariably, the captain would come by with a set of pilot's wings and in what I thought was a cowboy drawl, tell me that I had an important job to do — to keep watch on the exhaust flames coming out of the engines at my window. If the flames stopped, he said, I was to let him know immediately. This caused me to roll my eyes as even then I knew that the steady exhaust flames were a characteristic of the Connie's Wright R-3350 engines.

The stewardesses' pins simply said they were Susie, Nan, or Debbie. That any one of them could actually operate the aircraft's controls was to my ten-year-old mind incomprehensible. It would have been like my sisters attempting to work my Lionel electric train set! Even now, fifty years later, I gasp at the thought. For those too young to remember, it would only be a slight overstatement to say that stewardesses were to glamour then what the movie stars who adorn the red carpet at the Oscars are today. As I was usually the only unaccompanied minor onboard, these perky Doris Day lookalikes sat beside me and talked about the wonders of television which I had yet to see or rushed over to point out sights below like the Pyramids or Parthenon. They introduced me to root beer that I had read about in "Archie" comics and passed out "View Masters", along with "magic slates" (you drew on them and then lifted the transparent plastic cover to erase) and postcards of TWA's fleet for my collection. Responsible for my life in an emergency, I did not know (or care) that the movie star stewardesses had been hired mainly for their figures. I had no idea then how special it all was.

For all our nostalgia about the "Golden Age of Air Travel", it was more mythical than we like to think. As with other forms of transport, until the 1970s, commercial and military aviation were strictly gendered racist divisions of labour, both in the flight deck and cabin. Piloting was a lifetime career for white men, "stewardessing" a temporary one for women. Western culture was built upon images of men as chivalrous knights, cowboys, and soldiers — all living rugged manly lives, their greatest joy the comradeship on cattle drives, or men-of-war or in the trenches. In reality, by the beginning of the twentieth century, few males had ever been cowboys or seen active military service. Nevertheless, fueled by paperback novels and later Hollywood, the mythology persisted. National identity was defined by masculinity — in the United States it was the cowboy, in Australia the "digger" and in Canada, the lumberjack, the Mountie and after the Great War, the air ace.

Women in pulp fiction and movies were either the faithful forgiving wife and mother, the schoolmarm — or the dance hall prostitute. Pilots were defined by their training, professionalism, and their courage in the air. To frightened passengers — and that was everyone then, whoever sat in the cockpit was omnipotent. Women were defined by their domesticity and airlines recruited them to be substitute mothers, wives, and daughters to look after male clientele.

At a time when culture and masculinity combined to gender-code professions, society firmly disapproved of females as pilots. The reasons cited were that they were weaker in terms of physical strength, more susceptible to motion sickness than men — and then there were the old standbys of menstruation and pregnancy. Airlines and air forces held that their presence would affect a male flight crew's cohesion, or 'bonding' and reduce morale and mission effectiveness. Men are pre-programmed to believe that they will excel as pilots because, from the Wright brothers onward, there have been thousands of male pilots. Women, on the other hand, have seeds of doubt planted in them because female pilots remain a rarity. "The association of commercial flying and maleness" wrote Albert James Mills in *Sex, Strategy and the Stratosphere: The Gendering of Airline Cultures*, "was largely achieved through the exclusion of women."

The exploits of the female "aeronauts" in the ballooning years, and the wing walkers of the 1920s, all gaiety and desperate bravery, deserve their places in history. The women who first ventured into aviation were not to be taken seriously — they were "lady birds" and "petticoat pilots". The media and marketers leveraged their sex to sell advertising, airshow tickets and aircraft. The "flying flappers" were succeeded by misogynistic hostility during the Depression, when female pilots in commercial aviation were seen as taking men's jobs.

In the 1930s, nurses were hired to bring femininity to the fledgling airlines. Becoming a stewardess was an escape for young women, at best a short-term interlude between homework and housework, with perks like the social cachet of a distinctive uniform, companionship with others of their sex in aviation and most tellingly, the independence that a pay cheque brought during the Depression.

It was only during the Second World War when a manpower shortage forced governments to allow women to build and ferry aircraft did they cross the gender line at the hangar — always aware they would have to give this up when the men returned home. Female independence was exemplified by the ferry pilots of the ATA (Air Transport Auxiliary) in Britain and the WASPs (Women Airforce Service Pilots) in the United States. It was followed by a mandated return to domesticity in the 1950s with stewardesses fulfilling that role in the skies. Not until the mid-1970s did feminist militancy make inroads against the sexualization, the no-marriage rules and age ceilings for stewardesses, and female pilots could prise open the flight deck door. It was finally accepted that a woman could do everything a man could — backwards and in heels.

Much of this narrative takes place in a black and white world literally and figuratively, when gender and racial bias were not just conscious, but the norm. Bosses were always white males, their secretaries fetched them coffee, policewomen did the filing and little girls were told that marriage was their goal in life. A woman working outside the home (let alone in aviation) was an aberration to society, threatening to destroy its very foundation. Her role was to be looked after and (she hoped) cherished for her delicacy and ineptness for all things mechanical. If she chose to enter a male world, especially a testosterone-filled cockpit, gender discrimination and sexual harassment were to be expected — something (it was felt) she had brought upon herself and now had to silently endure. This does not even consider the discrimination and abuse that non-white pilots and stewardesses suffered.

As appalling as it is to us today, the aviation industry was hardly alone in patronizing their female employees. Sociologists will point out that the plight of the early aviatrix and stewardesses was not that different from other working women at the time. The medical, legal, and engineering professions were equally closed to them. When aviation began, women did not steer ships or streetcars or engage in labour activism. Stalin boasted that in the Soviet Union, women drove tractors and flew fighter aircraft, but none were ever admitted to the Politburo and millions were murdered.

With men doing all the hiring and setting of standards,

women had few occupational choices — nursing, retail, typing or teaching — all poorly paid, stringently controlled and without security. Female applicants in aviation were evaluated against the ideal standard for pilots — which was male and white. What those in power were looking for were copies of themselves.

This is a giant topic to cover in a single book and understandably, I have had to do some skimming and slicing. Written during the pandemic when according to the World Economic Forum, Covid-19 set women back by a whole generation in terms of gender parity and pay gap, this is not a happily-ever-after story. I am hopeful that it does what every book should — creates characters with whom we can identify and for whom we care. Unlike other aviation histories, this is a book where I wanted to have strong female protagonists and some are. Anger is a great engine of change and as Amelia Earhart warned, "If and when you knock at the door, it might be well to bring an axe along; you may have to chop your way through." I hope I have avoided the pitfalls of simplifying the heroines (and villains) and learned to muddy the water with shades of gray. It is the only way in which actual life takes place.

It was impossible to write *See Jane Fly* without a growing sense of righteous anger. I took comfort in Isabel Allende's advice to authors, "Write what should not be forgotten." I have.

Peter Pigott
Ottawa

1: QUEENS OF THE AIR

Ever since he could walk the Earth, Man has wanted to leave it and until 1903 balloons — hot air and later hydrogen — were the only means to accomplish this. Travel by air began on November 21, 1783, when the first manned untethered flight of a hot air balloon took place: the culmination of work by two paper manufacturers, Joseph-Michel and Jacques-Étienne Montgolfier. What was above the blue bowl that covered the world was unknown and as it was commonly held that the clouds contained noxious gases, Louis XVI suggested to the brothers that condemned prisoners be sent up to test the atmosphere.

The product of Enlightenment science, balloons were the pinnacle of human ingenuity then and grand schemes about their uses abounded: they could carry mail over the Alps, bring nations closer together, improve cartography and in time of war, bombard enemy fortifications from above.

On the balmy summer afternoon of June 29, 1785, George Biggin and Letitia Ann Sage floated over London in a balloon. The vehicle belonged to the pioneer Italian balloonist Vincenzo Lunardi. He was to go up with them but because of the added weight, gave up his place to the couple (forgetting that he was the only one who had actually flown before) "with a polite liberality that did him credit".

15

The year before, the war with the former American colonies had ended in ignominious defeat and Georgian society hungered for diversion. Londoners were thus cheered by the giant Union Jack that covered the balloon's gas bag — and more so by its brave female occupant, the first woman to travel in the skies over England. The gossip sheets that passed for tabloid newspapers then recorded not only the historic event but its salacious details. Miss Sage "barely veiled in flimsy gauze" was "a voluptuous West End actress". She wore a low-cut plum dress and a large hat adorned with a plumage of white feathers. No mention was made of Mr Biggin's attire. Buoyed as much by the gossip as the heated air, the pair ascended from Southwark and floated over the city. They enjoyed a lunch of ham, chicken and "Florence wine", (which fortuitously hadn't been jettisoned with Lunardi to lighten the balloon prior to launch), tossing the empty bottle over the side.[1]

Biggin was to conduct experiments in flight and was equipped with a thermometer and hygrometer to measure temperature and humidity, respectively. He would have had a barometer, too, had Sage not accidentally broken it earlier. After two hours during which the balloon roughly followed the Thames, it began to deflate and descend, dropping towards a farmer's field near Harrow. Biggin called out to some farm labourers to grab on to the dangling anchor rope. They did so to be joined by the headmaster of nearby Harrow School with his pupils. Back on the ground, Sage and Biggin enjoyed an evening of local hospitality, 'many flattering attentions' and 'rustic compliments', before returning to London — this time, by land.[2] The expectation of the dainty Miss Sage fainting at such altitude had not occurred — if anything she had taken an active part in the flight, at one point fixing a tear in the basket. The accolade of entering the "Mile High Club" was still 200 years away but speculation then was that George Biggin and Letitia Ann Sage were its founders.

The French Revolution's excesses impeded further development in ballooning and not until 1798 did one Andre-Jacques Garnerin propose taking a female up into the heavens with him. The self-proclaimed "Official Aeronaut of France", Garnerin was the first person in history to parachute from a balloon and he reasoned that should anything untoward happen during this venture, he at least would survive. He chose Citoyenne Henri to accompany him. History records that she was young, pleasing to the eye and unattached (i.e., expendable) — the playbook that airlines would follow when hiring stewardesses. When Paris's Central Bureau of the Police heard about this, Garnerin was made to appear before them. Not only did the immorality of a married man sharing a basket with a single woman rather uncharacteristically concern them, but the police warned about the unknown effects of atmospheric pressure on her "delicate parts". Fortunately for Garnerin, Napoleon was then on his way to conquer Egypt and the Minister of the Interior, possibly to demonstrate his own boldness, overruled the police.

Before a crowd of onlookers at Parc de Mousseaux, Paris on June 4, 1798, Garnerin and Citoyenne Henri first drove around in an open carriage, milking the occasion for as much as they could before climbing into the basket. They then made a successful ascent in the balloon, travelling in the wind for 30 km over the countryside. Citoyenne Henri disappeared into history but on November 10, Garnerin's wife, Jeanne-Genevieve Labrosse, perhaps distrusting him with other young citoyennes, became the first woman to ascend solo in a balloon. A year later, she (or her niece?) would be the first woman to parachute from one.

The balloon mania that followed was commemorated in paintings, prints, on fans, snuff boxes and crockery. A legion of "aeronauts" male and female, toured Europe, and North America with inflatable gas bags. Untethered flights were suicidal — balloons unexpectedly deflated at height and all onboard fell to their deaths or drifted out to sea and drowned — or terrified peasants were known to tear apart a descending balloon and its occupants. As with the barnstorming airshows to come, it was because of their inherent danger that the flights became a form of Roman entertainment. Their own short lives precarious with disease, injustice, and war, the public flocked to see them, hoping that something would go wrong. Charles Dickens was so horrified with balloon ascents that he wrote these "dangerous exhibitions" were no different from public hangings. Public in Britain until 1868, hangings competed with balloon ascents for drawing a crowd. In both, the author noted, there was a good chance that someone would be seen to perish. As airshow promoters, newspaper editors and Hollywood producers would later realize, the promise of death and sex were sure-fire ways to attract an audience.

When her husband (who had abandoned his family to marry the young girl) suffered a heart attack and fell out of their balloon in 1809, Sophie Blanchard took control of her own career, paying off his debts by touring Europe. If lacking physical strength, female balloonists had their charms and supposed vulnerability and Sophie was adept at using both. In diaphanous costumes and with coiffured hair, she accentuated her performances with music and fireworks. Although Napoleon had said that women are "mere machines to make children", Sophie was a favorite of his and named the "Aeronaut of the Official Festivals", the Emperor even asked her advice about invading England with balloon-borne troops. Bird-like physically and professionally, she was newsworthy, her adventures were recounted in literary circles and her form exaggerated on theatrical lithographs. She was afraid to ride in a carriage and only felt at home in the air. She had no fear flying at night, sleeping in her balloon for hours. She crossed over the Alps to Italy and once fainted and nearly froze above Turin when ascending to avoid a hailstorm. She nearly drowned after dropping into a swamp in Naples. Each show she did, promised to be more reckless than the previous and, despite warnings, Blanchard would set off pyrotechnics beneath her balloon.[3]

It caught up with Sophie on July 6, 1819, the year Mary Shelley's *Frankenstein* was published, warning that science when mixed with Gothic horror would kill any modern Prometheus. That evening, an audience at the Tivoli Gardens, Paris had paid to watch her do the slow burning "Bengal Fire" demonstration from her balloon. In an elaborate white dress and matching hat accessorized with an ostrich plume, she began her ascent carrying a blazing torch. Once in the air, she lit the fireworks and dropped them by parachute so that the slow burning "Bengal" lights hung from beneath her balloon. The wind blew her away from the gardens and suddenly there was seen a flash, followed by popping and flames shooting up from the top of the balloon. On fire, it began to descend, with Sophie cutting loose the ballast to slow the fall. At first, it looked to the horrified spectators that she would land safely but when the balloon hit the roof of a house Blanchard fell out, tumbled along the tiles and onto the street, where, according to a newspaper account, "she was picked up dead." Her creation had killed her.

In her life, Sophie Blanchard had made 67 ascents. The first woman to die in a ballooning accident, she was also the first to take charge of her own career in aviation. She was buried in Pere Lachaise Cemetery in Paris. When the promoters at the Tivoli Gardens wanted to donate the ticket sales to her family, they discovered that she had none. Aeronautics and offspring, as many female aviators would learn, did not go together. Instead, they paid for a tombstone showing her balloon in flames, with the epitaph "Victime de son Art et de son Intrepidite".[4]

Through the 19th century, balloon attractions continued through the western world, increasingly sharing the fairgrounds with man-lifting kites, gliders and ornithopters. Outnumbered by promoters (who were regarded as one step above snake oil salesmen) were the genuine pioneers who held demonstrations for scientific observation or to patent their "steerable" balloons. Mary Myers of Little Falls, NY and her husband were the inventors of such devices.[5] On July 4, 1880, under the name of "Carlotta, the Lady Aeronaut" (the name Mary Myers wouldn't bring in the punters) she became the first woman in the United States to pilot her own balloon. Later she would operate a "balloon farm" to make and sell them.

As L Frank Baum popularized in *The Wizard of Oz*, balloons were unmanageable and useless for anything other than the country fair circuit. With the strong men, Wild West shows, pig races and bearded ladies, they were entertaining, and no July 4, Bank Holiday or Victoria Day was complete without a balloon launch. Typically, the balloonist would take a local lady up to prove how safe it was, and that even such a delicate creature could enjoy the experience. One of them was the future aviatrix, Katherine Stinson. The 11-year-old was studying to be a pianist but in 1908, when she ascended in a hot air balloon, she said that she never wanted to come back down.

"A male balloonist could be seen anywhere," wrote author Jonathan Vance, "but a woman — now that was an attraction worth seeing."[6] In 1884, a Madame Lowanda "an adventurous young aeronaut in full command of the unwieldy monster" thrilled an Ottawa crowd as she ascended alone in the balloon *Queen of the Air,* scattering the advertising leaflets of her sponsors as she did. Advertised as "a curiosity" at the Great Eastern Exhibition, Sherbrooke, Quebec in 1896, Miss Nina Madison, in trousers, not only performed ascents, but parachute jumps as well. A journalist drily noting that the crowds came to see both feats as well as that of a woman wearing trousers. It was the rarity of a female in such a dangerous profession that gave Madison the attention.

In Edwardian England, the young governess Lily Cove would take her charges to Hackney Downs in London to watch the balloonists ascend and parachute down. It was on such an occasion that Captain Frederick Bidmead noticed her. He was looking for what in showman's jargon was a "crowd puller." Her options limited to remaining a spinster governess or slaving in a factory, Lily must have leapt at the opportunity. She proved to be fearless and charismatic and (as Bidmead's posters proclaimed), being "a handsome young lady with a fine figure and long golden hair" helped pull in the crowds.[7]

The pair toured the country, becoming famous for "Leaping Lily Cove"'s specialty. It was to climb down from the balloon onto a tiny trapeze below, then tear off her skirt, revealing beribboned bloomers, and then parachute down. The bloomers were to shock or titillate the audience but also a safety precaution to prevent her long skirt from getting entangled in the trapeze or parachute harness.

On June 11, 1906, at the Haworth Gala in Yorkshire, while tearing off her skirt, Lily fell off the trapeze. Without the parachute, she cartwheeled through the air twice, and hit the ground, smashing her skull. Haworth had not seen such national attention since the Brontes died off and the gate proceeds were enough to bring Lily's father from prison in London and fit him with a new black suit for the funeral. To quash any rumors that this might have been a suicide, the coroner's verdict was "Death by Misadventure." Lily was 21 years old.

When balloonists began using hydrogen gas as the lifting agent instead of heated air, they looked for a fabric that would be impermeable to the gas's tiny molecules. Casamir Frederick Weinling from Alsace brought the solution with him when he settled in Islington, London. It was "goldbeater's skin" traditionally used to make condoms. From the lower intestines of a cow, it was lightweight, had great strength and was impervious to hydrogen. Like today's cling film, it also has the unusual property of sticking together without needing to be

sewn. When Weinling made toy hydrogen balloons for the Great Exhibition at Crystal Palace, his development came to the attention of the military. He began providing the skin for British Army balloons and, on his death, his wife Ann and daughters Matilda, Elizabeth and Eugene took over the business.

In the era when the head of a workshop could only be a man and there were strictly gendered lines whether the occupation was for women, the efforts of the Weinling women were kept secret. Bending over the vats to separate the skin from the salted guts and then gluing it to a cotton-based fabric was a laborious, poisonous process. Making the skin for military balloons used in the Boer War and Ashanti campaign, the women worked at Chatham in 1882 and at the Royal Balloon Factory, Farnborough in 1907. By the First World War, Eugene was supervising hundreds of women making skin envelopes for air ships, giving Britain a technological lead over its enemies. The development of rubberized cotton by 1922 made goldbeater's skin obsolete. Forgotten today, the Weinlings were the first women to work for the Royal Aircraft Establishment (RAE) and justifiably called the mothers of British military aviation.

By now, another form of aerial entertainment was replacing balloons, equally precarious to its promoters and pilots — the flying machine. It was the perfect vehicle for feminism — both potent symbols of modernity, the optimism of one feeding off the other. In the early 20th century, a woman's life was strictly structured, and her behavior regulated by men. The medical profession warned that the strain of riding a bicycle or flying in an airplane — or going to college — was too much for the weaker sex, especially if menstruating. The "unnatural aspirations" of women who agitated for equality in all things could only lead to hysteria, a sickness specific to their sex. But increasingly educated, a few women were ignoring their advice. This was of course, only a fraction of them: white, urban, and middle class. Ascending in or jumping from a balloon was tame. Now women wanted to fly. No activity better symbolized the freedom that was lacking in their daily lives.

2: COME JOSEPHINE, IN MY FLYING MACHINE [8]

We certainly can't complain of the place. We came down here for wind and sand, and we have got them — so Orville Wright wrote to his sister Katharine in late September 1900. She was born in Dayton, Ohio in 1874, the youngest of the five Wright children. Following her mother's death in 1889, with their father — a bishop in the United Brethren of Christ Church — away frequently, the teenage Katharine took over running the household. Her siblings grown, instead of remaining at home, Katharine (Kate or Katie to her friends) enrolled in Oberlin College to take a degree in classics. It was here that she met Henry J Haskell who was two years ahead of her. However, he was already engaged to a woman he would marry and so, on graduating in 1898, Katharine returned to Dayton to teach Latin at the local high school. It was she who opened that historic telegram on December 17, 1903, announcing Orville and Wilbur's triumph.

The complete opposite of her dour, shy brothers, Katie was lively and vivacious. Intensely loyal to the two of them, she put her own life on hold and when Orville was injured at Fort Myer, Virginia in the first aircraft crash in history on September 17, 1908, she gave up her teaching job to nurse him at the military hospital. Wilbur, then in France demonstrating the Flyer, could also have used her help. The decadent lifestyle of *La Belle Epoque*, typified by the cancan dancers at the Moulin Rouge was at its height, the inventions of the telephone, electricity, and moving pictures fueled an insatiable appetite for a celebrity culture. Long before Hollywood's impact, The Gilded Age created an emphasis on appearance and apparel, on scandal and consumerism.

The French admitted to being impressed with Wilbur ("Veelbur" the young Pablo Picasso called him) who on September 21, 1908, remained airborne for 41 miles. But what dumbfounded them was that the lanky hawk-nosed American showed no interest in capitalizing on his celebrity status — or the charms of the opposite sex. "Has he a heart? Has he loved?" questioned a Parisian magazine. Wilbur's only mistress was the Flyer and he lived with it in a shed, in the company of an ugly mongrel dog (also unimaginatively named Flyer). The paparazzi of the day hounded him, and a woman even bored a hole into the wall of his shed to watch him bathe.

Like the balloon craze, aviation was mass entertainment — a gimmick that had no discernable practical value other than to sell newspapers. Courting the media, local aviators had already taken female passengers up. Six months before the Wrights first flew, Alberto Santos-Dumont had taught Aida de Acosta, a young New York socialite, to operate his powered balloon (dirigible) in Paris. On June 29, 1903, she flew it solo for 15 minutes with Santos-Dumont cycling beneath her, giving instructions by waving his handkerchief. She landed it in the midst of a polo match and when the Brazilian inventor asked how she enjoyed the experience, she simply replied, "It is very nice, Mr Santos-Dumont." According to Acosta, an overly excited Santos-Dumont exclaimed, "Mademoiselle, vous êtes la première aero-chauffeuse du monde!"[9] Acosta's parents were mortified when they found out about the flight. They had brought her to Paris for "the season" and feared that all prospects for a good marriage for their daughter had disappeared because of her foolish act. They made Santos-Dumont promise that he would never reveal her identity — a promise he kept despite the loss of publicity. Acosta, the first woman to control a dirigible never flew again —or mentioned it until 1927, when she would marry Col Henry Breckinridge, a close friend of Charles Lindbergh, who would serve as Lindbergh's attorney in the kidnapping case.

When the sculptor-turned-aviator Leon Delagrange took Madame Therese Peltier up in his plane on July 8, 1908, the first female passenger to fly unexpectedly gave birth to the restricting hobble skirt, designed so that more women could now decorously sit in a plane. Aware that they had squandered their technical lead to Glenn Curtiss and Henry Farman, Wilbur wrote home, worrying that the French were losing interest in him. Against his principles, he would take Mrs Edith Berg, the wife of Hart O Berg his business agent in France, for a two-minute flight on October 7th, the first American woman to fly. He asked Orville and Katharine to join him in France for Christmas.

With Orville still recovering from the crash at Fort Myers, it was Katharine who took center stage in 1909, making a positive impression on the European public. As Jackie Kennedy would, in 1961, she dazzled all who met her. She spoke French almost fluently and dominated the social scene with her Midwestern charm and candor. Photographs show her in the latest fashion and artists drew her as a "Gibson Girl". She was invited to prestigious dinners, notably at the Aéro-Club de France, the first woman ever in attendance. Recognizing her importance in aviation history, she was awarded the Legion of Honour, by the French government, at the same time as her brothers.

Katharine was also in the forefront of the first wave of the feminist movement — the Dayton branch of suffragists especially militant — which sought to broaden women's prospects so that their lives could be lived free of socially sanctioned conventions. What were her views (she must have been asked), on the effrontery of Muriel Matters (below) who had just flown over the House of Commons, London in a dirigible decorated with banners reading "Votes for Women" and "Women's Freedom League" to drop leaflets? The Australian suffragist did not operate the dirigible herself but hired a Captain Spencer to do so while she unloaded 38 pounds of paper, much of it, because of the wind, ending up in Wormwood Scrubs. That Katharine did not espouse the suffragist cause while in Europe was because of her brothers' ambivalence to it. Not until 1914, with her brother and father in tow, would she organize a march down Main Street, Dayton that drew 1,300 supporters.

The French resort city of Pau, knowing it would attract royalty, pulled off a public relations coup by inviting the Wrights to perform their flights there during "the 1909 season". Once there, Wilbur continued to sleep in a shed next to the Flyer, but as guests of the city, Katharine and Orville moved into the luxurious Hotel Gassion. When King Edward VII arrived in Pau on March 17, the Wrights were presented to His Majesty. Katharine knew how to curtsey having practiced it before with the wife of a British baronet. The King turned down an offer for a flight, which given his overweight frame must have relieved them. The royal visit put a public relations spin on flying and to demonstrate how safe the aircraft was, Wilbur took Katharine up that day.

"The American Girl Whom All Europe Is Watching" proclaimed *The World* magazine of April 11, 1909, with a photo of Katharine talking to King Alphonso XIII of Spain who was dissuaded from flying by his wife. Tours in Italy and Germany followed with European royalty ("as thick as fleas" Wilbur drily commented) said to be charmed by Katharine's straightforward, outgoing personality and (as neither of her brothers spoke French) her grasp of technical details, in explaining the aircraft to the audience. Beginning a precedent for her sex in Aviation, she humanized her brothers, softening their image for the media and boosting their popularity.

The Wrights returned to the United States in mid-June 1909 to fulfill their contract to train pilots for the US Army. The three were invited to the White House to meet President William Howard Taft and it was here that that Katharine renewed her acquaintance with Henry Haskell, now a journalist who would one day be awarded a Pulitzer Prize.

The brothers were besieged with entreaties from women to fly with them, including one from Alice Roosevelt Longfellow, the eldest daughter of President Theodore Roosevelt. The Wright's test pilot Eugene Lefebvre was killed on September 7 in a plane crash and neither the brothers nor the military were pleased with a civilian going up, particularly a female. But on October 27, 1909, Wilbur was persuaded by Katharine to take Mrs Sarah van Deman, the wife of an army officer, on a four-minute flight over the parade ground at College Park, Maryland. Sarah van Deman would be the first woman to fly in the United States and when asked by the reporters what it was like, she said, "Now I know why birds sing when they fly through the air." But when the Wrights opened a flying school in Montgomery, Alabama, in 1910, they continued to reject all the female students on the grounds that they were notoriety seekers. The brothers were unaware that for a woman, flying a plane like driving a car or smoking cigarettes, was symbolic. It denoted empowerment and equality with men.

In 1910, the brothers advertised for a seamstress for the Wright Company factory in Dayton and Ida Holdgreve, a local dressmaker was hired. She had answered a Help Wanted ad in the local newspaper for "plain sewing." It was an understandable typo. The brothers were looking for someone to do "plane sewing." The first and for a time the only woman in the first airplane plant in the United States, Ida sewed the light cream-colored fabric into the Flyer's wings, fins, and tail. When their company became the Dayton-Wright Company and built hundreds of aircraft during the First World War, she supervised a team of women who sewed stronger canvas onto the DH.4s that it built.

Twenty years later, little had changed for women in aviation. *Western Flying*, a Los Angeles magazine, conducted a survey in 1930 of women employed in the aviation industries. That the industry was almost completely male was evident at the Boeing Company in Seattle where of the 852 employees, 17 were women. Besides the usual clerical jobs, it was noted that they worked in the wing and fuselage fabric covering departments with a few in light metal plating work. It came as no surprise that as in other industries, there was a disparity in salaries. Men in the fabric covering departments earned 60-65 cents per hour for an average of $30 per week; women doing the same work received 40-50 cents per hour for an average of $21.50 per week. In figures for overall salaries in the aviation industry, there was an even greater gap. The hourly average earnings for men were 66.9 cents, and for women 36.7 cents.

In Viking times, the women who prepared the wool, wove the fabric, and spun it into sails for the long ships were crucial to the warriors' battles and explorations — it took as long to create a sail as it did to build a long ship. But with the Norse sagas written by men, women's contributions were never mentioned. Even today, after decades of feminist influence, we too often assume that building and maintaining an aircraft was/is a male domain. In both world wars (and today), that proved untrue.

Ida Holdgreve left the aviation industry after the war to sew draperies at the Rike-Kumler Company in downtown Dayton — the same department store where the Wright brothers had bought the muslin fabric for the world's first airplane, their 1903 Flyer. Only years later did she realize the historical significance of what she had done.[10]

Wilbur died of typhoid fever on May 29, 1912, and his brother's spirit was said to have died with him. Aircraft designs by others were leaving the latest Wright Model "C" far behind. Katharine was now increasingly embroiled in her brothers' correspondence, especially fighting the Smithsonian Institute as to their patents.[11] At the age of 52, she bravely followed her heart by announcing that she and Henry Haskell (now a widower) were to be married. Her passionate letters to him demonstrate that they had been in love since their college days. Orville, who seemed oblivious to this, was furious, his male pride hurt, and he condemned her for her disloyalty to the family. He refused to speak to her again. Although it cost her the affection of her surviving brother, she married Haskell on November 20, 1926, at Oberlin College. Alas, their happiness was short lived. Katharine Wright, regarded as the First Lady of Aviation contracted pneumonia and died on March 3, 1929.[12]

The English Channel was the prize for aviators then that the Atlantic Ocean would be in the 1930s. The natural boundary between England and the continent, it had a significance out of all proportion to its 21 miles. Crossing it however, promised an influential audience on either shore. In 1908, the *Daily Mail* launched the "English Channel Crossing Prize". This incentive-based competition pledged to award £500 to the first pilot to fly an airplane across the Channel from the Calais region of France to Dover, England. Given the unreliability of engines then, Wilbur Wright and Glenn Curtiss (both of whom had flown further than 21 miles) refused to risk it. When no serious attempts were made, the prize money was doubled to £1,000 and the offer extended to the end of 1909. Louis Bleriot's successful flight across the Channel on July 25, 1909, allowed the French to regain their lead in aviation.

But if there was ever a moment when the traditional role of the genders shifted, it was on October 22 that year, when Elise Raymonde de Laroche lifted her aircraft into the air. She guided it for a distance of 300 meters before landing, becoming the first female pilot in history. The Aéro-Club de France issued her Pilot License No 36 on March 8, 1910, the first ever to a woman.

The "aero clubs" of each country had until recently been gentlemen's motoring or ballooning societies and pilot's certificates or "tickets" were issued more for prestige than competence. In 1905, the Fédération Aéronautique Internationale (FAI), or World Air Sports Federation was founded to "regulate the sport of flying". To attempt any world record, an FAI certificate was required. As there was no separate classification for women either by the FAI or any of the aero clubs, female pilots who broke records did not receive the recognition they deserved for their flights. What they did was listed under "Miscellaneous Air Performances."

The French nation initially took "La Baronne Raymonde de Laroche" (the title was fake — her father was a plumber) to heart. Beautiful, tall, and elegant, always photographed in the latest Parisian fashions at the opera, unmarried (but admitting to having an affair), the first female pilot brought independence and femininity to an all-male club (see image opposite). She disregarded the "hobble skirts" but had an eye to practicality and the camera. When competing at the Seconde Grande Semaine at Rheims on July 8, 1910, Raymonde wore a grey divided skirt and a chic white sweater with hood.[13] "Flying" she said, "does not rely so much on strength, as on physical and mental coordination." But fashion not flight was sought by newspapers who sent reporters to cover events where women flew. When Helene Dutrieu of Belgium (who took the name "Girl Hawk") won over 14 male pilots in the Italia Coppa del Re (King's Cup) in 1912, more space was given to the scandalous revelation that the former music hall performer preferred flying without her corsets which she said were too confining.

As other female aviatrixes would do, de Laroche set up a women's flying school to be run by Jane Herveux, the fourth female pilot to be qualified in France. When another machine cut too closely across her in the turn at the Reims Air Race, de Laroche's plane was seen to dive to the ground. She survived the crash, but with multiple injuries to her arms and legs. Initially sympathetic, the press now turned against her, pointing out that the crash was proof that women could not/should not fly. Female pilots were too "ladylike" for competitions, were unable to handle the stress, and allowing them to fly only endangered onlookers. As the media continues to do with actresses, female sports figures and politicians, women pilots were built up only to be destroyed — either way, it sold newspapers.

Opposition to women in the cockpit was not confined to France. Melli Beese became the first female pilot in

Germany on September 13, 1911, to receive a license — despite sabotage by her male classmates at the flying school who drained her fuel and tampered with her steering prior to the test.

Soon after recovery, de Laroche almost died in a car crash that killed her partner, Charles Voisin. When the First World War ended, her ambition was to be the first female test pilot and "la Baronne" took up aviation once more, breaking the women's altitude record on July 12,

1919, by climbing to 4,800 meters. It was her bid for salvation in a society that had already condemned her. On July 18, 1919, as a passenger in a machine being test flown, she was killed when it crashed. She had died doing what she loved, the newspapers said. History's first female pilot is honored with a statue at Paris's Le Bourget Airport. On March 6-12, 2010, the 100th anniversary of her earning a pilot's license, Raymonde de Laroche's life was celebrated at the airport when 225 women were introduced to piloting. The plumber's daughter would be pleased to know that both Women of Aviation Worldwide Day and International Women's Day are celebrated annually every March 8.

It was not only social restrictions that prevented women from entering aviation. Misogyny has ancient roots; all the stories having been written by men. We cheer Jason for getting the Golden Fleece but ignore his wife Medea's aid and betrayal when he leaves her for a younger wife. Heroism like piloting was exclusively a male occupation and its affirmation began at an early age. Written in 1911, Margaret Burnham's "Girls Aviator Series" are about the adventures of two "girl aviators" Peggy and Jess who help their brothers perfect their late father's aircraft design and foil his rivals. But it is the boys who fly the plane and the "girl aviators" who wave goodbye. Education was far from an interdisciplinary curriculum then and the segregation of the sexes began in school when girls were discouraged from studying science and technical subjects. For all her encouragement of girls to enter the field of aviation, Amelia Earhart would bemoan that they had no basic technical knowledge. Why would they? A hundred years before, most girls were not taught to read. It was considered a waste of time for the lives they were to lead.

As a child, E Lilian Todd took apart typewriters, weathervanes, and clocks to learn how they worked. Like Henry Ford, she was a self-taught inventor. Although technical journals and advice were unavailable to her, Todd designed and built an aircraft in 1906 — the first by a woman — "the entire construction a monument to feminine skill" acknowledged *The New York Times*. To do this, she had spent days studying a specimen of an albatross at the Metropolitan Museum in New York. At its completion, she had difficulties finding a pilot for her aircraft — all were male and didn't trust her competence. Finally, on November 7, 1910, Didier Masson flew Miss Todd's plane for 20 feet at the Garden City Aviation Field near Mineola, New York. Even five years before, this would have been historic, but by then, Georges Chavez had already flown a Bleriot monoplane over the Alps.

Brooklyn-born Elsa Gardner suffered multiple hip operations early in the 20th century and was confined to bed for long periods. It was this that stimulated her intellectual interest in math and languages. A partial scholarship to MIT in the aeronautical engineering department and her work for the US Navy in both world wars made Gardner one of the very few women elected to the American Society of Mechanical Engineers. Other female engineers in the United States in the 1930s were Mabel Rockwell, Dr Francis Hurd Clark, and Isabel Ebel.

Technical colleges and universities that taught aeronautical theory were closed to women. The indomitable Elsie Gregory MacGill, was the first woman to earn a master's degree in aeronautical engineering in 1929, even while crippled with polio. Her suffragist grandmother Emma Gregory had ensured that feminism was woven into Elsie's life at an early age. The first practicing Canadian woman engineer, in 1938, MacGill was made chief aeronautical engineer of Canadian Car & Foundry at Fort William, Ontario. The company had been contracted to build Hawker Hurricanes for the RAF and through her leadership, 1,451 aircraft were turned out. Elsie rejected the label "woman engineer". Her perspective was that she was an engineer, period. That she was a woman did not need to be highlighted. After all, she had proven time and again that her sex in no way impacted her ability to do her job. The media crowned her "Queen of the Hurricanes", causing the men in the foundry (already coping with an influx of female workers) to resent the attention.

When it was discovered that she and Bill Soulsby, the plant manager, were having an affair, despite their importance to the war effort, they were marched off the premises. The couple married two weeks later. A beacon of hope to female engineers, Elsie went on to have a successful career, both as an engineer and feminist. As the Canadian representative in the International Civil Aviation Organization, she was the first woman to serve as its technical advisor on aircraft airworthiness.

The few flight schools that did accept women had little confidence in a female pupils' abilities. "Instructors start in with a prejudice," aviatrix Louise Thaden said, "and the woman student labours under a decided handicap." At a time when the disparity between the salaries of men and women was enormous, flying lessons were also beyond their financial means as schools would ask female students for a large bond in advance (up to the value of the aircraft) in case they crashed it. Maintaining an airplane once the instruction period ended depended on a generous, supportive father or husband. Amelia Earhart would warn: "The hardest part is keeping on flying after the instruction period is over. Renting an aircraft is expensive and many a long day goes by before an employer can be persuaded to risk his airplane on a novice pilot's skill — much less pay him to fly."

Male students were able to work as mechanics at airports to pay off their flying lessons but aspiring female pilots were unwelcomed in such positions. "No one wants a feminine 'grease monkey' around the hangar," Earhart recalled from her own experience, "to do the odd jobs which may partly pay for a young man's aviation training". Before she became the first woman to fly solo from Britain to Australia, Amy Johnson hung around the London Aeroplane Club ("wormed her way in" as she put it) watching the mechanics work on aircraft in the hangar and questioning them. Because the men occasionally swore in her presence, she would inevitably be escorted out. When she showed up to begin her apprenticeship, Johnson was at first ignored by the other apprentices and engineers (all male). "At last, I asked outright for a job," and was told "You can sweep the hangar floor." She started sweeping "with such vim and vigor" that the foreman said: "Hi chuck it, you fool. Jim, show this angel from heaven how to sweep the floor." Jim fetched a bucket of water and sprayed the floor before beginning to sweep. After that, Amy was accepted by the men who gave her the nickname "Johnnie" which she preferred to her own. As many aviation-mad women before her and since, she endured long hours of standing on concrete, the aches in her arms from scraping carbon off pistons, the blisters and bruises, the humiliations, and curses. In spite of it all, Amy (below) later wrote, "I had never been so happy in my life!"

Men also had the advantage of joining the military which taught them to fly without charge. Seventy-one years after the Wright brother's first flight, women would finally be allowed to train as military pilots — in the United States Navy in 1974 and the United States Air Force (USAF) in 1976, with Captain Theresa Claiborne (overleaf) becoming the first African American female pilot in the USAF in 1981. In 1993, Jeannie Leavitt (below) became the USAF's first female fighter pilot and in 2012 the first female to command a fighter wing.[14]

In Australia, in 1988 the first female Royal Australian Air Force pilots were Flight Lieutenant Robyn Williams and Officer Cadet Deborah Hicks. In Canada, Captain Deanna Brasseur and Captain Jane Foster became the first female CF-18 fighter pilots in 1989 and in Britain, Flight Lieutenant Julie Ann Gibson was the first full-time female pilot for the Royal Air Force in 1991.

Blanche Stuart Scott had been taught to fly by none other than Glenn Curtiss himself, one of two women to do so. He had great reservations about a female pilot, anticipating the inevitable crash and the bad publicity for his company. To prevent her from becoming airborne while taxiing on her own, Curtiss inserted a block of wood behind the throttle pedal. But even with that, on September 6, 1910, Scott managed to inadvertently (and unofficially) lift off to about 40 feet in the air.[15] Although the flight was witnessed by the maintenance crew, Scott was not granted a pilot's license. The second woman that Curtiss also reluctantly taught was Julia Clark who then joined the Curtiss-Wright exhibition team as one of "The Daring Bird Girls", performing at fairs in the Midwest.

Bessica Faith Raiche from Wisconsin was studying

music in Paris in 1908 when she saw Wilbur Wright fly and later, she would meet de Laroche. Raiche was a stereotype of the 20th century's "New Woman" — confident in her interests, career-oriented and in control of her life choices. Already a linguist, businesswoman, medical doctor, dentist and an accomplished pianist, Raiche even wore bloomers which polite society considered "mannish in dress". She returned home with her new husband and moved to Mineola, Long Island, NY, near Hempstead Field, then a center of aviation.[16] Unable to buy an aircraft, the couple somehow built one (a Wright copy) in their living room with bamboo, silk, and piano wire, removing a wall to bring it out. In riding breeches instead of a skirt, Raiche made a solo flight of a full mile on September 16, 1910, the first by an American woman. The Aeronautical Society awarded her a diamond-studded gold medal inscribed: "First Woman Aviator of America on October 13, 1910."

As few flying schools accepted women, in 1912, Bessica organized one for them in Mineola. She and her husband are remembered for teaching Lucean Headen, the first African American to fly.[17] She would leave aviation to become one of the first female specialists in obstetrics and gynecology. As Raiche did not perform at airshows or seek publicity, she remains less well known than other pioneers.

No one knew the power of hype better than Harriet Quimby. Born into a destitute Michigan farming family in 1875, she was brought up by an ambitious mother who took eight years off her age and created a fake identity for her so she could pass off as a member of a wealthy Boston family. Tall and beautiful, Harriet acted in a silent movie called *Line of White on A Sullen Sea* with Mack Sennett and Mary Pickford. As a journalist for *Leslie's Illustrated Weekly* in New York, she wrote for women in articles like "Hints to Stage-Struck Girls" and "Can Women Run Automobiles?" Women were fascinated with flying she told her editor as it freed them however temporarily from their social restrictions. Promising exclusive accounts of her own misadventures in learning how to fly, Quimby got him to pay $750 for her lessons in the summer of 1911 at the Moisant School of Aviation at Hempstead.

When Denise Moore fell out of her plane on July 21 at Etampes, France, the first female aviator to die, the media callously reported that as a woman she had most likely "swooned" under the pressure of piloting — it must have given Quimby and her readers some misgivings. But she passed the Aero Club's test on August 1 and was awarded a pilot's license. The following month at an air meet, she earned a lucrative $1,500.

As a journalist and former actress, Harriet was aware of the media's power. She always had a good quote for reporters, posed for photographers and had the American

Tailors Association design a special purple satin flying suit for her. Her articles in *Leslie's* inspired a generation of girls. "Men fliers have given the impression that aeroplaning is very perilous work, something an ordinary mortal should not dream of attempting," she wrote, "but when I saw how easy men fliers handle their machines, I said I could fly. Flying is a fine, dignified sport for women, it is healthy and stimulates the mind."

With popular culture daring young women to become "cloud kissers" (away from chaperones) and the gramophone playing *The Airplane Rag* — "Come girlie in my airplane. Come girlie and do that dip again," the sport was romantic, promising young women freedom from society's restrictions. No one it seemed, knew this better than the randy inventor, Laurence Sperry. His autopilot not only made flying safer but allowed pilots to do other things with their hands — and bodies — as he discovered. Legend has it that in late November 1916, while piloting a Curtiss Flying Boat C2 at 500 feet above the coast of Long Island, NY he had sex with one Cynthia Polk (her husband was driving an ambulance at the Front). During their airborne antics, they unwittingly managed to disengage the autopilot, sending their plane into Great South Bay, where they were rescued, both stark naked, by duck hunters. A gallant Sperry explained that the force of the crash had stripped both fliers of all their clothing, but that didn't stop a skeptical New York tabloid from running the famous headline "Aerial Petting Ends in Wetting." Sperry is generally considered one of the founders of the Mile High Club.

Harriet contacted Louis Bleriot's representative in New York early in 1912, and shortly after booked a passage under an assumed name for Britain. Charles Stuart Rolls had conquered the English Channel with a round trip on June 2, 1910, and John Moisant (who took with him his mechanic and cat) did so on August 23. But no female had attempted it and Quimby wanted to be the first. A title like "Queen of the English Channel" would catapult her to stardom. Unlike Moisant, she wanted to do it from England to France which given the prevailing wind was far more difficult. She had never flown long distances, nor over water, and there would be no support ship below.

She was also unfamiliar with the use of a compass. British aviator Gustav Hamel who handed her one warned that a false reading would cause her to disappear over the Channel and drown (Ironically, Hamel himself would vanish over the Channel on May 22, 1914).[18] The Bleriot XI shipped over to Dover in great secrecy was the 50 hp model and not the 70 hp one she had bought and because of fog, Harriet was unable to do a test flight with it. She must have also been aware that the French government had ordered all Bleriot planes grounded in March for two weeks until their structural problems were fixed.

At 5:30 am on April 16, 1912, the 37-year-old climbed into the unfamiliar aircraft. What struck her most was the doubt on the faces of onlookers that a woman could do this. Both Rolls and Moisant who might have helped had been killed in plane crashes two years before. With a hot water bottle strapped to her waist for heat, the young woman took off, disappearing within minutes into the fog. In an article for *Leslie's* she described what took place. "I was up fifteen hundred feet within 30 seconds … I could not see ahead of me; nor could I see the water below." She flew for the better part of an hour in deep fog, her neck aching from staring at the compass. Deciding to descend, when she lowered the nose, gasoline flooded into the Anzani engine which began backfiring. She was going to ditch in the Channel, she thought. "To my great relief," she wrote, "the gasoline quickly burned away, and my engine began an even purr." She looked at her watch, the only other instrument she had besides the compass. France had to be nearby — and it was. Quimby landed on a white sandy beach near Hardelot where Bleriot had his hangar and was soon surrounded by fishermen.

Sadly, because two days before the "Titanic" had sunk with more than 1,500 lives lost, her achievement would be overshadowed in the press and almost forgotten by history. There were no banner headlines or victory parades or prize moneys. Ominous too, was the news that Curtiss's former pupil, Julia Clark, who had just received her license on May 19, tumbled out of her plane on June 17 at the fairgrounds in Springfield, Illinois and was killed when the aircraft fell on her.

Nor did Quimby live long to enjoy her fame. On July 1, at the Boston Air Meet, she took its manager William Willard up in her all-white two-seater Bleriot. The aircraft was notorious for being unsteady and circling the airfield at 1,500 feet, onlookers saw its tail rise sharply and Willard fall out. Without him in the back seat, the aircraft became completely destabilized and Quimby was also thrown out — neither of them had been wearing of seat belts. *The New York Sun* noted that "Harriet Quimby's death showed that women lack strength and the presence of mind and courage to excel as aviators".

Aviation, in the last sepia-tinted days before the First World War was, for ordinary people, a continuation of ballooning — just summer fair entertainment. Two recent inventions were shaping the public's hunger for news of the notoriety of aviators: the rotary printing press (which printed on both sides of paper) which created a voracious demand to fill space and the newsreel camera invented in France by Pathé, which came to the United States in 1910. Exhibition teams at "air meets" jostled to attract media attention and financial backers. It must have been difficult for the public to distinguish the true visionaries who believed that this mode of transport had a commercial future from the daredevils who gave it a bad name — and there was a surplus of those including Eugene Ely, Omer Locklear, and Lincoln Beachey.

But they did inspire a generation of women to enter aviation, combining as it did youthful recklessness with feminist aspirations. When she saw Locklear land his plane on the roof of the St Francis Hotel, San Francisco in 1919, the hotel receptionist Viola Gentry thought,

"It seemed very easy … if a man could do it, certainly a woman could." She decided to take up aviation, working as a cashier. Performing a stunt to get noticed, on March 14, 1926, Gentry rented a Curtiss Oriole, took off from Curtiss Field and flew under both the Brooklyn and Manhattan bridges. An unimaginative reporter dubbed her "The Flying Cashier."

The only employment for a pilot male or female, was to join a "flying circus". Billed as "The Tomboy of the Air", as the only female with the Curtiss exhibition team, Blanche Stuart Scott was noticed more for her gender than flying skills. In this male vocation, to see a woman attempt equality and possibly die doing so, could only increase gate receipts. At air shows, Blanche's teammate Lincoln Beachey known as "The Man Who Owned The Sky" would dress up as her and in a "death dive" pretend to be out of control, causing a screaming terror from the audience — before pulling out in time. Scott (who is remembered for breaking 42 bones), went on to set so many long-distance records that *Aeronautics* magazine grudgingly reported that she "flies like a man."[19] Seeing no other option for women in aviation then, she would give up exhibition flying in 1916 before it killed her.

The first female aviatrix that Canadians saw was Alys McKey Bryant. She began taking flying lessons in the summer of 1912 after answering an ad stating, "Wanted young lady to learn to fly for exhibition purposes." Alys was hired and fell in love with her instructor Johnny Bryant. They married, but like many husband-and-wife teams, both kept their own names for publicity purposes. She was billed as "The Iron-Nerved Aviatrice" and Johnny "The Death-Defying Aviator" and the pair toured the Pacific northwest blissfully happy, from California to Oregon and Washington. They came to Vancouver, British Columbia on July 13, 1913, where at Minoru Park, Alys became the first female to fly in the Dominion.

In August, the city of Victoria paid the pair the vast sum of $1,000 to perform and attract attention to the races. Taking off from the Willows racetrack on August 5, Alys delighted the crowd with dips, rolls, and figures-of-eights but spectators saw that she had difficulty controlling the Curtiss plane. She cut short her performance, complaining of the "treacherous winds". The next day, the winds were even worse but as they had been paid in advance, Johnny took off to give the audience a show. Four hundred feet above the city, his plane was seen to go into a dive, lose a wing and crash into the Lee Dye building, killing him. After the repairs to the building had been paid for, Alys was left with $300 to take his body back to California. Telling reporters that she had "a fatalistic belief" that she would meet the same death as her beloved Johnny, she gave up exhibition flying. Aviation she later said, had given her everything — and taken it all back. Bryant taught aviation during the First World War, dying in 1954 at the age of 74.

Her fear was well founded. Exhibition flying was a hand-to-mouth existence that ended when either the aircraft fell apart or the pilot fell out of it. Undertakers would actually follow daredevil pilots from show to show to claim their bodies. In a macabre accolade, there were also morticians who would display the body for a fee.

To increase gate receipts, poorly designed aircraft were being flown in suicidal spirals by pilots who believed their own billing. *The New York Times* calculated that since the newspaper began keeping track in 1908, 308 people had died in crashes, 85 (including Bryant's husband) in the first eight months of 1913 alone.

The first woman parachuted from a plane on September 16, 1912, the first man, Capt Albert Berry, had only just done so on March 1, that year. Considering how few women flew, it was extraordinary — as was the woman who did it. When Charles Broadwick's "World Famous

Aeronauts" troupe arrived in Henderson, NC in 1908, Georgia Thompson was a fifteen-year-old single mother of two, working 12 hours a day in a cotton mill — as she had done since she was eight. After seeing the show, Georgia remembered, "I knew that's all I ever wanted to do!" She left her children with family and convinced Broadwick to take her on to jump from his balloon. Barely 5 feet tall and weighing about 80 pounds, her diminutive size worked to her advantage and Broadwick was enough of a showman to see the potential. Legally adopting her, he billed Georgia as the "Doll Girl," dressing her in ruffled bloomers, a silk dress, ribbons in her ringlets, and a bonnet. On May 15, 1910, she dropped from a balloon over Knoxville, Tennessee, to make the first parachute jump in the United States. Although "Tiny" Broadwick hated the "Doll Girl" name and the costume, she soon became the star of the show. Thinking they were seeing a little girl falling to her death horrified audiences — who then cheered as she floated safely down by parachute.

Hanging from a trapeze-like swing from aviator Glenn L Martin's plane on September 16, 1912 "Tiny" Broadwick would make the first jump from an aircraft. It wasn't the jumping or free falling she said, that was dangerous but what she fell onto: trees, lakes, power lines or roofs. After 1,100 jumps in shows from Mexico to Canada, she quit in 1922 to become a nurse in Los Angeles.[20] Forgotten until the 1970s, "Tiny" Broadwick was made an honorary member of the 82nd Airborne Division at Feet Bragg, NC.

Katherine Stinson (who as a child had been so stimulated by a balloon ascent) took the title "The Flying School-girl". Her publicity lied that she had been sixteen when she got her FAI license — she was nineteen. The first woman to carry the US Airmail, doing so in a publicity stunt on September 27, 1913, Stinson is credited also as the first female "skywriter" and the first woman to fly in China and Japan.

In Britain, the Women's Aerial League was begun in 1909 to further the development of aircraft technology and also presciently to "raise awareness of the airplane as a weapon for war." Although it was a strictly non-political body, its members included noted suffragists, Emmeline and Christabel Pankhurst. The League held annual Ladies' Aviation Days at Hendon Aerodrome.

At the Ladies Aviation Day on July 6, 1912, event, it was deemed too windy to allow ladies to compete as pilots. The organizers ruled that weather conditions meant that women could only take to the air as passengers. The silver cigarette box designed by Mappin and Webb to raise the profile of women in aviation was thus awarded to Major Lewis Turner — despite his lack of female credentials.

Piloting a plane was very much an avocation for wealthy sportsmen like Charles Rolls, Claude Graham-White and John Moore-Brabazon. The Royal Aero Club

issued certificates for pilots on behalf of the FAI, and on August 18, 1911, one Hilda Beatrice Hewlett, received Ticket No 122, the first British woman to be awarded one. The flight test had been at the new Brooklands Aerodrome and after it, the forty-seven-year-old said, "I did not feel a bit nervous, only happy. My dream was fulfilled."

Born in 1864, Hilda was one of the first women in England to cycle competitively and drive a motor vehicle. In 1888, after nursing in Germany she re-turned home and married Maurice Henry Hewlett. Maurice did

Mrs. Maurice Hewlett,

England's first airwoman. Mrs. Hewlett is the wife of the well-known novelist. She drives a biplane, Farnham type, with 50-horse-power engine. She won her license a few months ago, and is now interested in an aviation school in England.

not support his wife's interest in flying. "Women will never be as successful in aviation as men," he asserted. "They have not the right kind of nerve." They separated amicably in 1914.

Hilda went to France in 1910 to take flying lessons at Mourmelon-le-Grand where she met the pilot and engineer Gustav Blondeau. They opened the first flying school in England at Brooklands. The Hewlett-Blondeau Flying School advertised itself as "The only School which has never had a crash nor damaged an airplane." Thomas Sopwith and Geoffrey de Havilland were among its pupils.

Adopting the pseudonym "Grace Bird" for airshows, Hewlett also partnered with Blondeau to begin an aircraft manufacturing business called "Omnia Works" at Battersea, building Farman, Caudron and Avro aircraft under license. In 1912 with a contract to build BE 2cs, the company moved to Leagrave, Bedfordshire.

Affectionately nicknamed "Old Bird" by her family, Hewlett and her children left England in the 1920s and settled in the city of Tauranga on the North Island of New Zealand. As she explained, "The urge to escape from the three Cs, crowds, convention, and civilization, became strong." When Jean Batten toured New Zealand in 1934, she was hosted at Tauranga by Hewlett. The "Old Bird" died in 1943 at the age of 79. The life of Britain's first female pilot recalls the words of William Shakespeare: "Things won are done; joy's soul lies in the doing."

In the United States and elsewhere, opinions on women piloting planes ranged from amusement and condescension to outright hostility. The New Woman might wish to fly but without financial independence, it was impossible for her to buy a plane or learn to fly it. When twenty-one-year-old Ruth Law asked Orville Wright for flying lessons, he refused because, as he said, women were not mechanically inclined. When she wanted to buy one of his Flyers, Wright would speak only to

Charles Oliver, her husband in her presence. With Oliver as manager, she formed "Ruth Law's Flying Circus", a three-plane troupe that worked the county fairs by racing with cars and flying through fireworks. She specialized in car-to-plane transfers, around speedways or racetracks.

Dependent on empathy from a public that was mainly anti-suffragist, female fliers had to walk a fine line. Law's ties with the women's suffrage movement were known and when she flew from Chicago to New York on November 19, 1916, setting a long-distance record, she was asked by reporters if she was in favor of women suffrage. She fielded the question with: "Me a suffragist? Oh, I don't know. I move around so much that if I ever vote it would probably have to be from some upper-air polling place." The militant campaign for equal suffrage decreased significantly during the First World War, as Emmeline and Sylvia Pankhurst were convinced that Germany posed a greater danger to humanity than misogyny.

The Stinson sisters, Katherine and Marjorie instructed Canadians at their family's flying school in San Antonio, Texas so they could join the Royal Flying Corps. They had trained thirty pilots, when the United States entered the war, and civilian flying was forbidden. Refused permission to fly in France, Katherine went on a promotional tour for the Red Cross War Fund in 1917, flying from city to city picking up cheques and pledges, finally landing on a white canvas cross near the Washington Monument. She then came to Canada, holding aerial demonstrations on the prairies. "There is nothing about flying that makes it unsuited to a woman." Stinson told disbelieving audiences. "It doesn't demand size or strength."

The first war in the air had a cultural significance that solidified male dominance in aviation for much of the 20th century. With Zeppelins and Gothas now bombing civilians, aircraft were no longer rich men's toys or carnival attractions but viewed with malice and dread.

Like poison gas and the submarine, they symbolized the worst of the Industrial Age.

Along with other aviatrixes, when war began, de Laroche offered her flying services to the government but was turned down. She spent the war as a military chauffeur, driving officers to the front. Gladys Sandford drove an ambulance in Gaza and France for the New Zealand Expeditionary Force. In 1924, she would be the first woman in New Zealand to get a pilot's license. Amelia Earhart, deeply affected by the hundreds of disabled soldiers she saw in Toronto, volunteered as a nurse with the Voluntary Aid Detachment. Watching pilots train at the Armour Heights airfield near Spadina Military Hospital, she caught the "aviation bug" that would literally consume her life.

If they could not fly in history's first aerial war, women had other opportunities to demonstrate that their capabilities were equal to those of men. But even in wartime, they encountered misogyny. Female nurses for example, were acceptable — but at a time when medical practice was structured according to gender, race and social class, female doctors were not. Under the claim that men would not want to be examined by them, in 1915, the U.S. Army Medical Corps rejected all female physicians applying for duty. The women served instead in the Red Cross, the French Army, and the Medical Women's National Association.

With the majority of men in the military, women took over many jobs in the new aviation industry. In Britain alone, hundreds were employed at Claude Grahame-White's aircraft factory at Hendon, at Sopwith's at Kingston-upon-Thames, Handley-Page at Cricklewood and the Royal Aircraft Factory at Farnborough. Barred from apprenticeships pre-war, they were at first restricted to lower grade tasks. But as the conflict continued beyond Christmas 1914, so eager were companies to keep them that more women's toilets, creches (and flowers!) appeared in factories and advanced training for females was begun. As in 1945, women were forced to give up their jobs to the men returning home. The "Restoration of Pre-War Practices" Act was stringently enforced by the trade unions and companies that attempted to keep women on were prosecuted.

All combatants upheld the idea during the two world wars that women in combat of any form was abhorrent — forgetting that in the past, in many cultures and nations, women had been warriors — and for thousands of years. Little known outside Beauvais is the French heroine Jean Hachette (Joan the Hatchet) or Mary Hays, the first woman to receive a soldier's pension in the United States, because nineteenth century historians assumed that all women in war were either servants, camp followers, or prostitutes and, therefore, unworthy of mention in historical text. The examples of Queen Boudica the warrior queen of the Iceni, and Eleanor of Aquitaine, who led an army of 300 women in the Second Crusade in 1147, were far removed from the First World War picture of the 'ideal woman' as a gentle, nurturing pacifist. A pamphlet allegedly written by "A Little Mother" in 1916 (which sold 75,000 copies in less than a week) stated that women were 'created for the purpose of giving life, and men to take it'. It argued that 'women were not warriors', their job was not to 'bear arms' but 'bear armies'.

The only female pilots known to have flown in reconnaissance during the First World War were the Russian Princess Eugenie Shakhovskaya, (image overleaf) and Nadezhda Degtereva, who disguised herself as a man to do so. Her sex was only discovered when she was forced to seek medical attention after being wounded over enemy lines. The Soviet Union, the first country in the world to proclaim legal equality for women, allowed them to fly in the Red Army until 1923. Marie Elisabeth

Marvingt (image overleaf), was the third woman to receive a pilot's license in France. In 1915, she somehow became a volunteer pilot who flew bombing missions to German-occupied Metz. Post-war, Marvingt would lobby for the creation of an air ambulance corps so that the wounded would be picked up by fast aircraft from the battlefield and brought to frontline hospitals.

To distract from the slaughter below, governments mythologized their fighter aces as chivalrous knights of the air, supposedly jousting each other according to a code of ethics unknown since the equally mythical King Arthur's Round Table. The opposite was true as air ace Billy Bishop wrote in his bestselling memoir *Winged Warfare*. To watch his opponent going down in flames gave a fighter pilot the greatest satisfaction and the quickest way to win a dogfight was to aim for the opposing pilot's head or body — before he could do the same to you.

But because of this adulation, no longer were aviators seen as crazy, reckless daredevils with suicidal tendencies. Now they were romantic, almost divine figures that

transcended time and space. In the cockpit, the pilot was a *deus ex machina* (the God from the Machine). Sharing that lofty pedestal with women was unthinkable....

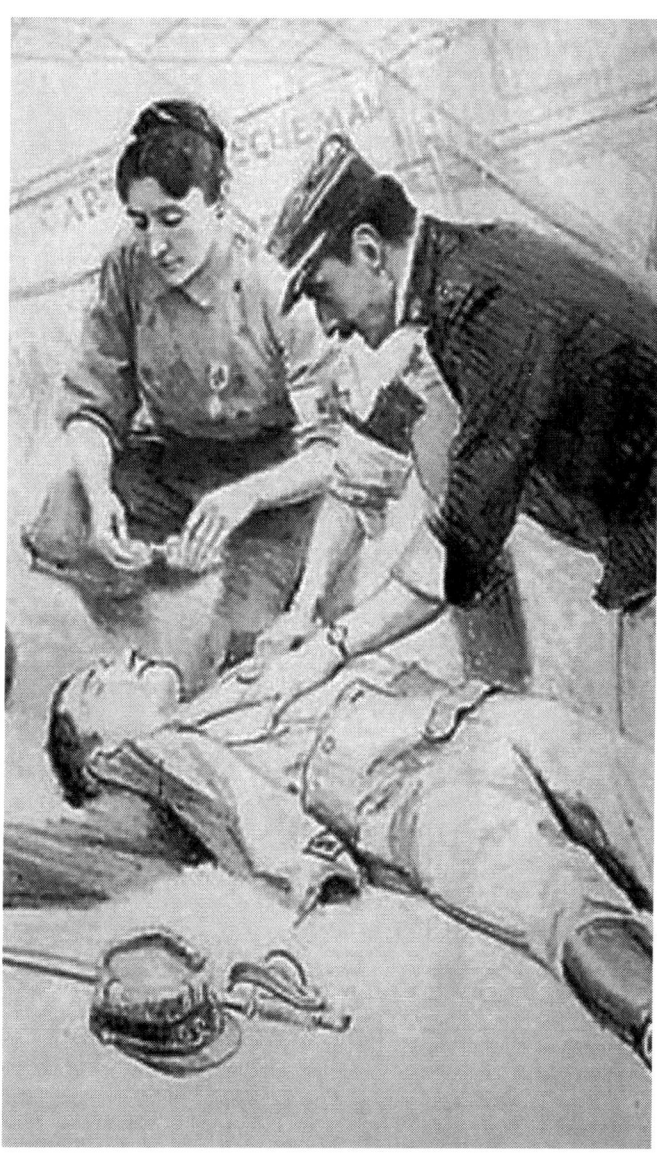

3: THE HILL WE CLIMB IF ONLY WE DARE

The euphoria of the end of the First World War was tempered by the effects of a brutal respiratory virus that invaded the planet, killing between 50 million and 100 million human beings world-wide. Adjusted for population, that would equal 220 million to 430 million deaths in 2020–21. The Great Powers had been drained of both their capital and a whole generation of their young men, while race riots in the United States and the threat of Bolshevik revolution worldwide had all torn at the social fabric of nations. The world was a dangerous place and North Americans took comfort in the two oceans that separated them from it. They felt safe in that no one could fly across either of them. With the present, too frightening to contemplate, nations looked to the future and aviation became the measure of modernity. As the space race would be, to fly longer, higher, and faster was seen as the measure of a country's strength. As their grandchildren would to astronauts, those who could shrink the planet were idolized, especially if they were female. The dew was still on the promise of flight — whether getting away from it all with a loved one, or braving the Atlantic.

The new woman of the 1920s bobbed her hair, frequented speakeasies, hiked up her hemlines, danced the Charleston, and necked in roadsters. The flapper flaunted cigarette smoking — in public! Once associated only with men (or prostitutes), imaginative marketing campaigns by the tobacco industry turned cigarettes into the 'torches of freedom' and women were convinced that by smoking they were demonstrating their equality with men.

In the hollow prosperity of the Jazz Age, more of her sex were earning their own keep (a fraction of what men were being paid for the same work), and if the celebrity culture in pictorial magazines and silent movies was anything to go by — engaging in gender-defying sexual freedom. Eve Adams' *Lesbian Love* was published in 1925 (with a limited distribution), and the first lesbian kiss appeared on screen in the movie *Lady of the Night*.[22]

Thanks to the suffragist campaign and the contributions of women to the war effort, with the 19th Amendment of the Constitution, on August 26, 1920, women in the United States were granted the right to vote — unless they were black, indigenous, Latino or Asian Americans. As with aviation, voting was an elitist form of feminism, reserved for the privileged. More relevant female issues like the pay gap, sexual harassment, reproductive health, and childcare were a century away. What women really wanted was the acknowledgement that they were the equal of males in rights and remuneration. But in 1920, there was nothing more symbolic of their cause than becoming an aviatrix.

Once almost hand-tooled, aircraft during the conflict had been mass produced and hundreds were now surplus. Pre-war only wealthy sportsmen could afford them, but now, like Henry Ford's ubiquitous Model Ts, they were within the price range of most people. For demobilized pilots, with airlines far in the future, entertaining the public by stunting was their only hope. In patchwork Curtiss JN-4s (Jennies) barnstormers male and female (and sometimes as husband-and-wife teams) traversed North America, selling rides, and thrilling rural audiences with aerial feats like stepping from the wing of one plane to another or climbing by rope ladder from a moving car to a plane overhead. As the 19th century balloonist had done, once local interest (and spare cash) was exhausted, the barnstormer moved on.

To escape the drudgery of farm work however briefly, there was a feminine fascination to flying and Slats Rogers, a barnstormer of this era, reminisced about it. "It was funny as hell watching the people go up for the first time. Here would come some middle-aged man and wife, and they would fight anybody who wanted to horn ahead of them, but they were scared white all the time. About the time it was their turn, the man would want to back out. But the woman would argue him into it. Almost every time it was that way — the man was the one that had to be talked into going up — the woman did the talking."[23]

Writing in the 1920s, journalist and pilot Margery Brown agreed. "Why do I want to fly?" she wrote, "Because halfway between the earth and sky, one seems to be closer to God. There is a peace of mind, a satisfaction which walls cannot give." Flying to men was merely mechanical, Brown thought, but for women, whether passenger or pilot, "it seems to signify rising above their environment in one way or another, symbolizing freedom from the irking limitations that have hedged them about for so many centuries."

The American poet-pilot Louise Thaden would explain:

> *Flight is abiding peace.*
> *Absolute serenity.*
> *It is faith and compassion.*
> *Purest joy.*
> *It is a spirit totally free.*
> *Flight is yesterday's yearning.*
> *The fulfillment of today's dreams.*
> *Tomorrow's promises.*

The economic fizz of the Roaring Twenties gave fast-growing, ambitious American cities like Cleveland and

Los Angeles the impetus to stage air races and, beginning in 1920, Ralph Pulitzer, the publisher of the *New York World*, to attract publicity for his newspaper, began sponsoring them. More than negotiating pylons or closed circuits, air races like the Schneider Trophy symbolized a nation's technological and military prowess. But because of the skill and physical strength required, they were limited to men. Women, everyone knew, could never win such a competition. But even losing, by her sexuality, she would take all media attention away from him.

Aerial exhibitions and barnstorming were the only entry women had to flying, and they began as wing walkers and parachutists. As soon as the ban on civilian flying in the United States was lifted, in 1919, twenty-two-year-old Laura Bromwell learned to fly by joining the New York Aerial Police Reserve. She became the first woman after the war to receive her pilot's license from the Aero Club of America. Wearing her police uniform, Bromwell looped-the-loop an astounding 199 times at Mineola, on May 16, 1921, breaking Adrienne Bolland's record of 25 consecutive loops made that year.

The first woman to fly over the Andes between Chile and Argentina, Adrienne Bolland, did so on April 1,

FRANCE   Adrienne Bolland 1895-1975

1921. With aviation, she had found her path in life, saying "I became a different person in an airplane. I felt small, humble. Because on the ground, the truth is, I was totally insufferable." Called the Goddess of the Andes, in the Second World War, Bolland was a heroine of the Resistance.

No one in Des Moines, Iowa would take Phoebe Fairgrave seriously when she graduated from high school in 1920 and said that she wanted to learn to fly. Ten hours of flying lessons cost $500 then and the purchase of a used plane between $2,000 and $3,500. Renting hangar space on the airfield was $25 to $50 monthly — all beyond the means of a recent high school graduate. Her parents must have pointed out to Phoebe that aircraft were built by and for men, not young women. Brakes and starters were designed according to the reach of male hands and foot sizes, which made it difficult for small women to operate. The controls were unwieldly and to reach them, a girl would have to sit on pillows.

Undaunted, Phoebe cashed in a small legacy and bought her own aircraft. The only way she could pay for flying lessons and maintenance on her plane was by wing walking and making parachute jumps. Joining the Glenn Messer Flying Circus, she established a world's record for women on July 10, 1921, by jumping from 15,200 feet. Phoebe married her instructor, Vernon Omlie, and they continued to perform until they had saved enough money to start their own flying school and aviation business, Mid-South Airways in Memphis, Tenn.

Few girls were as fortunate as Ellen Church who could watch service men learning to fly from the airfield neighboring her father's farm in Cresco, Iowa. She was mesmerized by the wailing engines, the endless take-offs, and landings. Realizing there was little chance of employment in aviation, Church studied nursing at the University of Wisconsin but also took flying lessons to become a licensed pilot. Qualifying as a Registered Nurse in 1926, she moved to San Francisco where one day the Boeing Air Transport office caught her eye.

When teenage Eileen Vollick in Wiarton, Ontario wanted to learn how to fly, she was firmly rejected by the local flying club. "Each day" Eileen recalled, "as I drove my car past the aerodrome a small, still voice whispered, 'Go ahead, brave the lion in his den and make known your proposition to him.'" The Canadian government ruled that a woman could not be licensed until nineteen years of age (rather than seventeen as required of men) because maturity came later to women. The Superintendent of Air Regulations in Ottawa had gone on record as saying that women were physically and mentally unsuitable to be pilots. A national magazine conceded that a woman might be a capable pilot under normal circumstances, but "when it comes to meeting the unexpected, she is far more likely to lose her head."[24]

Finally accepted at the Hamilton, Ontario flying club, the nineteen-year-old Vollick proved to be a better pilot than the men in her class (although at 5' 1" she had to sit on pillows to see outside the cockpit). She would make history on March 13, 1928, when she took off from the frozen surface of Burlington Bay, Ontario to perform three three-point landings on the ice, passing her test to be the first Canadian female licensed pilot. *The Hamilton Spectator* would taint the historic event with petty sexism. "Wonder what the local girl who has received her aviation license would do if she found a mouse in the cockpit?"

Vollick became a barnstormer in the United States, before marrying and settling down in Elmhurst, NY. She is the only female in Canada to have an airport facility named for her — the passenger terminal at Wiarton-Keppel Airport, Ontario.

The pretty and petite teenager Ethel Dare transitioned easily from trapeze artist at the Barnum and Bailey

Circus to wing walker. She joined Myron "Fearless" Tinny's company where she was billed as the "1920 Aerial Sensation" and "The Flying Witch". The newspapers reported that when transferring between planes by rope ladder, the "winsome aviatrix first used her teeth, then hands, then elbows to climb the ladder." Her boss Myron Tinny was killed doing this stunt on September 7, 1920, at the Michigan State Fair before seventy thousand spectators who at first thought it was part of the act. The tragedy doubled next day ticket sales and Ethel did not disappoint the sell-out crowd, coolly performing the same plane transfer perfectly. Having cheated it so often, on November 15, 1924, she would misjudge the jump between planes and fall to her death.

Lillian Boyer was a waitress in a Chicago restaurant when two barnstormers offered to take her up for an airplane ride. Potential female wing walkers were sought after as they were lighter than men, did not drink as much, were paid less — and were sure to attract publicity. Boyer accepted and made her first flight on April 3, 1921. On her second flight, on April 7, she climbed out on the wing, beginning her career as an aerial exhibitionist. Lillian dazzled crowds at fairs in the United States and Canada, taking to the air in a Jenny piloted by First World War veteran Billy Brock — she admitted to being in love with him. The headlines named her: "The Girl of Nerve", "The Aerial Sensationalist, and "The Fair Devil of the Air" as Lillian hung from the lower wing by one hand or two, by her knees or her toes, and even stood fixed on the top wing while Brock looped the loop.

What pleased the crowds the most was her hanging by her teeth. Reminiscing years later, she called it, "'The Breakaway'. It was the surprise. When I'd leave the cockpit, I would take a strong thin cable with me and attach it to a strut." Her mouthpiece was on it, and Brock could reel in the cable from the cockpit. But the spectators, watching

from below, did not know that. "After I'd do a few things on the tip of the lower wing, I'd put the mouthpiece in and climb over the wing to the skid, do one thing and another and then hang there a minute and let go. The 'Ahs' and 'Ohs' would start. They thought I was falling. Then, the cable would go taut, and I'd hang here under the plane, do a spread eagle and other tricks. As long as my weight was on the cable, there was no way I could open my mouth. Then, Mr Brock would lower the ladder and I'd grab it, let go of the mouthpiece, and do a few more tricks on the way up."[25] When Brock died of cancer, Lillian gave up wing walking and worked as a hat check girl. She did not trust any other pilot for her tricks, she said. What finally killed her was old age: Lilian Boyer died at the age of eighty-five. The weaker sex? That's always been a joke.

As the balloon launches had been, barnstorming for women was a competition of one-upmanship. Falsely claiming she was Buffalo Bill Cody's niece, Mabel Cody perfected climbing from a speedboat or a car up to a plane. When she grabbed the last rung with one hand, the plane would dip, causing the crowd to cry out, as if her extra weight might cause it to crash. Then it would level out and she would head up the ladder accompanied by cheers.

Viewed from a century's distance, the 1920s seem to be a decade of vulgarity and violence, both lurking beneath the surface of unrestrained affluence. For the women who took to aviation, it was a time of liberating freedom from society's restrictions — and stomach-churning fear. The Curtiss Jenny, as placid as an old dog, taught hundreds to fly, but the unreliability its OX-5 engine (which had a habit of shattering in flight), also taught them, as one barnstormer recalled, to "pat your shoulder to make sure your angel was still there".

In the exuberance of the decade, barnstorming allowed young women to escape the suffocation of rural or small-town North America and Europe. Where else could they meet dashing pilots (as played by actor Robert Redford in the movie *The Great Waldo Pepper*) or attract journalists and Hollywood talent scouts? Where else did they have such freedom but in the sky? Nellie Zabel Willhite who refused to be hindered by her deafness, did balloon racing, making the sharp turns flying into balloons floating in the air. Gladys Ingle, the only female member of the "13 Black Cats" exhibition troupe, went one better by shooting arrows at a target on the top wing of a "Jenny". Gladys Roy who played tennis and danced the Charleston on a plane's top wing, would also star in the silent movie *The Fighting Ranger* in 1925. Posing for photos for a "Miss Ohio" beauty competition on August 15, 1927, Roy would jump down from the wing of her plane — to be killed by walking into the still spinning propeller.

People came to see Sex and Death and there were female barnstormers who could at least give them the former. They realized, (as the aeronaut Sophie Blanchard had), in a male world, it was fortune and men's eyes that mattered — that they would be noticed more for spectacle than their courage. Of Swedish descent, blonde and blue-eyed, Florence Klingensmith (below) was said, as male pilots observed, to "have the curves." When she leapt from a plane with a parachute or stood on its wing, she wore only a smile and a bathing suit.[26]

For twenty-one-year-old Helen Lach, parachute jumping at exhibitions was more exciting than waiting tables. Wearing a two-piece bathing suit and heels, she would obligingly pose for photographers on the wing of her plane. Interviewed by the press about her jumps, Helen gave them good copy, "I get a wonderful thrill as I sail down to earth from the clouds, or I wouldn't take such a chance."

Of all the female exhibition fliers who had butterfly-short lives, the saddest was the first. Laura Bromwell was killed on June 5, 1921, when at 1,000 feet, the engine on her borrowed Jenny cut out, sending her crashing into the ground at Mineola, where she had triumphantly looped-the-loop 199 times, a month before.

SEE JANE FLY

In the decade of flagpole sitters, bootlegger massacres and marathon dancers, the public felt they were entitled to even more dangerous thrills. They wanted airshows with heart-stopping, near-death experiences — as they saw in movies. In 1923 alone, there were 179 barnstorming accidents, in which 85 were killed and 126 injured. While this was a fraction compared with the thousands who died in car crashes that year, it reinforced the belief that aviation was too dangerous for commerce. Tabloids and news reels delighted in displaying the gory details of any air crash, their reporters usually the first on the scene. The glorious dream of flight killed men and women, novices, and experts equitably, and not only in barnstorming. Capt John Alcock, who had conquered the Atlantic, died on December 19, 1919, when he crashed in fog. Between 1918–1926, thirty-five pilots hired by the US Post Office Department were killed flying the mail across the United States. That he survived the "Suicide Club" as it was called, gave Charles Lindbergh his nickname "Lucky Lindy".

No wonder pilots were known to drink heavily. As the author Stella Murray wrote in 1929, a major consideration for employing women pilots was that they would drink less than men. They would also withstand cold altitudes better, the author thought, "because of years spent enduring chilly temperatures while dressed in wispy dresses."[27]

The competition for stunt flying were the "serial" silent movies. Cheaply churned out by directors like Mack Sennett and D.W. Griffith, they were affordable for the urban poor, particularly immigrant and African American audiences. With more exposure than the all-white suffragist movement, by demonstrating what the weaker sex could do — silent movies were a social phenomenon and the origin of our virtual world today. As in stunt flying, here too, there was flagrant discrimination against women and non-whites, unequal pay, no insurance, or safety standards, and to "keep the crew happy" sexual harassment was the norm.[28] But for many women, it was the only way into movies. Louis Gasnier who directed *The Exploits of Elaine* series commanded his scriptwriters, "Put the girl in danger" — and they did so, again and again.

Aerial stunt women who shattered gender roles were those like Mary Wiggins who flew her own planes, crashed cars, and rolled down staircases enough times until the director yelled "Cut!" During the Second World War, Wiggins would serve in the WASPs as a flight instructor. Tragically, for reasons known only to her, in December 1945, she would commit suicide in her backyard by shooting herself. Mary Wiggins played her last scene alone.

Seat belts and the cumbersome parachutes were scorned by female pilots and wing walkers alike. Not only was it considered "sissy" to use either, but they were a nuisance in the cramped cockpits, and as routines were done within sight and height of the audience in the bleachers, parachutes were of little use. The only safety device in stunt sequences was a wire tied to the plane's strut and the ankle of the performer. And even when parachutes were used, there was no guarantee they would work. Jumping from the plane her husband was flying, Ruth Garner plunged to her death on October 13, 1924, in Wichita, when her parachute failed to open.

The first woman to save herself with a parachute was the stunt jumper Irene McFarland. On June 28, 1925, during a routine aerial exhibition, her Thompson chute failed to detach and open when she jumped. Fortunately, she was wearing an emergency chute and was able to disentangle herself from the Thompson chute and drop safely. McFarland would become the first female member of the Caterpillar Club. Not until 1936 was wing walking below 1,500 feet forbidden by the Bureau of Air Commerce and stunt performers required to wear parachutes, whether it was part of their act or not. By then, the eyes of the world were on women navigating the oceans.

If it was hard for white women to break into aviation, it was almost impossible for Bessie Coleman. African American and indigenous, she refused to be defined by her sex, color or race and would be the first black woman in the United States to receive a pilot's license.

Bessie was born in Atlanta, Texas on January 16, 1892, her father George Coleman was part Choctaw Indian. With her birth, there were now six children living in the sharecropper's one room cabin and later there would be seven more. Bessie grew up in a violent era of American history. In the early 20th century, with Jim Crow laws, white supremacist riots and lynching, the Southern United States were in the midst of an orgy of extrajudicial racial killings. Bessie, barefoot and illiterate, picked cotton as a child, learning her numbers so that the white overseer would not cheat her family. Joining thousands of African Americans, the twenty-three-year-old left for the North as soon as she could, settling in Chicago in 1915. She survived the race riots in her neighborhood four years later, but 38 African Americans did not and 537 were injured.

Coleman's eureka moment came when her brother, who had served in France with the Illinois National Guard, teased her. According to Doris L. Rich in her biography *Queen Bess: Daredevil Aviator*, he talked about the superiority of women in France over those of Chicago's South Side. "I know something that French women do that you'll never do," he said "fly!"

Local flying schools turned her down because of her sex and/or skin color, but Bessie was determined to get a license. Robert S Abbott, the African American publisher of the *Chicago Defender*, advised her to go to France for flying lessons. Black American writers and artists like

Richard Wright, Josephine Baker and James Baldwin had found in France the freedom that they were denied in the United States. There would be less racism there, Abbott said, offering to sponsor her. She began taking French language lessons and on November 20, 1920, boarded the SS *Imperator* for France. Bessie learned to fly at Rouen, Normandy where in 1431 another feminist, Joan of Arc, had been burnt to death for heresy, for leading an army and wearing men's clothes.

Coleman completed the ten-month course requirements and on July 15, 1921, received her FAI pilot's license, the first ever awarded to an African American woman. Although news of the horrifying Tulsa massacre that summer by white mobs jealous of black success must have reached her, Bessie Coleman returned to the United States in August. For her first exhibition, at Garden City, Long Island, NY, on September 3, 1922, the Glenn Curtiss Company lent her one of its airplanes. "Beyond question, this event will be the greatest attraction ever staged in America," the *Chicago Defender* promised. She arranged a show that appealed to both white and black audiences by playing on American patriotism in general and on the promotion of African Americans in particular. She staged the show in honour of the now disbanded 15th New York Infantry, the first African American regiment sent to France during the First World War, which had been comprised primarily of jazz musicians and theatre practitioners. Former members of its band came together and played *The Star-Spangled Banner*, while Coleman, in breeches and a French military jacket with a Sam Brown belt, went up twice, the *Chicago Defender* reported "to the delight of the hundreds of enthusiasts of both races."

Her skin color, which had prevented her from getting flying lessons, now became her drawing card. In 1925, a US Army War College report decided that African Americans "a sub-species of the human family that performed poorly as soldiers due to their cowardly, subservient, superstitious, amoral and mentally inferior nature" were unfit to fly. To see one — and a woman at that, doing so, attracted audiences. But to gain any credibility as a black female, Coleman had to walk a fine line. She had to earn the respect of the African American community but simultaneously not displease white aviation backers and media. She organized her shows to appeal to both black and white audiences, signing contracts with white managers only if African Americans were allowed to attend the show. "The air is the only place free from prejudices," she said. Coleman also lectured at black theaters and gave interviews. She told a reporter that as "Queen Bess", her greatest ambition was to make "Uncle Tom's cabin into a hangar for a flying school for African Americans."

When the Orlando Chamber of Commerce, Florida hired her to perform for a real estate convention, she discovered that African Americans would not be allowed to attend as they required a special pass to be out after dark.[29] Not only did Bessie threaten to cancel the show but when the Chamber rescinded, she dropped anti-segregation leaflets from her plane. Using borrowed aircraft, she performed throughout the South, including her hometown of Waxahachie — always drawing large crowds of the curious, both black and white, who at a time when it was thought that black women were incapable of driving cars, wanted to see if one could actually fly an aircraft.

Bessie wrote few letters and posed for fewer photos, and always aware of the times she lived in, kept her personal life private. As an aviator, she was a threat to whites who cherished their racial superiority in aviation, and as a female pilot, she threatened the ego of black males. Her marriage to Claude Glenn, one of her brother's friends, in 1917, was kept so secret that not even her close family members knew. Known to have had lovers black and white, at a time when many states prohibited miscegenation and interracial sexual relations, she ensured that no one knew.

As with all females in aviation, the media played a major part in Coleman's career — but with a difference. The femininity of white female pilots was emphasized in the press by calling them "lady fliers", "angels", "sweethearts of the air" or "flying flappers". When they did notice her at all, white newspapers made pointed references to Coleman's racialized identity and not her femininity. White female fliers marketed breakfast cereal, clothing, cigarettes, and cars. The only marketing that Bessie Coleman could get was posing with a huge tire as the "Business Booster" for the Coat Tire and Rubber Company. Marginalized, African Americans had little buying power so why publicize her attributes? Headlines such as "First Colored Aviatrix", "Negress an Air Pilot", "Colored Woman a Licensed Pilot" or "Negro Aviatrix Arrives" were enough.

Perhaps because of this, Coleman could not attract sponsors like aircraft distributors, clothing companies or even an aviation philanthropist like Vincent Bendix to expand her activities. In the mainstream media of the day, marketers and passengers linked "whiteness" to the modernity of aviation and African Americans to their servility on the railways and minstrel shows. Being white, W E Du Bois wrote, gave workers a psychological advantage of racial superiority. White pilots and stewardesses did what racial stereotypes would not allow black males and females to do: signal to fearful passengers that they were safely in the hands of those who understood this new technology.[30]

Bessie planned on retiring from barnstorming in April 1926 to open a flying school for African Americans, needing a plane to do so. As no one would sell her one in Florida, with $500 from Edwin Beeman whose family owned Beeman Chewing Gum, she bought her first aircraft, a well-used Jenny from a company in Dallas. The Negro Welfare League was counting on her to appear at May Day celebrations in Orlando. It was delivered to Jacksonville by William Willis who warned her that because of its poor condition, he had to make two emergency stops on the way. At 7:15 am, on April 30, 1926, at Paxon Field, Jacksonville, Willis took Coleman up for a test flight. When he put the plane into a dive at about 3,000 feet, it suddenly flipped over. Bessie, who had neither fastened her seat belt nor worn a parachute, was thrown from it, and fell to her death. Willis, who had his seat belt on, survived the plane crash only to be trapped in the wreckage. When a spark from an onlooker's cigarette ignited the petrol fumes, he burned to death.[31]

Five thousand mourners attended a memorial service for Bessie in Orlando and an estimated 15,000 people paid their respects in Chicago. Since 1931, each year, on April 30th, the Challenger Pilots' Association of Chicago fly over her grave at Lincoln Cemetery.

Also from South Side Chicago (where Michelle Robinson Obama grew up) in 1992, Mae Jemison was the first African American woman to go into Space. She wrote, "I wished I had known her while I was growing up, but then again I think she was with me all the time." In one way Coleman was indeed with her when she left the Earth. Jemison carried her picture into Space, flying far higher than the little girl picking cotton in Waxahachie had ever dreamed. The US Postal Service issued a "Bessie Coleman" stamp in 1995, commemorating "her singular accomplishment in becoming the world's first African American pilot and, by definition, an American legend."

Aviation was as much all white as it was all male. African Americans were dissuaded from flying or finding employment in aviation — a resumé that had black flying schools or Tuskegee University credentials in it disclosed the applicant as non-white. The Civil Aeronautics Act of 1938 prohibited discrimination of airline passengers on the basis of their race, but it could not help Africans Americans competing with white men for jobs.

Janet Waterford Bragg encountered discrimination because of her sex and skin color, the latter by those who should have accepted her. Through the 1930s, Janet worked as a nurse in several hospitals to afford flying  lessons and helped found the Challenger Air Pilot's Association.[32] In the spring of 1934 with 35 solo hours, Bragg passed the test for her private pilot's license. She passed the flight test for her commercial license but was denied it, encountering sexism at the Tuskegee black pilot training school. In 1943, when Bragg finally received her commercial license, she tried to join the WASPs. Ethel Sheeny, Jackie Cochran's assistant refused her an interview and a few weeks later Cochran sent her a rejection letter. Like Mildred Hemmons Carter, another qualified African American female pilot, Janet was turned down because of her skin color.[33]

It was difficult enough for Jackie Cochran to fight one prejudice without taking on two. Employing so many black women in her Washington office that it was called "Little Harlem", she was adamant about not allowing black female pilots into the WASPs. Scrutinized by bigots and the media, Jackie decided that she wasn't going to challenge the status quo. "I'm having enough troubles," she said, "without adding blacks to it." The women were training in the South, and integration in "Whites Only" towns would have posed too many problems for her.[34]

Besides, it had been impossible for black pilots to ferry aircraft when many American airports, especially in the South, were segregated and would remain so until the 1960s. Integration was achieved only because airports depended upon the funds they received through the Federal Aid Airport Program (FAAP), which was earmarked only for integrated airports.

In 1939, Chicagoan Willa Brown became the first African American woman to receive her commercial pilot's license. By now, with hostilities in Europe and the Far East, the government realized that it had a serious shortage of experienced pilots and Brown won grudging approval to open a flying school for African Americans on Chicago's South Side. The purpose of the Coffey School of Aeronautics, the "Chicago Tribune" reported, was to test whether (contrary to the 1925 US. Army study) African Americans were really fit to fly. The school trained two of the initial ten pilots and fifteen mechanics for the 99th Pursuit Squadron, better known as the Tuskegee Airmen.

If barnstorming demonstrated that flying was lethal, female pilots by their sexuality made it into a commercial industry. Advertisers realized that a woman — be she a housewife, movie star or wing walker — if photographed next to a plane, drew attention. Beginning in 1922, women were allowed to compete for the first time in the Olympic Games — in croquet and tennis, sports that were compatible with their femininity and fragility. Manufacturers paid well for product endorsements from well-known athletes — and female pilots. After her English Channel crossing, Harriet Quimby was hired by Vin Fizz as its spokesperson — replacing Calbraith Perry Rogers who had just been killed when his aircraft hit a flock of birds. Elinor Smith, the stunt pilot who, at sixteen, was the youngest ever to receive her license was the first woman to be featured on a "Wheaties" cereal box. Kendall Oil published testimonial letters from Phoebe Fairgrave Omlie, and Kinner Sport Aircraft took out full page ads that said: "Read what Miss Earhart has to say after flying a Kinner Airster." At the height of her fame, Earhart endorsed cars, airlines, luggage and trunks, chocolate bars, malted milk, tomato juice, collector cards and the Longines watch.[35]

But endorsements could backfire as it did with Amelia Earhart and cigarettes. Although she did not smoke, Amelia became the face of Lucky Strike cigarettes. After her historic transatlantic flight in 1928, Lucky Strike ads debuted, claiming she smoked their brand "all the way from Trepassey to Wales to lessen the strain." Earhart was angry at this, but George Putnam saw an angle. She agreed to a rewritten endorsement: "Lucky Strike were the cigarettes carried on the *Friendship* when I crossed the Atlantic." She then donated the $1,500 the tobacco company had paid her to Commander Byrd for his Antarctic expedition — Putnam ensuring the media heard about her generosity.

Before hundreds of spectators at Vero Beach, Florida, on April 18, 1926, twenty-four-year-old Jewell Bell fell off the bottom wing of a Jenny and died — her death ending the Wild West days of wing walkers and barnstormers. On May 20, the United States government began regulating the industry with the Air Commerce Act. Whether it was the lobbying of the fledgling airlines who wanted to prove that travelling by air was safe or the carnage at airshows, oversight by Washington was long overdue.[36] In France, pilots had been required to be licensed since 1909, in Britain since 1919 and in Canada a year later.

The first woman in the United States to earn a pilot's license from the Department of Commerce (Aeronautics Branch) was Phoebe Fairgrave Omlie who received Transport License No. 199 on June 30, 1927. She would also be the first woman appointed to a federal aviation post when, from 1933 until 1936, she served as special assistant for air intelligence with the National Advisory Committee for Aeronautics (the predecessor to NASA). With the war, in 1941, Omlie would develop a program for training women flight instructors and under her supervision, the Tennessee Bureau of Aeronautics opened a special school, funded by revenues from the state's aviation gasoline tax.

The United States was not alone in its restraint of licensing female pilots. Hilda Hope McMaugh took flying lessons in Britain in 1919, becoming the first Australian female licensed pilot but she was unable to fly in her own country. Women were, however, allowed glider pilot licenses in Australia as early as 1909 when Florence Taylor was awarded one.

As soon as she was allowed to do so in Australia, Millicent Maude Bryant became the first woman to earn a pilot's license, at Mascot, Sydney on March 23, 1927. The forty-nine-year-old separated mother of three was a pioneer in more than aviation. An excellent horsewoman, Bryant was one of Australia's early female motorists, a business entrepreneur and property developer. Her accomplishments in aviation were sadly cut short on November 3rd that year when the Sydney ferry Bryant was on collided with a steamer and she drowned.

In 1935, Nancy-Bird Walton became the first woman in Australia to get a commercial license. She began flying lessons at Charles Kingsford Smith's flying school on August 11, 1933, and got an "A" license by September 27. But she had to wait until she was 19 years of age and had 200 solo flying hours before she could sit for the transport license.

Nancy was fortunate to get a job in the 1930s, let alone in flying. The Far West Children's Health Scheme hired her to fly nurses around the outback to help mothers and babies — the first time a female pilot had worked commercially in Australia. She operated her own aerial ambulance service, navigating with a watch and a compass, following road maps because there were no aviation maps. She often asked people on the ground to drive a truck over a prospective landing strip ahead of her so she could judge the wind, and make sure there were no stumps in the way. Once, the stench of a dead horse was powerful enough to reach 450 metres above ground, telling her she was on course for Cunnamulla, Queensland. The title of her autobiography *My God, It's A Woman!* was the response of a shocked grazier, trapped on an outback property, when told that the pilot flying to his rescue was called Nancy. Not for nothing was Nancy-Bird Walton known as "The Angel of the Outback." In 2019, the Australian government decided that the Western Sydney Airport would be named Nancy-Bird Walton International Airport.

As British boys would devour Capt W E John's "Biggles" series well into the twentieth century, the generation of American boys growing up between the wars, had no doubt that aviation — like crossing the Sahara or hunting big game or any adventure — was theirs exclusively. Eddie

Rickenbacker and Jimmy Doolittle's exploits filled their comic books — and imaginations. At Saturday matinees, they thrilled at *The Perils of Pauline*, silent movie serials in which actress Pearl White (who had grown up as a bareback rider in a circus) was constantly having to be rescued by the leading man from speeding trains, torture-loving Mexican bandits, logjams, and edges of cliffs.

Charles Amory Beach's books for American boys then had a well-defined theme, typically: "Two chums learn how to fly, then journey to France and tender their services to the Lafayette Escadrille. In thrilling scenes on the battle front, the chums unmask a traitor and then rescue a pretty girl (is there any other kind?) from her dastardly German uncle." In movies, books and magazines, the culture was driven by the helpless damsel-in-distress narrative (never were men rescued by women) with repercussions for generations of men and women after.

A girl on the other hand, had to wait like the sleeping princesses in fairy tales, for a handsome prince to awaken her, her life fulfilled only when he kissed her.[37] The popular culture of the day didn't help. The female characters were only there to cheer the men on or scold them for their mischief. William Wellman's classic *Wings* in 1927 (in which Clara Bow goes to wartime France as an ambulance driver to find her hometown boyfriend) and Howard Hughes's *Hell's Angels* in 1930 (with Jean Harlow informing the hero that "she is not that innocent ...") reinforced the trite image that there were only two types of women — the mothering angel and the slut.

The only woman above universal reproach was chemistry teacher Evangeline Lindbergh. After her son's triumph in 1927, she was lauded as the epitome of "air minded" motherhood. While later events would prove the canonization of her son precipitate, Charles was seen as a farm boy, portraying clean cut masculinity, his only love his aircraft. Evangeline had even travelled with him when he barnstormed across the mid-West. Combining a career of teaching science with motherhood, she was an example to women everywhere. In 1928, the National Education Association unanimously awarded Evangeline Lindbergh honorary lifetime membership to their organization.

In the heady prosperity of the decade, flying was a recreational pastime — like owning a sailboat, racehorse, or a sports car and it did not take aircraft salesmen long to figure out that shaming male customers would sell planes. If women — mechanically inept, frivolous, and scatterbrained as they were thought to be — were shown operating a plane easily and safely, it obviously required little strength or brain power to do so. Advertisements aimed at private aircraft buyers headlined "So Easy that Even a Woman Can Fly It." "Petticoat pilots" were ideal to sell planes to potential male customers, demonstrating their simplicity of control and safety in flight. On demonstration flights, the male customers would force

the plane into harrowing situations to prove themselves and reaffirm their masculinity, with the poor saleswoman having to regain control.[38]

"Nothing impresses the safety of aviation on the public quite so much as to see a woman flying an airplane." Louise Thaden ruefully commented. "If a woman can handle it, the public thinks it must be duck soup for men."

4: THERE'S MORE TO LIFE THAN BEING A PASSENGER

In the Roaring Twenties, at a time when women's ambition was met with anxiety and contradiction (more so than today), a record number of trail-blazing aviatrixes appeared. As little girls, clutching umbrellas, they had jumped off the roof of barns, or been daredevils on snow sleds. For Elinor Smith, propped up on pillows in the cockpit, flying lessons began at age seven. As teenagers, they ignored the social norms of the day as Evelyn "Bobbi" Trout did when her Aunt Edna admonished, "Young ladies of good families do not fly airplanes."

In the madness of the decade, the cast of characters who consciously or unconsciously advocated feminism in aviation included Ruth Nichols, Amelia Earhart, Ila Fox, Laura Ingalls, Elinor Smith, Louise Thaden, Florence Klingensmith, Anne Morrow Lindbergh, Evelyn "Bobbi" Trout, Helen Richey, Viola Gentry, Jessie Maude Keith-Miller, Mary von Mach, Florence Lowe "Pancho" Barnes, Marvel Crosson, Thea Rasche, Gladys O'Donnell, Blanche Noyes and Frances Marsalis — all wanting to show the world that as Klingensmith said, "A woman can handle one of these things as well as men."

With rare exception, female aviators were unmarried. Remaining single was empowering for many and a lot of them chose to be so. Besides its danger, aviation was a jealous lover that demanded autonomy and once a woman married, she lost her rights to sign a contract, to own property, to sue — in effect to live by her own moral compass.

All the women came of age in a rich and transitional period in the history of aviation, as it evolved from barnstorming into the business of commercial airlines. On its fringe, they were excluded from being military, commercial or racing pilots, leaving only the suicidal challenge of attempting the oceans on either side of the American continent.

Then as F Scott Fitzgerald wrote: "In the spring of '27, something bright and alien flashed across the sky … and for a moment people set down their glasses in country clubs and speak-easies and thought of their old best dreams."

At 10:24 pm. on May 21, the *Spirit of St Louis* landed at Le Bourget Airport, Paris — having flown 3,614 miles from New York, non-stop, in thirty-three hours, thirty minutes, and thirty seconds. In that moment, everything changed — for the ex-airmail pilot, for flying and for the planet. Interest and confidence in aviation soared — Tin Pan Alley was quick off the mark with: *Lucky Lindy! Up in the Sky.*

Thirteen-year-old Nancy Harkness Love (overleaf) was actually at Le Bourget Airport to witness the *Spirit of St Louis* touching down. Three years later, she earned her pilot's license. By 1937, she was competing in air races and working as a test pilot, helping to develop the first tricycle landing gear. During the Second World War, Harkness Love and Jackie Cochran formed what became the Women Airforce Service Pilots (WASP) to ferry aircraft from factories to bases.

Even before Lindbergh's flight, radio, radiographs, and the Bartlane Cable Process could transmit images and voices around the world within seconds. Movies had just mastered the synchronization of sound, allowing historic events

to be seen world-wide, almost instantaneously. With the new technology, the celebrity industry exploded, becoming the century's religion, even crucifying the aviator gods like Lindbergh that it created.

In his best-known work, *The Great Gatsby*, Fitzgerald would explore the slippery ties between the very wealthy and those who hovered, and generally died, in their money's glare. With the noblest of intentions, these men put up prize money in aviation that attracted the hopeful and the desperate of both sexes to attempt oceans and/or win air races. When Lindbergh landed at Le Bourget, Raymond Orteig, then in the south of France, rushed to Paris to award him the prize of $25,000. The Orteig Prize had been created by the French American hotelier in 1919 as an incentive for the first person(s) who could perform a non-stop flight between New York and Paris, either way. In attempts to claim it, aviators more experienced than Lindbergh had failed — some fatally — Stanton Hall Wooster, Noel Guy, René Paul Fonck, Philip Payne, Richard E. Byrd, James DeWitt Hill, Lloyd Bertaud and in the first East-West crossing, Charles Nungesser, and Francois Coli. Handing over the cheque on June 16, Orteig was said to have been relieved that no one would die trying to fly across the Atlantic anymore. Aircraft of the day did not have the power to carry the necessary fuel, radios were too weak and too heavy, radio navigation was in its infancy and the unpredictability of the ocean's weather made it close to impossible.

If so many men and women attempted to emulate Lindbergh, one wanted to be the next Orteig. Immediately after Lindbergh's flight, Hawaii pineapple millionaire, James D Dole, put up $35,000 in prizes for the first civilian pilots to make the Pacific crossing. The 2,400-mile distance between San Francisco and Hawaii was 1,200 miles less than Lindbergh's flight to Paris (although the distance over water was 600 miles farther) and Dole hoped that Lindbergh himself would enter the Derby. "The Lone Eagle" was then on his goodwill tour sponsored by Harry Guggenheim, visiting 48 states, and 82 cities (including my hometown, Ottawa, which named its new airport after him).

The Children's Crusade of 1212 was a misguided adventure by innocents with heartbreaking results, but what occurred in the mad summer of 1927 was no less tragic. On the foggy morning of August 16, before an estimated crowd of 75,000 people at Oakland Airport, San Francisco, eight aircraft were lined up in a semicircle at the 7,020 feet long runway — the longest in the world then and built in just 21 days to meet the start of the Dole race. Fifteen men and one woman were going to brave the Pacific Ocean and attempt to find the island of Oahu which was 2,410 miles away.[39] Before the race even began, three aircraft had crashed, resulting in three deaths. What buoyed everyone with false hope was that Lt Albert Hegenberger and Lt L Maitland had successfully flown from this very airport to Honolulu on June 28/29 in the Fokker C-2 *Bird of Paradise*.

Mildred Doran was a spirited twenty-two-year-old schoolteacher in Flint, Michigan. Her mother had died when she was 14 and Mildred spent her youth bringing up her large family by herself. When she heard that Lindbergh had flown the Atlantic, she innocently mentioned (as many must have that year), that she wanted to be the first woman to fly across the Pacific Ocean. And why not? The hit song of the day was "I'll fly to Hawaii. Someone's calling me. My heart's on fire. I'll fly 'cross the sea." In Mildred's case, it was exactly what family friend Bill Malloska wanted to hear. The former carnival owner realized the publicity that a woman with Doran's good looks and personality crossing the Pacific Ocean would bring to his company, Lincoln Oils. He bought a locally made Buhl Airsedan CA-5, christened it *Miss Doran* and had large Lincoln Oils logos painted on both sides. Two flying circus pilots, Slonnie Sloniger and Augie Pedlar, neither of whom had experience in long distance flying, were hired. With navigator Manley Lawing (later replaced by V P Knope), and Mildred as passenger, the four took off from Flint for Oakland. Along the way, engine trouble forced them to make an emergency landing at Mendota in the San Joaquin valley. "The Flying Schoolmarm" attracted so much media attention that Hollywood starlets begged the other Dole Derby entrants to let them fly with them as well.

The wisdom of the day questioned a woman doing this, even as a passenger. Mildred shrugged it off, saying "A woman should fly just as easily as a man … Women certainly have the courage and tenacity required for long flights."[40]

Three of the aircraft were so overloaded with fuel that they couldn't take off, but one of the remaining five that did was *Miss Doran*. The Airsedan returned 12 minutes later with a misfiring engine. As the only damsel in distress in the race, Mildred instantly attracted the media's attention. Augie was heard to plead with her to stay behind as the danger that it would happen again

was too great. She would have none of it. Teary-eyed and angry, she reacted to the reporters' questions, "Scared? Frightened? I should say not. If they force us down seven times, I'll go up again the eighth." As she had told the *Flint Journal*, "Life is nothing but a chance." And this was Mildred's.

Miss Doran took to the air once more and was sighted passing the Farallon Islands. As it had no radio, no one heard from its crew after that, and it was never seen again. For months after, bits of aircraft and bodies thought to be from the Derby washed up on Hawaiian and California shores. The Dole Derby cost the lives of eleven aviators, one of whom was "The Flying Schoolmarm."

In 1927–28 why did so many women run towards almost certain death in aviation? Was it the spiraling stock market? (Or that no one had had a stiff drink for years?) Susan Butler, whose mother was a pioneering pilot, recounted this era in *East to the Dawn: The Life of Amelia Earhart* (1997). Flying, she wrote, was still a magical experience for everyone. "To women, though, flying was something more. Still hemmed in by all sorts of restrictions, still valued for looks and decorative skills, still steered toward passive accomplishments, for women it was the ultimate escape: total freedom, total mastery — no interference. Total liberation. Women who became pilots won something additional along the way: respect." This was especially true for marginalized women who, in their lifetimes, had experienced none of that.

At a time when "westerns" teemed with racist images of "merciless Indian savages," (as in the words of the Declaration of Independence), Eula "Pearl" Carter Scott, half Chickasaw and half Choctaw, became the second indigenous female to earn a pilot's license. She was taught by Wiley Post who was just beginning his aviation career and in 1929, the thirteen-year-old Eula became the world's youngest pilot. She married at sixteen and soon with two children, left aviation to become a social activist. Eula Carter Scott served as a Chickasaw Nation legislator and later was a charter member of the Smithsonian's National Museum of the American Indian.[41]

Mary Riddle of the Clatsop and Quinault tribes was the third indigenous woman to earn a pilot's license. Her cries at birth reminded her grandmother of the kingfisher's call that she was named "Kus-de-cha" after the bird. As a seventeen-year-old while visiting San Diego, Mary saw a woman crash to her death in an airplane and the consensus that women would never be pilots prompted her to prove that they could. Riddle earned her private pilot's license at the Tex Rankin School of Flying in

Portland, Oregon. Rankin would teach James Stewart, Errol Flynn, and Edgar Bergen to fly as well as Dorothy Hester, the first woman to pull off the difficult airborne maneuver known as the "outside loop". Mary soloed on May 19, 1930, appearing at the Portland Rose Festival in tribal costume, riding a horse up to her plane.

She attracted nationwide attention when she announced her plans for a transcontinental flight to deliver gifts from Native American tribes in the Pacific Northwest to President Herbert Hoover in Washington, DC. With the Depression, this did not occur, and Mary became a stunt parachutist. In 1937, when her parachute failed to open correctly, she was injured in the fall and retired from aviation.

Rankin would also teach Leah Hing, the first Chinese American woman to fly. At a time when the Chinese Exclusion Act was still in force and discriminatory practices like banning Chinese children from public schools were in effect, a newspaper photograph of Lee Hing in aviator headgear shaking hands with Rankin under the headline "Chinese Girl Flying Pupil Quick to Acquire Knack" was historic. Called the "Chinese Miss Lindy," Hing's ambition was to go to China to fight the Japanese. Unfortunately, the Chinese Air Force (as with all other air forces), did not allow women to fly. Unable to join Portland's Aero Club, a social club for private pilots and aviation enthusiasts, because she was Chinese, she worked there until she retired as a "hat check girl".

On August 31,1927, the newspapers reported "British Fliers Over the Atlantic Ocean Enroute to Canada", and it looked as if the first woman to succeed would be a *grande dame* socialite. She and her two pilots were competing for the London to London, Ontario prize of $25,000 offered by the Carling Brewery of London, Ontario.

Princess Anne of Löwenstein-Wertheim-Freudenberg was a British widow whose German husband had died in the Philippines, fighting for the Spanish. "The Flying Princess", even at sixty-three years of age, Anne was no stranger to aviation, having already flown with Capt Leslie Hamilton, a stunt flier known as "The Flying Gypsy" in the King's Cup.

Unknown to her family, Anne financially backed Capt Hamilton and Col Frederick Minchin for an East-West crossing, this time to Canada, provided they secretly took her along as a passenger. A former air ace in the Royal Flying Corps, the thirty-seven-year-old Minchin was an Imperial Airways pilot who in 1924 had surveyed the air route from Britain to India. As the second son of an Anglo-Irish noble family, on his father's recent death, he could not inherit the estate in Ireland and "allowed himself to be cheated by rich and unscrupulous friends, took the blame in a messy divorce, and was, for a time, reduced to penury and declared bankrupt."[42]

In *The Razor's Edge*, W Somerset Maughan would write of a First World War pilot trying to find meaning in his life while coping with the devastating effects of post-war trauma. Minchin had been arrested at Croydon Airport, having been drunk "while in charge of a motor-car." Police Inspector Burke said he found the colonel at midnight, stooping by his car (we've all been there). "His behavior throughout" added the inspector, "was that of a gentleman." The chairman, in dismissing the case on payment of costs, said that as the colonel was not driving at the time, there had been no danger to anyone.

On the day of their flight from Uphavon airfield, Wiltshire, the princess told her long-suffering family that she was only going to cheer Minchin and Hamilton on, promising not to be flying with them. Disbelieving her, they put a watch on her home and local inns, to no avail. When she suddenly appeared at the airfield and, it was noted, dressed for flying, the princess explained that she was wearing royal purple to demonstrate what style of clothing women should wear on a transatlantic flight. Her wardrobe consisted of purple leather knee-breeches, a matching jacket, a black crush hat, black silk stockings, and high-heeled fur-lined boots. The rumor was that the princess was also carrying $200,000 worth of jewelry to sell in the United States. Anne posed before the blue Fokker F.VII she had bought and then dramatically discarded her coat and stepped into its cabin where a wicker chair had been prepared for her.

With Minchin at the controls, the aircraft lumbered off, fighting strong headwinds, narrowly missing a hangar at the end of the airfield. It was seen plodding slowly over Ireland — proof that the headwinds were in the Atlantic — but without a radio, no one heard from the three again.[43] Princess Anne of Löwenstein-

Wertheim-Freudenberg would be the first woman to die attempting to fly the Atlantic. Those who knew Minchin were dumbfounded that such an experienced aviator had attempted such lunacy. Perhaps, like the Irish airman he was, Frederick Minchin had foreseen his own death.

A week later, on September 7, *Sir John Carling*, a Stinson Detroiter sponsored by the same Canadian brewery and flown by Terrence Tully and navigator James V Medcalf, two ex-Ontario Provincial Air Service pilots, disappeared after refueling at Harbour Grace, Newfoundland. The same day, *Old Glory*, a Fokker sponsored by Randolph Hearst with the best crew he could hire, left Old Orchard Beach, Maine and also vanished. With aviators killing themselves almost daily, the Canadian and United States governments were called on by the public to forbid more flights. The US Weather Bureau stopped issuing its Atlantic forecasts on October 8, the official explanation was for budgetary reasons, but everyone knew that without them, it would be suicide to attempt such a flight.

They reckoned without four women: their ignorance of the dangers involved, surpassed only by their vanity. The oceanic expanse between Cape Chidley, Labrador and the Blasket Islands, County Kerry had swallowed the city of Atlantis, countless seafarers, and ships, and most recently the unsinkable *Titanic*. It was not for science, or money that the four women wanted to risk their lives (and those of their crews), but in the unbridled hedonism of the Jazz Age, for fame. Despite the approaching winter storms, for the first of their sex to conquer the North Atlantic, even as a passenger, meant instant stardom.

There were two pairs of contenders in the grip of this suicidal obsession. Used to being chauffeured about were wealthy matrons Mabel Boll of New York and Amy Phipps Guest of Philadelphia — each wanting to snatch the attention that such a flight would bestow on the other. Ruth Elder and Frances W Grayson on the other hand were out to prove as Grayson said, that they were no longer "little nobodies".

The divorced Frances W Grayson was a serious feminist who had convinced a Danish woman, Aage Ancker, to invest $40,000 in the purchase of a S-36 amphibian, the second one that Igor Sikorsky would build. Now she was looking for a female pilot and navigator — it was to be a feminist flight. The ultimate connection between feminism and flying was soaring above an ocean without regulations telling her what she could or could not do. At thirty-five years, Francis was older than the other aviatrixes and plain and severe with a toothy smile, the media dubbed her "The Flying Matron."

Her opposite was beauty contest winner Ruth Elder. The daughter of a farm laborer. As soon as she could, Ruth escaped her hometown of Anniston, Alabama and worked her way up from modelling lingerie to becoming a dental assistant in the real estate boom town of Lakeland, Florida. "I want to do something that will make people notice me," she would say.

Elder's second husband, Lyle Womack, a former professional boxer and lion tamer, somehow convinced enough "snowbird" millionaires in Florida and West Virginia that his young wife could fly the Atlantic to be "Lady Lindbergh". The backers put up $35,000 for an orange Stinson Detroiter and Elder was taught to fly by the barnstormer Captain George Haldeman, who was also persuaded to go with her on the flight. Marketed as "America's Aviation Sweetheart", Ruth's soft Alabama drawl and her femininity won over the public with women copying her signature gypsy scarf. On landing at Roosevelt Field from Florida, she must have felt like she had fallen down the proverbial rabbit's hole. Elder posed for a voracious New York press and met their questions with flirtatious non-feminist answers, "Why did she want to go to Paris?" "For the dresses they had there of course, and to get all dolled up".

91

It is a truism in the science of advertising, as airlines would demand of their stewardesses, that married women are less marketable than unmarried ones — who supposedly are naïve, available, and virginal. The Stinson had been christened not *Mrs Lyle Womack* but *American Girl*, invoking the image of the desirable, single girl next door. And there in lay the rub. At twenty-three, Ruth had already been married twice. Ill advisedly, she announced to reporters that to be single once more, she was in the process of divorcing Womack. This was akin to throwing bait to sharks and rather than flying the Atlantic — which they assumed was never going to happen — they hounded her about her marital issues. Ruth wept prettily, and with a naïveté that demonstrated her ignorance of the press, asked for their understanding and sympathy.

Everyone that she might have looked to for support now began to bail: the backers who, after the Dole disaster, were wary of her success, and the husband who discovered that he was to be divorced through the national media. Lindbergh, who had flown the ocean for $25,000 now piously said he was opposed to such flights being conducted for "publicity purposes", Eddie Stinson, who had built Elder's plane, and even Ruth's mother (reporters were quick to search her out) who had sent her the family Bible, begged her not to go. With the encroaching winter, Elder and Haldeman were advised wait it out until 1928. Only the fear that Grayson or Mabel Boll might beat them to it kept them at Roosevelt Field.

When J J Lanning, the owner of Roosevelt Field, ruled that anyone using his premises to fly the Atlantic now had to have a multi-engine amphibian with a radio and navigator, Grayson qualified — but Elder did not. Ruth knew what to do, having charmed obdurate men before. She had a private meeting with Lanning — and the next day the restrictions were dropped.

The summer of 1927 was an opportune time to be a

celebrity in New York, still dazed by the riots that the late Rudolph Valentino's mourners had caused. The city has always loved its "characters" and its mayor, the flamboyant "Gentleman Jimmy Walker" was that. His critics claimed that he was running the five boroughs from a casino in Central Park, but "Beau James" (known for his dapper suits) knew what New Yorkers wanted. Besides keeping the price of subway tokens at 25 cents, to distract from municipal corruption and his affection for speakeasies and chorus girls, Walker lived by Oscar Wilde's advice that nothing succeeds like excess.

That summer, he had staged lavish ticker tape parades through Manhattan's "Canyon of Heroes" for Lindbergh, Cdr Richard Byrd, Clarence Chamberlin and Charles A Levine. As the first female flier, Elder could see herself in a ticker tape blizzard of a parade on her triumphant return. With "The Lone Eagle" even then drowning in offers (marriage and movie), book deals, speaking tours, sponsorships, and seats on company boards, for a small-town girl who said that she had been nowhere, it was Elder's one chance at the golden ring. Attempting the Atlantic and possible death, or returning to Lakeland to forever be a dental assistant and married to Womack, was a fate worse than ... She was determined to go.

Frances Grayson on the other hand was methodical in preparation. She monitored the building of the Sikorsky amphibian and christened it *Dawn* for the birth of feminism in Aviation. The logic for such an aircraft was inescapable — if there was trouble, it could land on water and wait to be rescued. Unable to find a female crew, she hired Wilmer "Wild Bill" Stultz as pilot. When the Gates Flying Circus arrived in New York in 1925, Stultz had flown through the canyons between skyscrapers, creating a name for his fearlessness. The other crew she hired were Frank Koehler, an expert on engines and radio operator/navigator Brice "Goldy" Goldsborough who had calibrated the compass on the *Spirit of St Louis* for Lindbergh. Although the point was to demonstrate that a woman could do anything Lindbergh could, Grayson would fly only as a passenger but with the rank of "Commander". Tired of competing for attention with Elder's coquettish charm, Grayson, who had all the appeal of a wet weekend, left Roosevelt Field for the jumping off point of Old Orchard Beach, Maine.

There began several attempts by her to take off into the Atlantic. Each time, they were thwarted by the weather. On October 10, the Sikorsky refused to climb above it because of a strong headwind and "Wild Bill" contrary to his name, wisely returned to the beach. Like many pilots of the day, Stultz was known to drink, and Grayson feared that the waiting for better weather was having an adverse effect on his nerves.

Hearing that Grayson was in the air, despite equally poor weather at Roosevelt Field, Elder and Haldeman took off the next day. The reporters who continued to treat the young woman as a joke, duly reported that she was carrying a complete vanity case, and when asked why, Ruth was quoted as saying: "I want to get out of the plane at Le Bourget as cool and neat as I did at the start. Surely, I'll powder my nose whenever I feel like it — flying or not flying." It was femininity not feminism that Elder represented and whether she succeeded or more likely disappeared into the Atlantic, the press had their story.

Oil troubles forced them to ditch after 2,623 miles and, spotting a Dutch tanker, Haldeman (who unlike Lindbergh, had sensibly chosen to fly along the shipping routes), ditched by it. The pair climbed out on a wing from which a lifeboat rescued them while *American Girl* caught fire and disappeared beneath the waves. The Azores was still 360 miles away, but it was the longest non-stop flight until then by a woman. When the headlines proclaimed: "Ruth Elder Safe on Ship", *The*

New York Times with the rest of the media did an about-face: "Everybody in France is eager to see this audacious girl succeed in proving that she is no weak woman. If she does succeed, this lovely American will have a triumph as great as that of Lindbergh. The daring and self-confidence of this American girl have imbued public opinion with the conviction that she will succeed."

Grayson, who had been so long at Old Orchard Beach that *Dawn* had become another seaside attraction, gallantly sent Elder a congratulatory telegram. Asked if she would give up now, she snapped, "There's plenty of room over the Atlantic for two women." On October 17, they tried once more, only to have Stultz again turn back because of weather. Furious, Grayson replaced him with Oskar Omdal of the Royal Norwegian Navy. He had flown with both Roald Amundsen and Lincoln Ellsworth on their polar flights and his expertise was unquestioned.

Fourteen days after having left Roosevelt Field, Elder stepped on the mainland of Europe. She was feted in Lisbon and Madrid and flown to Paris to shop.[44] "Paris Welcomes Ruth Elder and Aide as Sky Conquerors" headlined the expatriate *New York Herald Tribune.* The French who had taken Lindbergh to heart because they said he was some mother's son, pegged Elder as a "midinette", a silly young girl.

Disembarking in New York, she was met by Mayor Walker himself who gave her and Haldeman the ticker tape parade. She had proved that she was more than a pretty face and Walker could not restrain himself from observing, "Pulchritude is no bar to courage." And he was not speaking about Haldeman. Ruth went to Washington and met President Calvin Coolidge with Lindbergh. Sweetest of all, she was mobbed in her hometown of Anniston.

Womack, jealous of her fame — particularly when the media called him "Mr Ruth Elder" disparaged her and agreed to the divorce on the grounds of cruelty.[45] Other critics were Eleanor Roosevelt and Winifred Sackville Stone, (the founder of "The League for Fostering Genius") who sniffed: "This girl came out boldly and said she cared nothing for scientific advancement but wanted to be the first woman to fly across the Atlantic. But anyone can sit in a machine while there is someone to guide it."

Ruth Elder's "noble failure" (she is pictured above) as it became in the media, impressed the Honorable Elsie Mackay, a British heiress, movie actress and daughter of James Lyle Mackay, Viscount Inchcape of Strathnaver and chairman of the Peninsula & Orient shipping line. Over her father's objections, the madcap Mackay married an actor, only to be disowned by her family. Now divorced, the gossip columnists noted that besides driving her Rolls-Royce at alarming speeds down country lanes, she was flirting with airplanes — almost literally. When Elsie got her pilot's license, the tabloids were sure that aviation would be just another caper in the breathless life of Lord Inchcape's naughty scamp of a daughter. At thirty-five years of age, Elsie had already lived a life far more imaginative than any of her movie roles. As one of the first pilots in Britain, she had almost fallen to her death when in an "outside loop", her safety strap broke, and she clung to the bracing wires as her body swung outside the plane.

Its characters out of P G Wodehouse's England, and a plot twist worthy of Agatha Christie, this attempt to cross the ocean had all the ingredients of a good story, especially that author's *And Then There Were None*. Elsie's family were not to know that she planned to fly the Atlantic against the prevailing winds and that she had persuaded Capt Walter G R Hinchcliffe to accompany her. "Hinch" had already flown from East to West in *The Columbia* with Charles Levine when he replaced Clarence D Chamberlin in September 1927. Now working for Imperial Airways, the one-eyed former air ace had just bought a house in Purley near Croydon Airport. Elsie offered him a good salary and an insurance policy of $50,000 if they did not return. She reassured "Hinch" that the policy had been paid in full. On her instructions, he went to the United States and forgetting its oil troubles, bought a Stinson Detroiter and shipped it home. Christening the aircraft *Endeavour* after Capt James Cook's ship, Elsie flew it well under his guidance as the pair waited for early 1928.

For Elder, the money now came rolling in. She signed contracts for news rights ($17,000), and was paid to go on a speaking tour ($100,000) where she protested to mainly female audiences that now she "just wanted to settle down to a simple life". Ruth flew once more in the 1929 Women's Cross-Country Derby, placing a creditable fifth. The Atlantic flight and her beauty helped get her parts in two movies, *Moran of the Marines* and *The Winged Horseman* with Hoot Gibson.

With November, cold rain and grey fog enveloped Old Orchard Beach, soon to be followed by snow. After a Sikorsky engineer estimated that if ice formed on the *Dawn*'s wings, it would be two hundred pounds heavier, Grayson and her crew argued about attempting the trip that year. But she was determined to go, saying they would be spending Christmas in Denmark. When she showed reporters the small pistol she carried, they asked if it was a badge of authority as the plane's commander? Instead, she spoke of "the horror of a prolonged period of suffering ... before death intervened." They returned to New York and at 5:07 pm, December 23, *Dawn* took off from Roosevelt Field, making for Harbour Grace, Newfoundland where they were to refuel.

That Christmas Eve of 1927, the death toll of those who had tried to fly the North Atlantic was eighteen with five injured. Two had died trying to cross the South Atlantic and eleven had perished in the Dole Derby. Their desire for immortality far outweighed that of their morality. As listeners waited for news of Grayson's flight on the radio, the hit tune that day was Bessie Smith's *Christmas Blues*.

The crew of a French cable station at Orleans, Cape Cod saw *Dawn* at 7:10 pm. Supposedly, there was a single radio message from it and depending on where it was picked up, it was either "Plane down", "Can't exist long" or "Where are we?" Grayson and her crew were never seen again.

As to her competitor, by 1955, Ruth Elder had gone through not only all her money, but four more husbands as well. When Howard Hughes found her, she had been hospitalized for a sleeping pill overdose. He had known Elder in their youthful days, and there may have been a relationship between them. To keep her from poverty, Hughes made her a secretary at Hughes Aircraft.

"America's Aviation Darling" died in 1977 and according to her wishes, was cremated, her ashes scattered by plane over the Golden Gate Bridge, San Francisco. Her pilot, George Haldeman would take part in the 1928 New

York to Los Angeles race and later set an altitude record of 30,458 feet. He would die in 1982, living long enough to consult on the design of the B-1 bomber.

In the New Year of 1928, the Atlantic remained unconquered by a woman and Amy Phipps Guest and Mabel Boll each determined that they would be the one to do it — if only as a passenger.

Mabel Boll had hawked cigars in speakeasies until 1922 when she and her costume caught the eye of the Columbian coffee king, Hernando Rocha, who married her. A self-promoter, she gave herself the title "The Queen of Diamonds" (the media closer to the truth, dubbed her "The $250,000-a-day Bride"), and phoned *The New York Times* to announce that she now wanted to be "Queen of the Air". Coveting the fame that went with a transatlantic flight, Boll offered $50,000 to anyone who would fly her across the ocean. She initially had approached Capt Hinchcliffe who, with his own secret agenda, had turned her down. Mabel did manage to get on the front page of newspapers on March 5, 1928, when Stultz and Oliver LeBoutillier took her in *The Columbia* on the first non-stop flight from New York to Havana, Cuba.

An heiress to half of the Carnegie fortune, Amy Phipps was married to "Freddie" Guest, the former British Secretary of State for Air, and a cousin of Winston Churchill. She sought adventure as a suffragist, philanthropist, aviation enthusiast and big game hunter — her courage on safari in Kenya had impressed big game hunter, Baron Bror Von Blixen. Although a feminist, that a one-time speakeasy hostess was planning to be the first woman to fly the Atlantic, was too much for Amy's Anglo-American affectations and she resolved to be the first to do so.

In 1899, Donald Woodward's father paid $450 for the formula to make Jell-O and then mass-produced it. The family was soon rich enough for Donald to keep horses and hounds — while living off the bones of their less fortunate brethren. Woodward's Jell-O ads, which featured in women's magazines, came at the right time in history as between 1920 and 1930, the number of women working outside of the home increased by 35 per cent. The "Jell-O Girl" advertising copy emphasized the product's ease of convenience, not for only for secretaries and nurses but matrons who had recently lost their housekeepers to more lucrative factory work and were unaccustomed to cooking for themselves. Sponsoring a woman to fly the Atlantic was a match made in heaven for Woodward and he bought Commander Richard E Byrd's Fokker VII trimotor for $62,000, leasing it to Guest. It was christened *Friendship* to commemorate the Anglo-American symbolism and floats and extra fuel tanks were installed. Before Boll could, Amy hired as pilot the invaluable Wilmer Stultz for $20,000 and Louis Gordon as mechanic for $5,000. The aircraft was kept in Boston in secrecy in case her archrival heard of it.

Meanwhile, in England, muffled beyond all recognition, Elsie MacKay (under the name of "Gordon Sinclair"), and Capt Hinchliffe took off from RAF Cranwell in great secrecy.[46] Knowing they couldn't use a public airfield because of the media and her father's reach, Elsie went to Sir Samuel Hoare, the Minister for Air and begged for the covert use of the RAF College airfield. "Hinch" had trained there and knew its runway.

Hoare had once been in MI6, and as British Ambassador to Spain during the Second World War, would smuggle downed Allied aircrews to Gibraltar. The subterfuge must have appealed to him and as the founder of the RAF College at Cranwell, he had the influence to do this.

On March 9, Hinchcliffe and MacKay received a telegram from the Air Ministry stating that they had overstayed their welcome at RAF Cranwell and to depart immediately. In actual fact, the newspapers had uncovered the misuse of a military airfield for a suicidal venture and threatened to expose the flight. Before questions could be asked in Parliament, overstaying their welcome by four more days, the pair disappeared into the heavy snow clouds above Lincolnshire on March 13. Hinchcliffe left a note for his wife, but Mackay's involvement was still secret — fearing her father would stop her. The poignancy of it all, caused in part by social restrictions, was of a life lived on Elsie's terms and not her gender's.

They were spotted over Mizen Head on the Irish coast — and then nothing. Two hours after their departure, a letter arrived at RAF Cranwell addressed to Miss MacKay. When opened, it stated that an additional $10,000 would have to be paid before the insurance company accepted the risk on Hinchcliffe's life.[47]

Seven months later, the Air Ministry confirmed that part of an aircraft undercarriage had washed ashore in County Donegal and was identified as from a Stinson Detroiter. The finding was consistent with a sea landing in which water or ice had sheared off that part of the plane.[48]

Nor was Amy Phipps Guest destined to fly the Atlantic. Her son, Winston Frederick Churchill Guest, phoned from Yale to say that if she did so, he would leave the University and devote his life to playing polo — as he would anyway, captaining the US polo team to victory in the 1936 Olympics. With such a threat, Amy gave in and looked for a young aviatrix to take her place. She was very exacting about who she wanted, and it had to be a lady of "true womanhood". An American girl who knew how to fly, she had to be educated, with manners that would allow her to fit in with the British society that Amy had married into, and also be physically active and attractive. And if this woman bore a resemblance to Charles Lindbergh, all the better.

Enter George Palmer Putnam, the dilettante son of the famous publisher who had acquired the rights to

Lindbergh's autobiography titled *We*. Married to Crayola heiress Dorothy Binney, George was known to be a "star maker". He loved publicity, often doing stunts to promote his publishing ventures. He once faked his own kidnapping to gain media attention for a book he was writing called, *The Man Who Killed Hitler*. When George heard about this, he had his contacts look for what he called "the right sort of girl."

For Amelia Earhart (opposite), the flight to Howland Island began with a phone call to Dennison House, Boston where she worked. Hilton H Railey, a former military pilot now employed by Putnam, asked her if she would be interested in doing something in aviation that might be hazardous? If so, could she pay her own way to come to the publisher's office in New York for the interview? When she did, Putnam kept her waiting for over an hour but when asked, "Why do you want to fly the Atlantic?", her answer, "Why does a man ride a horse?" must have impressed him. Besides, with a haircut, she did look like Lindbergh.

In movie jargon, the part is known as "You play the girl" — sit there and look pretty while the men take center stage and all the applause. Was Amelia insulted that the only reason Putnam had invited her to join was because of her gender? She was to be the passenger — a sack of potatoes, she later said. Unlike Schultz and Gordon, there would be no pay nor publicity for her. This was evident when the pre-flight all-male party took place, and she was hidden from the media in the next room. As humiliating as that was, Railey and Putnam placated her by saying she would be the map reader and also the "commander". It was all going the way of Grayson's doomed venture.

Because of the secrecy, her fiancé Sam Chapman was the only person Amelia talked to about the flight. Making her will was easy — all she owned was a yellow roadster. Her memories of the whole experience were waking up at

3 am to get to the harbor and boarding the *Friendship* as they tried several times to take off in the rainiest summer in memory. When they finally did lift off on June 5 and landed at Trepassey Bay, Newfoundland to refuel, they were stuck there for two weeks because of the weather. Stultz, increasingly moody, found alcohol and was hung over, which for Amelia brought back memories of her father. While the two men were out scouring whatever fleshpots there were in Trepassey — Amelia, wearing the only clothes she had, scribbled in her diary, lived off canned rabbit stew and scandalized the nuns at the local school by appearing in pants to talk to the students. Only the thought that Mabel Boll was on the same island, also waiting for good weather, kept them there. Little did Earhart know that the two weeks at Trepassey Bay were the last quiet time she would ever have.[49]

Shocked to discover that Stultz had taken an unknown social worker instead of her, Mabel hired stunt flier Oliver LeBoutillier and Canadian RFC veteran Arthur Argles. She also leased the by now well-traveled *The*

Columbia — and renamed it *Miss Columbia*. They took off from Roosevelt Field on June 12, only to be stuck by the same poor weather on the tiny airstrip at Harbour Grace, Newfoundland. The villagers had never seen anyone quite like Boll, and "The Queen of Diamonds" reveled in the attention, thinking it a rehearsal for Paris and New York. Instead of taking off when there was a break in the weather, *Miss Columbia*'s crew decided to wait and see if the *Friendship* was really on its way across and not just on a test flight. Later, Mabel would blame the Weather Bureau for not sending her reports (they were available if asked for as Putnam had for the *Friendship*), but photographs show her in bright sunshine, attending receptions, even going to St John's for a cocktail party on June 15.[50] This blasé attitude spelled disaster for her, as on June 18, the news wire reported that Amelia Earhart had landed safely at Burry Port, Wales. Boll was said to have been heartbroken, and they decided to return to New York on June 20.

Amelia thought the transatlantic flight "a mess". In front of reporters, she and Stultz had argued about going at all. She did not have the skill to take over the controls and had to pull rank (and hide Stultz's alcohol) to get them in the air. They got lost and missed Ireland completely. They landed a half mile off the coast of Wales, with too little fuel to go further.[51] But that was good enough for the first-woman-across-the-Atlantic record and the Putnam publicity machine went into high gear.

All she had done was sit painfully between the fuel tanks on the cabin floor (the cushions having been jettisoned to save weight), but the thirty-one-year-old Amelia had morphed into a marketable commodity. For Putnam, it all fell into place. Everyone loves an underdog and unlike Elder and Boll, Earhart earned $35 a week, and had a socially acceptable job caring for immigrant kids. Like Lindbergh, she was Mid-Western "wholesome" and had a loving mother. Most important of all, even in slacks and with short curly hair, she was tomboyishly feminine and unlike Grayson, shyly charismatic.

Once in England, there were rounds of media appearances and parties for her — Mrs Guest met Earhart in Southampton with a suitcase full of Parisian gowns — while Stultz and Gordon went to Croydon Airport to look at aircraft. Amelia stayed at the Guest's Park Lane home, dined with Lady Astor, Winston Churchill, and Lord Lonsdale, and even bought an Avro Avian from Lady Mary Heath, shipping it home with *Friendship*. What must have pleased the feminist in her was watching Helen Wills win at Wimbledon, the first American female to do so.[52]

With the flowers, letters, and the offer of a car, she also received a marriage proposal to which she replied perceptively that she was caught in a situation where "there is little of me that is free." On her own accord, she told the British press that she had undertaken the whole trip to pay off her family's mortgage, which she would later do.

On July 6, Mayor Jimmy Walker met their ship with his yacht and gave Earhart, Stultz and Gordon a hero's welcome with a ticker tape parade down Broadway. Guest then paid the men off and they were happy to disappear. For Earhart, as she later wrote, "It was evident the accident of sex — the fact that I happened to be the first woman to have made the Atlantic flight — made me the chief performer in our particular sideshow." She downplayed her "passenger" role in the flight, sending a telegram to President Calvin Coolidge saying: "Success entirely due great skill of Mr Stultz." As a feminist, she consoled herself by describing it as a "feminine expedition" because Amy Phipps Guest had initially conceived and financed it to "emphasize what her sex stood ready to do". But ever after, her watchword was: "There is more to life than being a passenger."

Life would never be the same for Amelia Earhart (opposite). Putnam had orchestrated a whirlwind triumphant tour of a dozen cities including Washington, Boston, Toledo, and Chicago. Waving from a Pontiac convertible with Chapman on the running boards, Earhart rode down Medford's packed main street — the same one that Paul Revere had in 1775 to warn that the British were coming. As he did with Lindbergh, Putnam had her begin on a book about the flight called *Twenty Hours and Forty Minutes* and she moved into his Rye estate to do so. It was from there on November 23, 1928, that she would announce that her engagement with Sam had been broken. As America's darling, she now belonged to the nation — for doing nothing — and it must have eaten away at her. Admittedly, crossing the Atlantic by air in 1928, even if only as a passenger, was heroic. Guest, Railey and Putnam had pulled this off in the nick of time. On October 29, Clara Adams became the first female passenger on the *Graf Zeppelin*'s inaugural flight from Lakehurst, NJ to Germany. With that, any moneyed woman could fly the Atlantic — as a passenger.

Of those who had taken part in that transatlantic race, Capt Arthur Argles would be killed on May 21, 1929, over Roosevelt Field, trying to teach a student the mysteries of the spin. Stultz would be killed with two friends on July 1, 1929, when he crashed near Roosevelt Field. An autopsy revealed that he had been intoxicated when he made the flight and the consumption of alcohol within 5 miles of the airfield was banned. Louis Gordon, the last of the trio who crossed the Atlantic in *Friendship* would later work for Trans World Airlines (TWA) and die in 1964. As to the ocean itself, it continued to claim the ambitious. In February 1931, the wreckage of Beryl Hart and Lt W MacLaren's aircraft was found 270 miles from Horta, Azores. That one flew by 'dead reckoning', wrote an aviator of the era, only emphasized the word 'dead'.

Claiming that she had "got aviation out of her system," by 1931, Mabel Boll, was onto her third husband, Count Henri de Porceri. As the Countess Porceri, she would buy in her own name a custom-built Duisenberg Berline limousine. She would make headlines once more years later, when her young boyfriend shot himself on her lawn. Mabel Boll would die at the Manhattan State Hospital for the Mentally Ill in 1949, where her fourth husband had committed her. The bartender's daughter would achieve some of the immortality she had craved in 2016, when the Queen of Diamonds' Duisenberg was auctioned off by Sotheby's for $715,000.

5: THE RIGHT STUFF, THE WRONG GENDER

For eight days in September 1928, Los Angeles hosted the National Air Races — the city of dreams and fantasies making aviation one of them. The Disney studios put Mickey Mouse in an aircraft with his girlfriend Minnie in the silent cartoon *Plane Crazy*, later adding sound. The Academy of Motion Pictures and Science met for the first time at a banquet on May 19 and honored the director William Wellman with a gold-plated statuette for his aviation extravaganza, *Wings*. A life size statue of Lindbergh was erected by the city, hoping he would show up. A beacon light flashed on top of City Hall tower — which confused aviators who mistook it for the airfield. To cash in on the momentum, Warner Brothers released *On with the Show* a musical comedy and the first technicolor "talkie" film.

More enduring than any of these was the levelling of Mines Field, (named by William W Mines, the real estate agent who had been trying to unload it) known to the world today as LAX. Although three hundred thousand tickets were sold, so many more came to the races that pews from the local church were pulled out to accommodate them.

For its organizer Cliff Henderson, the Los Angeles air race was a success — but as always, it was an all-male competition. Earhart flew out with Putnam in her Avro Avian to publicize her book, only to embarrassingly crash in Pittsburgh — it had been a while since she had flown. The only women involved in the air race had been moonlighting starlets selling aviation-related merchandise or posing with the fliers. To Elizabeth Lippincott McQueen, the formidable, wealthy, and eccentric proponent of women in aviation — that was a travesty. Devoted to achieving world peace and feminism, she believed that aviation could be a key instrument to both. Cleveland (Henderson's hometown) had won the bid to host the races in 1929, and she focused on getting him to approve an all-women's derby there.

When the National Exchange Club, a men's service club elected to sponsor a women's race as their publicity project for 1929, Henderson agreed to organize it. Elated at the news, women signed up to race — Thaden, Nichols, Elder — and Earhart, her celebrity status attracting national attention.

Air minded women could barnstorm and attempt oceans, but competitive air races, like commercial aviation, was firmly a male preserve. "The sexism was blatant — and everywhere." wrote the author Keith O'Brien. "Male pilots belittled the women. They did not want them flying in the air races — and the women knew it. The press often disparaged the women too, with demeaning comments and headlines." The men feared that allowing women to compete would accord them less status, value, and financial reward — fears that were not unfounded.

The race organizers (all men) doubted the lady birds had the endurance for the proposed eight-day flight of 2,400 grueling miles from Santa Monica, CA, to Cleveland, OH, over deserts and mountains, navigating by dead reckoning and reading roadmaps — it was hard enough for a man. They proposed instead a gentle two-day trip to Cleveland during daylight hours — "a pink tea affair" Thaden said with some contempt. They also proposed that each of the women fly with a man to look after her.

Sometimes history, as Vladimir Lenin said, needs a push, and for those who believed that women couldn't fly solo, this came in the form of McQueen and Earhart. Thanks to lobbying by McQueen and the British aviatrix Lady Heath, both of whom had approached the FAI in Paris that year, a separate category for officially acknowledging women's record flights was created at the FAI Conference in Copenhagen in June 1922.[53] Besides founding the Women's International Aeronautical Association, McQueen would be the first aerial policewoman in the world (she was deputized by Police Chief Charles Blair of Beverly Hills in 1929) ready to assist civil authorities in times of emergency. The City of Beverly Hills had an ordinance that banned "stunt flying", in reality aerial "paparazzi". Officer McQueen would intercept offenders, forcing them to land and issue the pilot a citation. The Beverly Hills Aerial Police program ended in 1934 when the Bureau of Air Commerce took over air traffic control.

Leveraging her fame, Earhart stated that unless they flew the full 8 days and alone, she and all the women would boycott the air race. This was the first collective and militant action taken by female pilots. The sacrifice of those of their sex who had attempted to fly the oceans through 1927–28 (even if only as passengers), demonstrated that women had earned their place in aviation.

As if proof were needed, on October 21, after several weeks of checking tide tables for bridge clearances and practicing low-level flying around the masts of boats in Manhasset Bay, plucky seventeen-year-old Elinor Smith took off from Curtiss Field and flew her Waco 10 under all four of New York's bridges — the Brooklyn, the Manhattan, the Williamsburg and the Queensboro. She then circled the Statue of Liberty, after which every ship in the harbor blew their whistles in salute. No man had done that — or ever would.

In 1930, the American Society for the Promotion of Aviation asked the nation's licensed fliers to name the best male and female pilots in the United States. When the ballots were counted, Smith — who'd assumed Earhart would take the title because of Putnam's lobbying — was stunned to learn she had won. "It was such an honor to know that my peers considered me the best,"[54] she said. However, the *New York Sun* tabloid chose to focus instead on Smith's attire with "Girl Flyer Appears Wearing Real Shorts. Roosevelt Field's hard-boiled aviators were goggle-eyed yesterday at the appearance of a flier in warm weather 'shorts'. The latest advocate of the cool garb was Miss Elinor Smith, holder of the woman's altitude record. Elinor wore a white, short-sleeve shirt, open at the neck, white slippers, and socks. The shorts were of white duck and came within an inch of her knees." Her courage and expertise did not rate a mention.

The citizens of Cleveland were bereft at news of the female boycott of the derby — especially local businessmen Louis W Greve and Frederick C Crawford who had played major roles in bringing the air race there. Cleveland had built the first municipal airport in the country, its terminal and hangars only just completed and what's more, the *Graf Zeppelin* on its round the world trip was expected to visit that summer! With Greve and Crawford's persuasion, the race organizers compromised. The women could race — as long as they satisfied the entrance requirements (100 hours flying time and 50 hours cross country) and they could fly alone. But to remind all who was in charge, they ruled that a woman could only fly an aircraft with horsepower that was "appropriate" for her. Though Opal Kunz, whose husband owned Tiffany & Co, flew her own 300 hp Travel Air, it was disallowed as the organizers deemed it "too fast for a woman to fly." Opal rented a lesser-powered airplane and competed anyway.

The entrants would have to carry emergency rations and wear parachutes and cope with overnighting at stops for rest, fuel, and repair. These were San Bernardino, Yuma, Phoenix, Douglas, El Paso, Pecos, Midland, Abilene, Fort Worth, St Louis, and Cincinnati, each with their own rough airfields and local reporters who wanted to see the phenomenon of women fliers. The men doubted the women had the "moxie" or the money — they first had to find race planes — and how many aircraft manufacturers were going to trust women to fly their creations? And as to cooperating with each other, general opinion was they would fight like cats. In short, they expected the women to quit this insanity.

By August 1929, seventy women held Department of Commerce pilot's licenses but only 40 met the race requirements. Of those, twenty signed up. They would operate an assortment of race planes — mainly

Lockheed Vegas and Travel Airs. With the nationwide media coverage, here was their chance to prove the men wrong. But if even one of them crashed, all would face condemnation as being just 'petticoat pilots'. Besides the $25,000 prize money, each woman was imbued with the determination to overcome the entrenched prejudice in an industry that had barely begun, but in which men (and popular opinion) already thought was no place for them.

Marvel Crosson began flying in 1922 while living in San Diego. She and her younger brother Joe bought a wrecked Curtiss seaplane for $150, put in an old OX-5 engine and flew it. Joe was allowed lessons at a local airfield, but not his sister. As soon as he obtained his license, Joe taught her to fly, and she followed him to Alaska where the pair flew commercially. Joe would become an Alaskan legend, flying as far as Siberia, and become the first person to land on a glacier. Marvel would set an altitude record of 23,996 feet on May 28, 1929, in a Travel Air.

Ruth Rowland Nichols (below) was from Rye, NY "old money", (her father had been one of Teddy Roosevelt's

"Rough Riders"). A Wellesley College graduate and on the Social Register of New York, her family expected that she would marry suitably and settle down. With such a background, the press called her the "Flying Debutante", a name she hated. Nichols held License No 2, signed by Orville Wright himself, and was the first woman to earn a hydroplane license. In January 1928, Ruth and Harry Rogers, her flying instructor, flew the first non-stop flight from New York to Miami. Nichol's life was one of "what might have been". Instead of a social worker in Boston's grubby Chinatown, in 1928, Putnam was more likely to have chosen her, a blue blood from the same Rye neighborhood. She might also have thwarted Earhart in flying the Atlantic solo had she not crashed and was severely injured attempting to do it on June 22, 1931 — no one had checked the suitability of the landing field in Saint John, New Brunswick. It was as though there was always one piece of a jigsaw that didn't quite fit. In 1940, Ruth would begin "Relief Wings", an air-rescue service of female pilots and volunteer medical professionals connected to a network of medical facilities. Its slogan was "Humanitarian Service by Air." It would become an adjunct relief service for the Civil Air Patrol (CAP) during the war.

Late in life, Nichols was turned down by NASA for its Mercury program in 1959 — only Jerrie Cobb was accepted. Although NASA eventually cancelled the female astronaut program, it must have been the final indignity for her.[55] On September 25, 1960, suffering from severe depression, the fifty-nine-year-old Ruth Rowland Nichols was found dead in her home in New York. The examiner ruled that it was suicide caused by an overdose of barbiturates.

Farm girl Florence Klingensmith from Clay County, Fargo, ND, financed her flying lessons as a wing walker. She would somehow convince the hardnosed businessmen of her town to back her as an air racer. "If you are willing to risk your neck," said one, "I'll risk my money." Nicknamed "Tree Tops" because she flew that low, Florence loved the spotlight and would be the first woman to compete against men in a tight pylon speed race.

Anne Morrow Lindbergh had been taught to fly by her husband and at media presentations deferred to him in every way, acting as was expected of her — a housewife in the cockpit. The first woman in the United States to earn a First-Class glider pilot's license, in 1934 she was also first woman to win the National Geographic Society's Hubbard Medal for serving as a radio operator and co-pilot for her husband's two flights which spanned five continents. Yet, married to a controlling man who cheated on her, Anne patiently endured reporters' questions about domesticity in the air like where she kept the lunchbox in the cabin.

In two books, *North to The Orient* and *Listen to the Wind*, no other female pilot popularized flying as much as Anne Morrow Lindbergh. Although written for the general public, both inspired generations of girls to become pilots. Anne was one of the 20th century's leading feminists — as a wife, mother and pilot — and echoed many of her gender's concerns with observations such as this: "What a circus act we women perform every day of our lives. Look at us. We run a tightrope daily, balancing a pile of books on the head. Baby-carriage, parasol, kitchen chair, still under control. Steady now! This is not the life of simplicity but the life of multiplicity that the wise men warn us of. It leads not to unification but to fragmentation." Her later book *Gift from the Sea* inspired by her own struggle for identity in a difficult marriage, anticipated the contemporary feminist movement by decades.

Evelyn "Bobbi" Trout first flew in an aircraft when she was sixteen on December 22, 1922. But it was not until January 1928, after saving enough money and being able to take the time off from managing her father's filling station, that she had her first flying lesson. She soloed on April 31, 1928, and accepted aircraft manufacturer R O Bone's offer to demonstrate his Golden Eagle to set records.

Born Bessie Lee Pitman, Jacqueline (Jackie) Cochran (below) was an adopted daughter of a dirt-poor family and spent her childhood dressed in sacking and running around barefoot in Southern sawmill towns. At six, she went to work in a Georgia cotton mill, earning six cents an hour for a 12-hour day. By age seven, she was cooking and cleaning for pregnant women around town. Pregnant and married at fourteen, her break came when she presented herself to a local beauty parlor owner, pretending she knew what to do. Erskine Caldwell was writing *Tobacco Road* about the dehumanizing effects of Southern poverty around him — just as Bessie climbed out of the abyss she had been born into.

A pretty young mother, Bessie smoked, was loud, and divorced her husband but kept the Cochran surname.

Her greatest tragedy was when her four-year-old son, Robert Jr, alone in the backyard playing with matches, set some paper on fire and within moments his clothes were ablaze. He was badly burned and died from his injuries. For many years, it was too painful for Jackie to remember. "I added and subtracted information at will, as it suited me," she said years later. "I didn't see it as lying, so much as survival."

Like Baroness de La Roche and Harriet Quimby, Bessie reinvented herself, moving to New York and taking the name "Jacqueline" from the beauty shop. Throughout her life, Jackie had a single-minded determination to get what she wanted. She made a fortune in the cosmetics business and in 1932 on the advice of Floyd Odlum took up flying to promote it. Her lack of any education prevented her from map reading or instrument flying but through sheer force of will, she studied hard enough to get her license. She married Odlum, one of the wealthiest men in the United States in 1936 and began breaking records for speed and distance.

If the definition of a feminist is someone who champions equal rights, Cochran did so, for herself and the women in the WASPs. Women were there to share with men she said, not replace them. She was more at ease in male company — where the power was — than her own sex. But she was friendly with Beryl Markham and Amelia Earhart, and when the latter went missing, she used her psychic powers to try and locate her. In Jackie's future was the setting up with Nancy Harkness Love, plans for female pilots to ferry planes in wartime. It was a long way from that Georgia cotton mill.

At school, Helen Richey had been the only girl who wore pants and once she ran off to join the circus. By 1930, she was performing aerobatics at Bettis Field, Penn and the Bureau of Air Commerce granted her a limited commercial license, allowing her to carry passengers within a 15-mile radius of the airfield. With Frances Marsalis, Richey held the women's endurance refueling record of nine days, 21 hours, and 42 minutes. Helen would say, "I don't feel like living unless I'm in an airplane."

After Marsalis was killed in the 1934 Women's Air Meet in Daytona, Richey gave up stunt flying to begin her dream to be a commercial pilot. A few women had been granted the coveted "transport" (commercial) licenses. Edith Foltz, Oregon's first woman pilot and the fifth woman to hold a transport license, was one. "In the fall of 1928," she wrote in the *Ninety Nines* newsletter (March 15, 1933), "I had my first opportunity to fly as a co-pilot on a tri-motored Bach on West Coast Air Transport which operated between Seattle and San Francisco. I wasn't on the payroll then and just went when I was invited by one of the pilots. They took turns about giving me instruction. A woman flying alone was quite a novelty then, and at first these pilots, all former Army pilots, flew with me out of curiosity, thinking it impossible for a woman to fly decently. But after flying a while with me they decided that maybe I would be a pretty good pilot with more instruction. Finally, the chief pilot on the airline said that I handled the Bach as well as any of the male co-pilots and that I go with him on charter trips. Then Western Air Express bought the line and I thought I would lose out, but no, they retained me for charter trips. I got around 70 hours on Bachs and Fokkers and a few on Fords before Western Air sold the line to United. The argument most companies put up about hiring a woman flier is that the women passengers wouldn't trust another woman. I used to ask the women who were our passengers how they felt about me, and they all seemed pleased."

When Richey (oposite) was hired by Pennsylvania Central Airlines (PCA), its president admitted that he had done so to cash in on the 24-year old's beauty and racing fame. *The New York Times* and *Collier's* magazine seized on the story with: "This is Pilot Richey. Yes, she's a girl. She's young. She's pretty." It was only going to be for a few months, the airline president mollified his male pilots when they protested, and by then she would have given up. That wasn't enough for them, and the men threatened to strike if Richey wasn't let go. The pilot's union not only refused her membership but also lobbied hard to get her fired. She didn't have the strength to handle the Ford Trimotor, they claimed. More critically, the Bureau of Air Commerce objected to the airline entrusting its passengers to a female in the cockpit.[56] But whether it was her piloting skill or her novelty value, Richey proved popular with the public and 8 months later was still with PCA, flying the Ford Trimotor on the Washington-Detroit route. In August 1935, when the Bureau forced the airline to restrict her flying time to fair weather days only, she quit in disgust, frustrated that she had been duped into what turned out to be largely a publicity stunt for the airline.

Amelia Earhart who had flown with Richey in the Bendix Trophy Race of 1936, led a public protest, as did other Ninety-Nines, to no avail. Unusual for aviation matters, the affair achieved national attention with Alice Paul, the founder of the World Party for Equal Rights for Women, defending Richey. *The New York Times*

announced, "Feminists Stirred up over Woman Flier; Alice Paul agrees with Amelia Earhart that Sex not Inability, Cost Helen Richey Her Job". The pilots' union defended itself by explaining that "the big planes were coming and they would be too hot for a woman to handle." Besides, there were few enough jobs for men in commercial aviation. It was discrimination Earhart wrote, pure and simple.

In 1940, Richey, unable to fly commercially, became the first female to be awarded an instructor's license by the Civil Aeronautics Authority (CAA), the precursor to the present Federal Aviation Administration (FAA). As with other female instructors, she saw the men she had trained go on to fly commercial aircraft that she was forbidden to.

Florence Lowe Barnes was a force of Nature. Called "Pancho" because (it was said) she once outdrank the entire Mexican Army. The truth was even better. She had shipped out as an able-bodied seaman running guns and jumped ship in Mexico. It was no surprise that Pancho took up flying, qualifying in 1928. Her grandfather was Thaddeus S C Lowe, the pioneer balloonist for the Union Army. The first female stunt pilot to fly in motion pictures, she did much of it in Howard Hughes' *Hells Angels*. Moon faced, too large and loud mouthed for the media and without a Putnam to publicize her, Pancho fell on hard times in the late 1940s. She opened a restaurant outside Edwards Air Force base called *The Happy Bottom Club*. There she held court and it was where test pilots Chuck Yeager, Gus Grissom, John Glenn, and Buzz Aldrin hung out.[57]

Blanche Wilcox was pursuing a career in the theatre and the movies when she fell in love with the stocky red-haired Dewey Noyes and decided that she would rather fly with him than act. Dewey, a pilot for the US Airmail, taught her, and Blanche soloed after only 3 hours, 45 minutes of dual instruction.[58]

Thea Rasche was Germany's female stunt pilot. On July 7, 1927, American newspapers (as usual concentrating on her appearance) wondered if "the blond Fräulein who was sturdy not plump" might become the first woman to conquer the Atlantic. This did not occur, but Rasche would enter the Powder Puff Derby. She wrote about flying until the Nazis came to power and her books were banned for being too pro-English/American.

Louise Thaden grew up in Bentonville, Arkansas and paid for her flying lessons by selling aircraft for Walter Beech. On December 7, 1928, she would fly to a height of 20,260 feet, in a Speedwing, the first officially recorded woman's altitude flight. She would also hold the record of flying faster than any woman had done so before, attaining a speed of 156 miles per hour on April 13, 1929. In August 1932, Thaden and Frances Marsalis set a women's endurance record of 196 hours, 5 minutes in a Curtiss Thrush that the press called *The Flying Boudoir*. They exceeded by 74 hours the previous women's endurance record, which had been set by "Bobbi" Trout and Edna May Cooper the year before. In 1936, when women were first allowed to enter the Bendix transcontinental aeronautical race, Thaden did and won. Louise Thaden epitomized the radical notion that women are pilots. In her autobiography *High Wide and Frightened* she wrote, "A pilot who says he has never been frightened in an airplane is, I'm afraid, lying." The airport in Bentonville is named for her.

The Australian aviatrix Jessie Maude "Chubbie" Keith Miller was in Los Angeles with her partner, the former RAF pilot Bill Lancaster, both hoping to interest a Hollywood studio in doing a movie about their England to Australia flight in 1927. Hearing about the Derby and the prize money, "Chubbie" got her US license and asked Lawrence Bell (who would one day be awarded the Collier Trophy for the Bell X-1), to loan her a Fleet biplane for the race.[59]

The race was to begin at Clover Field, Santa Monica, where on March 17, 1924, four Douglas World Cruisers had taken off for the first circumnavigation of the globe by air. Mistaking a nearby field for the airport, Phoebe Omlie had put her airplane down in it and was hauled off to jail by the sheriff who thought she was a dope smuggler. The entrants were to be divided into two groups — light planes and heavier ones. The times between each stop were to be added up and the winner would be the woman with the fastest aggregate time. The day before the start, the route was changed to include another town, prompting the humorist Will Rogers to say that it was too bad Mexico City could not raise $50 or it, too, could have seen the lady birds. The women staged a late-night protest over a stop they deemed too dangerous, and a compromise was reached in the morning. Thaden would sum the general feeling up with: "We women of the Derby were out to prove that flying was safe; to sell aviation to the layman."

August 18, the morning of the start, was exuberant chaos at the airfield. With admission a dollar a car, there were hundreds of families, Hollywood stars, and the simply curious — including a shy Howard Hughes who wanted to see if women could really do this. The aircraft were lined up into two competitive categories, depending on horsepower. The women polished their planes nervously, wore their photo-op clothes and, if they were Ruth Elder and Amelia Earhart, handled the press with practised ease. This was the first time that they had met so many other female fliers, their loneliness in the all-male world of aviation evident in their "talking shop". In jodhpurs, with a sporty beret and smoking her standard black cigar, Pancho Barnes told the media that flying made her feel like a sex maniac. Earhart flew one of the two aircraft that had an enclosed cockpit, so she carried other pilot's luggage for them — even though the extra weight slowed her down.

On his nationally syndicated radio program, Rogers predicted that the women would last 60 miles before they came back. He also condescended that, "their female genes compelled each racer to take one last glance at her compact, along with a dab of powder on her nose. It looks like a powder puff derby to me!" The name stuck and the air race became "The Powder Puff Derby."[60]

At 2 pm, at the sound of the radio-relayed pistol shot, the white flag dropped, and 19 airplanes headed out at full speed for San Bernardino (Mary Haizlip left the next day). The first day was not without mishaps — so many of the spectators drove their cars onto the San Bernardino airfield that the dust they stirred up almost caused aircraft landing to hit each other. Day Two was to Phoenix with a stop in Yuma. It wasn't the terrain here that bothered the women as much as sabotage of their planes left unattended at night. Wires were cut, switches in the cockpit were turned on and gas lines mysteriously clogged. The district attorney in San Bernardino questioned the mechanics and found no basis in the claims of sabotage.

By dark on day three, 16 race planes had landed in Phoenix. All the missing airplanes were accounted for, except Marvel Crosson. Marvel had flown the entire course prior to the race, yet her Travel Air was found demolished in the mesquite jungle in the Gila River Valley. She had been thrown from the airplane and it was noted that she had pulled the ripcord on her parachute, trying to get out. They wrapped her body in her parachute, carried it out of the desert on horseback to put on a train to San Diego where she and her brother Joe had once built their own plane.

While the evidence suggested that she had endured carbon monoxide poisoning, "the biological deficiency that women suffer" came to the fore. Dr L H Bauer, the founder of American aviation medicine and editor of its *Journal of Aviation Medicine*, advised the Bureau of Air Commerce to inform female pilots that they should not fly during, immediately before or immediately after their menstrual periods. He warned that this inescapable fact of biology was the cause of a number of crashes by women. Menstruation then was considered an illness rather than an aspect of health. Seizing on this and without evidence, J G Noel, the Air Commerce inspector concluded that Marvel Crosson had crashed while in the throes of menstrual distress. In doing this, he eliminated any further need to investigate for mechanical failure, thus satisfying both the derby organizers and the whole aviation industry. It was what the media trumpeted as "The Curse of the Ladybirds". The concept of "the premenstrual syndrome" later used by the airlines, began here. Employing a female pilot was obviously a risk — she was too moody, irritable, and depressed to fly at certain times of the month.

As if on signal, there began the expected calls to stop the race because "these women have proven conclusively that they cannot fly." Across the country, newspaper columnists pontificated that Marvel's crash proved that air races were for men. Cliff Henderson and, ironically (and unfairly), the Cleveland race organizers, were blamed for allowing this fiasco to happen. Ultimately, the women themselves were held responsible for Crosson's death. When men died in a race, they were aviation pioneers — when women did, they were failures as pilots. Erle Halliburton, the founder of an oil company better associated today with his future successor Dick Cheney, wanted the race stopped immediately because, "Women have been dependent on men for guidance for so long," he said, "that when they are put to their own resources they are handicapped."

As to the women themselves, they decided that the best tribute to Marvel would be to go on — and they did. Their response was "We wish officially to thumb our collective noses at Halliburton." But fearful of possible recurring carbon monoxide problems, Travel Air mechanics arrived to modify all the Travel Airs.

"We did object to being made exhibits and more or less circus attractions." Louise Thaden would later write. At every overnight stop, throughout the race the pilots had to dress up for the banquets (invariably fried chicken) organized by the different exchange clubs. The media expected them to live up to their reputation as "sweethearts of the air" and thus they were kept up late every night to entertain the invitees and please the event sponsors. In the October 1929 issue of *The Women's*

Journal, Frances Drewry McMullen noted: "Everywhere at the banquets, they had to be 'sweethearts of the air,' 'flying flappers,' 'angels,' 'sunburned derbyists' and what not, when what they really wished and felt entitled to be considered was simply 'fliers' — 'women fliers,' if you must."

Race Day 5 was an all-Texas day from El Paso to Pecos, Midland, Abilene, and Fort Worth. The citizens of Pecos were so excited about the women racers landing in their town that they drove onto the landing strip for a close-up look. Pancho hit a car and while not injured, she was out of the race.

Leaving Texas on Day Six, they could now fly at lower altitudes, and the section lines straightened themselves out into neat square patterns. Crossing the Red River brought the red earth of Oklahoma under them, with lower visibility and forest fires to their east. In Wichita, home of the Travel Air Manufacturing Company, each racer was assigned a mechanic and the aircraft were hangared for maintenance, repair, and security. The sleep deprived women, changed into their now wrinkled dress-up frocks, and joined in the festivities. When they dutifully met with the friendly crowds, signed autographs, and responded to the press, their appearances and clothes gained more inches in print than their airplanes and standings. The sun had done its work on the pilots flying in the open cockpits. They had "farmer-foreheads" and owl-eyed looks, their sun-tanned V-necks showing up in their scoop-necked dresses. Fog on Sunday morning gave the racers a welcome breather, especially needed by Louise Thaden whose oil tank had accidentally been drained.

Monday August 26 was the last day of the race and was only from Columbus to Cleveland and everyone hung on for just one more leg to the finish. Ruth Nichols made an early test flight to Columbus. The new concrete runway at its

airfield was still under construction, and the first portion was closed. A steam roller was working at the edge of the runway, just about where the usable portion began. Ruth hit it and somersaulted, coming to rest upside down on the soft dirt. She was unhurt, but her third-place standing had ended.

Cleveland was only 120 miles and 44 minutes away for Louise Thaden. There were three cross-country races to that city underway: The Powder Puff Derby and two men's races from Portland, Oregon, and Miami, Florida. The *Graf Zeppelin* on its round-the-world flight was also nearing Cleveland, guaranteeing that every aircraft and balloon was in the sky to escort it. Each of the pilots flew the last leg with singular concentration. Thaden arrived over the finish line first. Blanche Noyes and Gladys O'Donnell were right behind her.

The frenzied crowd swarmed Louise's Travel Air and reporters and photographers engulfed her airplane. A horseshoe of flowers was placed around her neck — as the thorns hadn't been removed, it was quickly transferred to the airplane's propeller hub. Phoebe Omlie took first place in the lighter aircraft category. Louise dedicated her trophy to Marvel Crosson.

Immediately after the race, Earhart would call a meeting in her hotel suite to commemorate the Derby by forming an organization that would consolidate the gains made by the women in the race. She had once admitted, "I am lonesome for the companionship of women in aviation. When I want to talk shop in aviation, there are only men to talk to." But when she suggested that they should lobby to race with male pilots so they could compete for bigger purses, several of the women walked out.

A month after the stock market crash, on November 2, 1929, five Powder Puff veterans and ten other women pilots met at Curtiss Airport, Valley Stream, New York. Neva Paris and Opal Kunz were the key organizers of the meeting. A $1 membership fee was collected, and Amelia Earhart was elected president. As a name for the group "Angel's Club" was discarded because it was thought the men would laugh at them. It was decided that the number of charter members would determine the club's name and with more female pilots joining, it was called the "86s", which evolved later into the Ninety Nines. It was all low key; the women did not want to be seen as too powerful because it would threaten the old boys club that aviation was (is). There would be a newsletter to keep track the member's activities, with articles, recipes, and clothing hints. This was to be a social and professional organization and limited to licensed female pilots.

The fame of the Ninety Nines reached across the border to Canada and Margaret Fane, one of a group of female pilots in Vancouver called the "Flying Seven" flew to California to meet Amelia Earhart. She wanted to begin a chapter in Canada but there weren't enough women pilots to do so. The "Flying Seven" would continue to perform at air shows in British Columbia, the women in a uniform of culottes with a silk blouse beneath a wool jacket, topped by a Glengarry hat, all in gray.

Opal Kunz, disappointed in what she considered

the Ninety Nines' unobtrusive policy, founded, and funded a paramilitary air corps in 1931 for women called the Betsy Ross Air Corps. The Daughters of the American Revolution were delighted but at a time when paramilitary organizations in Europe were on the march, the government in Washington was less impressed.

An article in an early edition of the Ninety-Nines newsletter asked: "Are women fliers still superstitious? The Baroness de la Roche, first woman to fly a plane, always wore a bright green sweater for luck; Harriet Quimby, America's first woman pilot (sic) had a little brass idol as a luck charm, Mathilde Moisant, another American pioneer, had the number 13 as a good luck symbol; Helesei Dutreau of France carried a pair of her father's army gaiters in her plane for luck, while Jeanne Harvieu, French speed flier, carried a baby pig until he got so big, she had to keep him in the hangar and only had him put into the plane for a moment before she took off. Mrs Jimmy Martin took along a wisp of her husband's red whiskers when she went for a flight. Small wonder that Harriet Quimby said in 1912 'It is a curious thing, but all women fliers are superstitious.' Superstition, as many persons hold, having more to do with imagination than with any other human faculty, and fliers on the whole being an imaginative lot, the chances are that many of the women fliers today are as superstitious as the pioneers, Frances Marsalis, for example, carries a rabbit's foot on all her flights, Dorothy Hester takes a string doll, and Betty Huyler Gillies a pair of old white golf shoes with a black saddle vamp."

Chicago was to host the 1930 National Air Races and Henderson, living off his showmanship with the Powder Puff Derby, expected to count on the women fliers again. This time neither Earhart nor Thaden wanted to take part — which didn't prevent Henderson from exploiting their fame. The race organizers ruled that given what had happened with Crosson, a doctor and two US. Army Air Corp planes would escort the women across the country. Having just won their independence from patriarchal control, the Ninety Nines opted to boycott the air race.

By now, the carefree Twenties had given way to the grim Depression which, like a medieval plague, was laying waste to much of the country. While women who worked outside the home had always been marginalized — they were cheaper to employ than men and didn't complain of whatever humiliation they endured — with the Depression, they became the scapegoats for male unemployment — "Don't steal a job from a man" — and were let go. Those race goers who made it to Chicago's Curtiss-Reynolds Airport without being mugged on the way, did so past armies of bedraggled, starving men and women on city streets. The 1930 Air Races barely broke even. Cliff Henderson knew he needed the female fliers back.

His opportunity was the 1933 Chicago World's Fair which trumpeted the progress of Technology. This was especially so in aviation when 24 Savoia-Marchetti flying boats arrived all the way from Italy, recording the first formation flight across the North Atlantic.

For Henderson, Labor Day at the Fair was perfect for a woman to compete in the Philips Trophy Race. The co-founder of Phillips Petroleum, Frank Phillips had put up a $10,000 prize and trophy for the best time, around a 100-mile triangular course. Open to both men and women, it was to be 12 tight laps between large pylons over an eight and one third mile course. Combining Sex with Speed, Henderson not only invited the golden haired, blue-eyed Florence Klingensmith to race but secured for her a red-and-white Gee Bee Y, the most dangerous, unstable, overpowered aircraft then. Having once walked on wings in her bathing suit, Klingensmith must have been thrilled. Without a Putnam to publicize her, this was her only chance. She would emerge from the race as Elder and Earhart had, a celebrity — and with that sex appeal, a very marketable commodity.

At the airfield, reporters ogled her Nordic beauty and needled her with taunts about her social life. Saying before taking off "I'm going to give the boys a race", Florence was in control of the monster through the pylons — until the home stretch when fabric began tearing off its right wing. In getting it away from the crowds — she was too low to jump — they saw the red and white missile smash into the ground, killing her instantly.

In the subsequent investigation, the air deputy coroners targeted Klingensmith's pre-race physical and mental condition — not the obvious instability of the Gee Bee. Was she moody and irritable before the race? To men, that could only mean one thing. Had she been examined by a doctor before the race for her monthly period? As the other participants were male, all a doctor did was ensure that they hadn't been drinking.[61] If she were menstruating, would that make her lose control of the aircraft? Henderson was not around to answer these questions — he had left town. The verdict was that although being weakened by menstruation, Klingensmith had flown to prove that her sex could do it, selfishly putting her male competitors and all the spectators at risk.

Jackie Cochran would fly a Gee Bee in the MacRobertson race from London to Melbourne in 1934 (image overleaf) and crash in Romania. "The cute nickname is a sham," she recalled years later. "They were killers. There were very few pilots who flew Gee Bees and then lived to talk about it. Jimmy Doolittle was one. I was another."

Vilified in the media, Florence Klingensmith was abandoned by all. Henderson who had personally invited her to race in the Gee Bee, now said that Klingensmith's death proved that women really didn't belong in his races, and he would ban them from future ones. Her body, in the mangled form it had been extracted from the Gee Bee wreckage, was covered in newspapers, and shipped home to Minnesota in a cheap casket. Florence Klingensmith deserved better than this.

This was an opening salvo in the war over "The Curse of the Ladybirds". When the CAA, without medical evidence, attempted in 1940 and 1943 to prevent women in the WASPs from flying while pregnant or menstruating, Betty Huyler Gillies fought them. The mother of three children, she and a lot of other women had successfully flown through pregnancies and periods. And as to menstruating, that would be impossible (embarrassing?) for men to enforce. Every pregnant pilot military or commercial, who flies today owes a debt to a feisty 5' 1", 100 lb dynamo called Betty Huyler Gillies. No wonder in the WAFS, she was nicknamed "The Mighty Atom."

After Crosson's death, the poet pilot Louise Thaden wrote a eulogy which serves for Klingensmith — and all pilots who are killed in flight.

"If your time has come to go, it is a glorious way in which to pass over. Smell of burning oil, the feel of strength and power beneath your hands. So quick has been the transition from life to death, there must still linger in your mind's eye the everlasting beauty and joy of flight."

6: MY GOD! IT'S A WOMAN

The Great War had ended in victory, pyrrhic though it was, for Britain. With its share of former German colonies, the Empire was at its unwieldy height. This was to be the beginning of a prosperous era. New technologies like the 'wireless' and the 'talkies' were springing up. They might not run countries, wars, or companies but women now had fractionally more rights. Forty per cent of their sex were allowed to vote — if they had university degrees, were over 30 years of age and their husbands owned property. Their rising real wages while still less than what men earned, invigorated consumer culture, especially in leisure. Coco Chanel had popularized the dropped waist and creeping hem lines in women's fashions and the simplicity of the "Eton" crop for hairstyles. Gramophones, telephones, electric household gadgets appeared and motorcars, like the Baby Austin, were affordable. As in the United States, a celebrity culture had emerged. Royals, gangsters, and silver screen actors were tabloid fodder, existing as they did in a glamorous world beyond the grime of everyday living.

Private aviation in Britain, like house parties and fox hunting, was for the wealthy. The feminist author Virginia Woolf had just announced that to express herself, a woman had to have money and a room of her own. The London Aeroplane Club, Edgeware, became that "room" for female pilots, many soon to be famous. The airfield was also where the amateur entomologist Geoffrey de Havilland was then perfecting his line of Moths. In 1925, the government began subsidizing flying clubs, which brought aviation within the reach of men and women of moderate means, initially presenting each club with two Mark 1 DH Moths. The scheme was copied in Canada and other parts of the Empire. The subsidies gave members the opportunities to earn either an "A" license for amateur flying or a "B" license, the professional qualification.

Through inheritance, marriage or flirtation, a few air-minded women got the chance to pursue their independence. Like Hilda Beatrice Hewlett, at a time when society expected them, once married, to disappear politely, each discovered second acts for themselves.[62] Among those who graduated from the London Aeroplane Club were Lady Heath, the Duchess of Bedford, Lady Bailey, Winnifred Spooner, Amy Johnson, the Hon Mrs Victor Bruce, Joy Muntz, Pauline Gower, Dorothy Spicer, Joan Meakin and Jean Batten.

Mary Russell, the Duchess of Bedford (opposite) took up the pastime of aviation at the age of 60. During the First World War, she opened her home, Woburn Abbey, to convalescing soldiers, and through the 1920s, was associated with three other veteran's hospitals. Her Grace suffered from increasing deafness caused by typhoid fever as a child. Flying was an escape from the madding crowd and in the days before air traffic control and radio, it gave her complete freedom. She learned to fly at the London Aeroplane Club and on June 17, 1926, took her first flight from Croydon Airport to Woburn Abbey.

With Charles Barnard as pilot and Bob Little as mechanic, on August 2, 1929, she embarked on the first of her historic flights as a passenger — this one from Croydon Airport to Karachi, India and back in a record eight days. On April 10, 1930 "The Flying Duchess" using a single engine Fokker FVIII, once more with Barnard

and Little, flew from London to Cape Town in ten days. She would hire Flt Lt J B Allen (also suffering with deafness) as her personal pilot. They were about to set out for the Oasis Rally in Egypt in December 1933 when Allen, flying solo, hit high tension wires, and was killed.

By 1937, Mary needed just 56 minutes of solo flying time to reach the 200 hours necessary for her pilot's "B" license to be renewed. Fearful that her deafness would prevent this, she had been depressed for weeks and subject to fits of dizziness, worrying about not being able to fly again.

The seventy-two-year-old set out from Woburn Abbey in her DH Puss Moth on March 22 to earn the minutes. It was supposed to be an easy triangular course — Woburn-Buntingford-Cambridge and back. She was never seen again. The Puss Moth's struts washed up on shore, but her body was never recovered. For many years, the mystery surrounding her last flight has been speculated on as suicide. The sentiment in an entry in her diary after Allen's death suffices. "For him, it has been the best of deaths for an airman to die."

Mary Westenra, born in 1890, was the daughter of Derry Westenra, the fifth Baron Rossmore of Rossmore

Castle, Co Monaghan, a sportsman and rake. After a childhood of hunting, shooting, and fishing, in 1911, the twenty-year-old Mary married Sir Abe Bailey, a South African diamond mine financier who was 27 years her senior. Becoming a licensed pilot in early 1927, Lady Bailey flew across the Irish Sea (with an inflated a motorcycle inner tube around her midriff, in case she had to ditch) the first woman to do so. She set an FAI World Record for altitude of 5,268 meters (17,283 feet) on July 5, 1927.

The following March, she began a solo flight in a DH.60X Cirrus II Moth from the aerodrome at Stag Lane to Cape Town, via Malta and Cairo. Her plane was locked away in Khartoum by order of the Governor-General of the Sudan to prevent her from continuing. Women were not allowed to fly alone across the Sudd, the great swamp in South Sudan that Beryl Markham described as "a prehistoric crucible that was sinister, eerie and treacherous." If they came down in it, the crocodiles alone would kill them. She contacted Dick Bentley (who had flown to the Cape a few weeks before) to escort her in his own aircraft. Lady Bailey's luck would run out in Tanganyika where she would crash, writing off her airplane. Abe paid for another DH.60 Moth to be delivered from Pretoria and she continued, despite having the flu.

The return journey was made via the western 'French' route — the Belgian Congo, Portuguese Angola, and the French Congo. She arrived back at Croydon on January 16, 1929, 10 months after leaving. These were the longest solo flights and the longest flight by a woman. Lady Bailey was awarded the Harmon Trophy in 1927 and again in 1928. The Royal Aero Club awarded her its Britannia Trophy in 1929.

Born in Limerick in 1896, Sophie Catherine Pierce Evans (opposite) had a violent start to her life. When she

was a year old, her father beat her mother to death and when the police arrived, they found the baby Sophie sitting beside her mother's lifeless body. Her father was sent to an asylum for the criminally insane and Sophie to her grandparents in Dublin.

During the First World War, Sophie served as a dispatch rider and ambulance driver. In 1916, she married Capt William Davies Elliot Lynn, OBE who was twice her age and abused her. On her maiden solo flight in 1925, Sophie flew to Prague to address the Olympic Congress, where she campaigned to have women's athletics accepted in all sports at the Olympic Games.

When her husband drowned in 1927, Sophie married Sir James Heath, receiving her title as Lady Mary Heath. Buying an Avro Avian, she set altitude records and became the first female ground engineer in Britain. She also earned a "B" license which allowed her to fly "for hire or reward." This was subject to frequent medical checks for her menstrual cycles.

On January 5, 1928, Lady Mary Heath left Cape Town in her Avro Avian for a tour of South Africa's airfields. A few weeks later, she flew from South Africa towards London.

The first person, male or female, to fly solo from Cape Town to London, she arrived at Croydon airfield on May 17 to wild celebrations. She sold her Avro Avian to Amelia Earhart and went to the United States. On December 2, 1928, Lady Mary Heath made the record height of 16,428 feet at Curtiss Field in a Gypsy Moth — the first women's altitude record under full supervision of the National Aeronautic Association.

Looking forward to competing in the 1929 Powder Puff Derby, tragically, before she could, Lady Mary Heath crashed her plane into a roof on August 29, 1929, while practicing a dead-stick landing. With a fractured skull, broken nose and internal injuries, her aviation career ended. To add insult to injury, she was served with divorce papers on the way home.

With her third marriage to a Trinidadian jockey, she encountered racism in England as her supporters fell away. Divorce and alcoholism followed, and on May 9, 1939, Sophie died at the age of 42 after falling down the steps of a tramcar in London. Remembered today as the Irish Icarus, her ashes were scattered by plane over Limerick.[63]

Pauline Gower was the daughter of a member of parliament who initially refused to pay for her flying lessons, and she gave violin lessons to do so. In 1931, she and Dorothy Spicer began Airtrips Ltd, an air taxi service, and later she joined the Crimson Fleet Air Circus to aid British hospitals. A member of the Women's Engineering Society, the first woman to be awarded a 2nd class navigator's license, Gower would write *Women with Wings*, about her life in aviation. Amid it all, there was no thought that a decade later she would be in a war. As Pauline said on a BBC radio program in 1940: "I looked on flying as one of those things which help unite the nations of the world … The men and women pilots of my generation really believed that we were increasing the world's happiness."

◊◊◊

"Amy Johnson? Isn't she the typist that flew to Australia?" Had it not been for a love affair in her twenties that ended badly, Amy would never have flown anywhere. He was a Swiss businessman that she had been infatuated with since the Sixth Form. Eight years her senior, Franz saw Amy whenever he was in her hometown of Hull. With his foreign accent, his motorbike and (in her eyes) Rudolph Valentino looks, she was besotted by him — especially when he taught her to smoke a cigarette — the symbol of female emancipation. The romance allowed Amy to visit his family in Switzerland which, for a daughter of a Hull fish merchant in 1926, was transformative.

It was an obsession more than a love story. Franz was critical of whatever she did — from getting a university degree to her "flapper" frocks. He belittled her Yorkshire accent and when she wrote to him in her high school French, he would return her letters with the errors marked in red ink. Yet, with wildly unrealistic optimism, Amy believed that they would soon hear wedding bells. Her sister Irene was happily married to Teddy Pocock and looked forward to a domestic life as wife and mother.

In March 1928, when Franz told her that he was going to marry someone else, Amy retaliated by replacing him with another obsession. "I'm going to learn flying!" she wrote to him. "I'm joining the London Aeroplane Club and then I can get tuition and always use their airplanes." She would show him.[64] If duchesses and wealthy men's wives could do it, why not the daughter of a Hull fish merchant? The twenty-five-year-old cast off what she called "her old maidness", went to the movies where she saw *Wings* (of course) and learned the latest dances — the Black Bottom and Charleston — Franz had only allowed her to do Viennese waltzes.

Unlike the Duchess of Bedford and Ladies Bailey and Heath, Amy was hard put to pay for her flying lessons. As a secretary earning £5 a week, finding the 30 shillings per lesson besides the club entrance fee of £3, meant sharing a "bed-sit" with a friend, walking to Stag Lane from the nearest Underground station and making the Club her entire social life.

In June 1929, just as she had decided to devote her life to aviation, her sister Irene committed suicide. She left a note to Teddy and then put her head in the gas oven. It was a shock to everyone as it was thought she had been incredibly happy. Mr Johnson, having lost one daughter, was disinclined to lose a second to aviation and wanted to forbid her flying. But Amy had just earned her pilot's "A" license — the thirty-seventh woman in Britain to do so — and it took Jack Humphreys, the club's chief engineer, to convince him that his daughter had the potential to be Britain's first female air engineer. When she became famous, Humphreys would say, "When that girl first came to Stag Lane, I knew I had a born engineer to deal with."

One day, as she was lamenting the restrictions that prevented her from becoming a commercial pilot, one of the men flippantly suggested that if a woman flew solo to Australia, it could only help her gender's case. Bert Hinkler, a test pilot at A V Roe, had been in the news for having done it in fifteen days.

By luck, a reporter happened to be at the Club that day for another event and its female engineer was pointed out to him. When he interviewed her, Amy (or "Johnnie" as she preferred) divulged wanting to fly solo to Australia in an imaginary "secret plane". Men had been flying from England to Australia since 1919. The only woman who had done so was Mrs Keith "Chubbie" Miller in 1927, but as a passenger (her boyfriend Bill Lancaster did the piloting) — and the flight had taken five months. The only woman to have flown across the Atlantic then was Amelia

Earhart — as a passenger. Amy's longest solo flight had been from Stag Lane to Hull. For a woman who had no long-distance flight experience to attempt 11,000 miles in an open cockpit without a man was inconceivable. The reporter recognized a good story and when "Girl to Fly Alone to Australia" appeared in *The Evening News* the next morning, there was a crowd of media including camera crews at Stag Lane, and Amy Johnson, like Cinderella, was transformed into a celebrity.

Applying the blind tenacity she had pursued Franz with, she gave up her typist job and began a publicity campaign — writing letters to and meeting with those who she thought could help like Lord Beaverbrook and the Director of Civil Aviation Sir Sefton Brancker. "Can you not do anything for me?" she begged. "I need between £1,000 and £1,500." She reminded them that Lindbergh wouldn't have flown the Atlantic without the support of the businessmen of St Louis.

With Brancker's influence, Lord Wakefield, the owner of Wakefield Oils Ltd, offered to provide some of the financing and all of the fuel for the flight. Amy bought a two-year-old DH Gypsy Moth "G-AAAH" (below) which

came with long distance tanks for £600, her father and Wakefield paying £300 each. She had it painted green and named "Jason", a contradiction of "Johnson", the trademark of the family business.[65]

The legend that she flew to Australia using a school atlas is false. Amy bought the latest strip maps fixed on rollers for the whole of her flight to Darwin — although over Southeast Asia, the maps were barely adequate. The 12 "stopping places" she was aiming for were: Vienna-Constantinople-Baghdad-Bandar Abbas-Karachi-Allahbad-Calcutta-Bangkok-Singapore-Sourabaya-Atamboa-Darwin. It was only when she did her research at the Air Ministry would she discover that there were rudimentary aerodromes as far as India (thanks to Imperial Airways and the Royal Air Force), but few after that. No wonder Alan Cobham had used a seaplane on his record flights.

On the chilly May 5 morning of 1930, after posing for photographers in her Sidcot suit, Amy Johnson took off from Stag Lane for Croydon, the club's aircraft providing her with an escort.[66] The 8-hour flight to Aspern, Vienna was perfect except that the fumes caused by pumping fuel into the gravity tank on the upper wing made her nauseous. When she got to Constantinople the next day, she put her engineering expertise to good use and cleaned the aircraft engine in a car's headlights. Waiting for her, was a cable from London — a poignant echo from the past: "Best luck and wishes — Franz".

Johnson dreaded overflying the Taurus mountains to Aleppo, Syria. Climbing above the cloud bank to 11,000 feet brought on an intense cold and she could no longer follow the railroad tracks because they ran through tunnels. With the aid and hospitality of French and RAF officers, Imperial Airways mechanics and British consuls ("I was so glad to see among the horde of natives rushing towards me, a white face" she would write) Amy made it as far as Calcutta by May 12. A crash landing the next day near Rangoon tore Jason's fabric and shattered several of the aircraft's ribs and for the first time, she considered giving up, the whole flight "a terrible failure." Although they had never seen a plane before, the locals helped as much as they could. The forestry officer rebuilt the spars, students from the government technical institute welded the broken metal and someone recalled that men's shirts were once made of airplane fabric. Twenty shirts were bought, torn into strips and the Rangoon seamstresses pieced them together to sow on the wing.

The delay cost her three days and when she got to Bangkok on May 16, Amy knew that she had lost out to Hinkler's record. She touched down at Seletar aerodrome, Singapore, on May 18, but thanks to Fleet Street, her fame had gone ahead of her. Hundreds of Europeans, the women dressed as if for a garden party, came out to see her. A local reporter was struck by the contrast: "Miss Johnson smiling through the oil on her face, in men's khaki shorts, oil-stained shoes and men's drill jacket, with her hands and face burnt brick red."

The flight from Sourabaya, Java to island of Timor on May 22 was 928 miles, the longest, as she said, and over shark infested waters but surprisingly all went well. On Timor itself, she landed in a field of ant hills, to be rushed by "a horde of natives, hair flying the wind, holding knives in their teeth." Amy pulled out her revolver to defend herself, but they were only welcoming her to guide her to the nearest European home. The next day, to help her "hop" Jason to the nearby Portuguese airfield at Atamboea, the same natives flattened the ant hills and held the wings up, letting go when she gave the signal to take-off. As no one had heard from her since Sourabya two days before, by now the newsboys were shouting, "Flying Girl Missing. Feared Dead". People across England began praying for her and in Hull, strangers consoled her parents.

Amy's troubles began over the Timor Sea. The engine was spluttering, the foreign matter from the poor fuel in Atamboea choking the carburetor. The Shell company had stationed an oil tanker halfway between Atamboea and Darwin in case she needed rescuing and when Amy saw it, it so cheered her up that she came down to a few feet of its deck, waving to the figures rushing around. She felt protected then, knowing that in half an hour she would be in Australia.

"Her fame will live forever" — "What a brave wonderful daughter to be proud of — "When I read of her safe arrival, I danced up and down the tram car" — "Endurance, courage, and skill — you're Britain's pride" — "The Queen and I are thankful and delighted to hear of Miss Johnson's safe arrival in Australia." Friends, relatives, royals, prime ministers, the Lindberghs, Louis Bleriot, Sir Sefton Brancker (who in four months would be killed in the R101 crash) — all cabled Darwin with their congratulations. The most remarkable feature of the rejoicing at her safety and adulation was its spontaneity. There had been no press hyperbole beforehand or professional publicity campaigns. Amy had the common touch and came across as a genuine, endearing figure, unashamed of her accent or her toothy grin. To the man in the street, she was one of them. If she could do it, any woman could, and flying clubs were suddenly flooded with enquiries from female applicants. When the media wanted to call her "The Lone Dove" after Lindbergh's "Lone Eagle", Amy delighted everyone by insisting they call her "Johnnie".[67] She had no experience in public speaking and the affectionate way she described Jason "But the engine was wonderful" became a catchphrase. She wasn't a titled lady but a lowly typist, a penniless nobody who had set off on an awfully big adventure — straight out of James Barrie. Dubbed "Australia's Sweetheart", the Australians wanted her to marry

one of the princes and return as the wife of their next governor general.

Fan letters from around the world were addressed to her parents simply as: "To the Parents of the Empire's Greatest Little Woman." Of all the songs composed about her, the most popular and catchy was "There's a little lady who has captured every heart, Amy Johnson, it's you!" The press outdid themselves with comparing her to Joan of Arc, Grace Darling and Edith Cavell. The *Daily Mail* gave Amy a payment for future services (not a gift as she thought) of £10,000 and de Havilland donated a Puss Moth. She was awarded the Harmon trophy and in the Birthday Honours, made a Commander of the British Empire — too young to be a Dame like the Duchess of Bedford.

Although she probably wouldn't have called them such, Amy Johnson betrayed strong feminist instincts. Made an Honorary Fellow of the Society of Engineers — an illustrious all-male institution — she was convinced that women shared with men the necessary qualities for aeronautical engineering — "patience, delicate fingers, and a fertile mind". During the First World War, women who stepped up as engineers so the men could join the armed forces, were let go when they returned. Begun in 1919 to resist this pressure, the Women's Engineering Society (WES) promoted engineering as a rewarding career for women. Johnson would be elected president of the WES in 1934, the youngest woman to hold the title.[68] In 1935 her friend Dorothy Spicer became the first woman in Britain to achieve the "D" License which authorized her to inspect, pass out, and repair both engines and airframes — women had never been allowed to study at such an advanced level — Johnson would write, "A man holding this license would have many excellent jobs at his command, but I doubt whether Miss Spicer will find the license of any practical use."

Beatrice "Tilly" Shilling was a WES member, being one of two women studying engineering at The University of Manchester in 1932 (the first year the program allowed women to join). The RAE hired her in 1936 as its only female engineer. In 1940, she worked on why the Merlin engines of Spitfires and Hurricanes would cut out when the aircraft were in a nosedive and the carburetor flooded. Shilling invented the 'restrictor', a small metal disk, which regulated the fuel flow, and prevented stalling. It helped win the Battle of Britain and got the nickname 'Till's orifice', for various reasons other than it had a small puncture in the centre of the disk.

With her mentor Jack Humphreys, Amy would fly from London to Moscow in a day in July 1931, continuing on to Tokyo after. At a time when bestselling books were David Garnett's *The Grasshoppers Came* about fliers stranded in the steppes and Evelyn Waugh's *Black Mischief* where African cannibals eat the lost female pilot, a young woman confronting her fears, as Amy had, distracted from the poverty and unemployment of the Depression.

In 1931–1932, the two great tragedies that philosophers warn of in life befell: a hysterectomy meant she lost her ability to have children — something she very much wanted when she met Jim Mollison.[69] His roguish charm covered a considerable number of flaws — he was known to drink heavily and had left the RAF in 1928 with unpaid bar bills. "Jim's long-distance flights differed from those of others," aviator Sidney Cotton would write, "in that others came down when they ran out of petrol, but Jim's ended when he ran out of brandy."[70]

When Lady Diana Wellesley heeded her mother's warning and broke off an engagement with him, in March 1932, Mollison left for South Africa, setting a record of flying from England. In his autobiography *Playboy of the Air*, he would write that on his return, he invited Amy to lunch on May 9, but his proposal of marriage during the meal was entirely unpremeditated. To the shock of her parents and friends, that same afternoon the pair called *The Times* to announce their engagement. They married on July 29 — her family were not at the wedding because Jim had insisted that no relatives were to be invited. As she had been with Franz, Amy was infatuated with the opportunistic Mollison, blindly making light of his debts, his drinking and reputation as philanderer. After the hysterectomy, he was the only family she could ever have. The press blithely dubbed the couple *Sweethearts of the Air* and Amy's celebrity, and monetary value has never been higher.[71] While vacationing in Florida, Jim forbade her from driving his new Buick — the same model that the Prince of Wales had, and she bought herself a Mercedes coupe.

Mollison shortened their honeymoon to make the first East-West transatlantic flight solo on August 20, flying from Portmanock, Ireland to Pennfield, New Brunswick, continuing onto New York. His Puss Moth was named *Hearts Content* for the Newfoundland village where he hoped to make landfall. In July 1933, on a dual transatlantic flight, Amy and Jim would fly from Pendine Sands, South Wales, to Stratford, Connecticut, while aiming for New York. They were given a ticker tape parade in Manhattan with Amy attracting more attention than Jim. By now, it was obvious that the pair were more competitors for media attention than companions.

◊◊◊

One of the women who attempted to best Amy's record time to Australia was the South African-born Australian Maude Rose "Lores" Bonney. She decided to fly from Australia to England "because in 1933, it was considered the ultimate test for the men. Amy Johnson had made headlines flying from England to Australia, and I wanted to be the first woman to fly the more difficult reverse route and beat Amy's time in the bargain." In 1932, Bonney had been the first woman to circumnavigate the Australian mainland by air. She left Brisbane on April 10, 1933. "I was ahead of schedule," she recalled, "until I landed in Singapore and overnighted at the Raffles Hotel. To this day, I'm sure I would have beaten Amy's record if I hadn't gotten food poisoning. Stupid me — I should never have eaten the fish." The record time no longer possible, Bonney would arrive at Croydon Airport on June 21. Jean Batten would claim that prize the following year and Bonney fell into obscurity. It would not be until 1991 that she was awarded the Order of Australia.

Amy and Jim entered the MacRobertson Air Race to Melbourne in October, 1934, buying a DH 88 "G-ACSP" naming it *Black Magic* — Jim's favorite color (opposite). Jeffrey Quill, one of the RAF officers who was on the starting line, remembered Mollison as noticeably drunk and Amy apprehensive.[72] The pair made it as far as India when their troubles began — the undercarriage failed to retract after Karachi, and they had to return there — then relying on the wrong maps, they got lost. When they made an unscheduled stop at Jabalpur, the only fuel available was motor car spirit which caused the DH.88's engines to seize up and the Mollisons to drop out of the race.

"Mollison was woman-mad" remembered a mutual friend of theirs, "and a great many women were Mollison-mad." When a woman friend teased Jim by remarking that he probably did not even remember their names he drawled, "My dear, I never ask their names." In February 1936, Amy escaped to Paris and was smitten by the wealthy and sophisticated Francois Dupré (an upmarket Franz?). That she would make a final record-breaking flight on May 4, flying a round trip solo in seven days from Gravesend, Kent to South Africa, said it all. In September, when Jim formally admitted to his numerous infidelities — he had met an heiress and wanted a divorce — she started proceedings against him. The sordid and cynical drama ended when Dupré discovered that Amy had also been sleeping with a friend of his and abandoned her. On August 24, 1938, Amy's divorce was granted.

With war inevitable, the little lady who "had captured every heart" tried to get a job as a senior advisor with the

Air Ministry (or as she would write "a dangerous mission in the Secret Service") to no avail. She was furious that Maxine "Blossom" Miles was chosen to represent the female pilots in the Civil Air Guard and not her. When she remonstrated with the Air Minister Sir Kingsley Wood, he told her that the position was voluntary and that with her expensive lifestyle, he knew she would have wanted to be paid. In June 1939, on her 36th birthday, Amy Johnson accepted a job flying for an air ferry company, earning £1 a day. She joined the Air Transport Auxiliary (ATA) in May 1940, at White Waltham, as did the now remarried Jim Mollison. While the press pounced on the possibilities of this new romance, Amy wrote to her sister that now "he bored her stiff."[73] With the other ATA women, she ferried planes — the pilots of the recipient squadrons in awe of her when she landed. Amy's family thought she had never been happier.

In June 1942, the movie *They Flew Alone* (renamed *Wings and the Woman* in North America) a "biopic" of Amy Johnson, was released. Given women's strides in aviation during the war, she is depicted as a visionary in the air — the ultimate feminist flier. The movie is dedicated to 'women who have driven through centuries of convention.' The actress Anna Neagle who had previous portrayed Florence Nightingale, played Amy as an independent young woman who wins fans around the world with her record flights but loses the love of her husband Jim Mollison (Robert Newton), a pilot who fears his own accomplishments are overshadowed by a woman's. Having sacrificed her marriage for aviation, Amy then joins the ATA and in the last scene, its female pilots are shown delivering Spitfires.

Amy did not live to see the movie as her plane had crashed into the Thames Estuary on January 5, 1941. Her body was never found and as with Amelia Earhart's disappearance, this has given rise to various 'conspiracy theories', the most popular that she was on a secret mission carrying a German spy. "Our Amy", the typist who flew to Australia has been commemorated in Britain with statues in Hull and Herne Bay, in lectures and on television. What she would have loved best was that in 1968, the University of Sheffield named a building that houses its systems engineering after her. The fame that Amy Johnson pursued in life continues to find her in death.

◊◊◊

"I closed the throttle and glided down to a landing, and as the wheels of the Gull came to rest, felt a great glow of pleasure and pride. This was really journey's end, and I had flown 14,000 miles to link England, the heart of Empire, with the city of Auckland, New Zealand, in 11 days, 44 minutes, the fastest time in history."[74] It was to be the high point of Jean Batten's life.

Soon after Jean was born in 1909 in Rotorua, New Zealand, her mother pinned a newspaper picture beside her cot of Louis Blériot, who had just flown the English Channel. A thwarted actress with strong feminist views, Ellen Batten would dominate her daughter's life, living out her own unfulfilled dreams through her.

When her parents divorced, in early 1930, her mother took Jean with her to London where she could learn to fly. Telling her father that she was studying at the London School of Music, Jean used his and her brother's money for flying lessons at the London Aeroplane Club. She was not a natural flier but like Amy Johnson, her perseverance got her noticed. On December 5, 1930, awarded her "A" license she invited her no doubt surprised father to watch her fly. He cut her off financially and sent her back to Auckland. On the ship home, Jean worked her wiles on Fred Truman, a New Zealand RAF officer serving in

India. He wanted to marry her and loaned her £500 (his entire life savings) to return to England and continue flying. She did so and as soon as she got her "B" License in December 1932, Jean had nothing more to do with him.

The men at the Club thought her a lesbian — no doubt because she spurned their advances — but Jean Batten had no time for romantic overtures — unless they served her purpose. Her (and her mother's) obsession was to better Amy Johnson's record flight to Australia and make a name for herself in aviation. In 1932, the German aviatrix Elly Beinhorn became the second woman to fly solo from Europe to Australia — a flight that had taken 110 days, because of sightseeing along the way. Jean knew she had to find an aircraft to do so — and soon. When she could no longer afford her Club membership fee, Victor Dorée, the son of a wealthy linen merchant paid it and loaned her his own Gipsy Moth to train in.

Dorée would buy her another Gipsy Moth (opposite) to make her first attempt to Australia on April 9, 1933. She crash-landed it near Karachi and tried to persuade him to buy her a second plane. When he refused, she ended the relationship with him. She tried again on April 21, 1934, the knight errant this time was Edward Walter, a stockbroker whom she even got engaged to. Unfortunately, she ran out of fuel on the Italian coast and returned to London. The press called her the "Try Again Girl" and with Lord Wakefield's sponsorship, on May 8, 1934, Jean took off once more. This time she made it to Darwin on May 23. Her time for the epic flight was 14 days, 22 hours, and 30 minutes, bettering by four days Amy Johnson's record. On landing in Darwin, Batten cabled her mother: "Darling, we've done it. The airplane, you, me."

The British media congratulated her as having won the war of the sexes, the Australians wanted to keep her as their own and the mayor of Auckland thought she deserved a good spanking "for being a naughty girl, trying to do what men do." Much of the success of her publicity was beauty — Batten was more photogenic than Johnson.[75] But critics were quick to point out that her flight had been faster because thanks to Imperial Airways and KLM, ground conditions along the way had improved since Johnson's flight.

With fees from the media, on her 26th birthday, Jean took delivery of her dream machine: a Percival Gull Six cabin monoplane. With it on November 11, 1935, she flew from England to Senegal, landing at Thies near Dakar to overnight. The next day, she crossed the South Atlantic, making it to Natal, Brazil. Her total flying time from England was 13 hours, 15 minutes, breaking all previous records for both sexes. All that remained for Batten now was connecting England with New Zealand. On arrival in Sydney in October 1936, she was shocked by the public resistance to her proposed flight. Batten was considered

"abnormal" for attempting what no man had done.

Inspired by Lindbergh's flight in 1927, two New Zealanders John Moncrieff and George Hood bought another Ryan monoplane and on January 10, 1928, attempted to fly across the Tasman Sea from Sydney to Trentham Racecourse, Upper Hutt, New Zealand. They were never heard from again. In her unpublished memoirs, Jean observed, "I was a woman flying alone and in those days Australia, like New Zealand, was very much a man's country." After being warned that if she came down in the Tasman Sea, Australian lives were not going to be put at risk looking for her, Jean took off from Richmond Aerodrome, Sydney, for New Zealand on October 16. Her arrival to a huge crowd ten hours later at Mangere airfield, (now Auckland Airport), she said was the greatest moment in her life — even her father was there. Jean Batten had set a record of flying from the heart of the Empire to its furthest outpost in eleven days and 45 minutes.

She returned to London and in the Second World War, hoped to fly for the ATA. But she failed her medical examination and her beloved Percival Gull was requisitioned by the RAF. In later years with her mother's death, Batten turned her back on her home country. She would die in 1983 unnoticed in Marjorca, Spain and was buried in a common grave. Today, the terminal building at Auckland Airport is named after her and Anthony Stones' statue of her stands outside it. Her Percival Gull (pictured with Batten below), no doubt unnoticed by the travelers purchasing their liquor, is now suspended above the airport's duty-free shop.

7: IT WAS AN ADVENTURE, A BRAND-NEW LIFE FOR WOMEN

I t will come as a surprise that not only does the flight attendant profession predate passenger-carrying aircraft but that the first one was male. Before fixed wing airliners, as early as 1912, German airships making scheduled flights between cities warranted someone to care of their passengers. Heinrich Kubis had learned his trade at the Ritz Hotel in Paris and in March 1912 was hired as an "air steward" on the airship *Schwaben*. Credited as being the world's first flight attendant, Kubis would later serve on both the *Graf Zeppelin* and the *Hindenburg*. On the former, in 1928, he would look after Clara Adams, the first female to cross the Atlantic Ocean. When the *Hindenburg* burst into flames on May 6, 1937, at Lakehurst, New Jersey, Kubis, in true flight attendant fashion, helped evacuate passengers and crew before jumping to safety himself.

As soon as the First World War ended, using aircraft that had been designed as long-range bombers, air companies in Europe began flying travellers about. European capitals were within easy reach of each other by air, the Alps being the continent's only geographic impediment. But travel by aircraft was not simply a means to get from London to Paris, but an exercise in bravado — or more realistically in utter stupidity. Wings folded in flight or fell off, engines seized and propellers broke off. The aircraft's lightweight wooden spars and fabric that had made flight possible, rotted away with regularity. Disoriented in rain and snow squalls, the pilot attempted to navigate through fogged up goggles — in short — to travel in an aircraft was exorbitant suicide. "The passages were expensive," wrote Nathan Heller "plane tickets in the twenties cost up to fifty per cent more than first-class fares on trains and ocean liners, yet the trips could not be called luxurious. Cabins were as temperate as a meat freezer, and skull-numbingly loud."

In contrast, there were the well-established railroads. Who would give up beginning a journey at an imposing railway station downtown — for a muddy airfield in the outskirts? At the station, one was met by porters who whisked your luggage onboard without weighing it — or you. You looked forward to enjoying a multi course meal in the dining car followed by drinks and convivial conversation in the parlor car. Finally, you retired to a turned-down bed in your snug roomette to be woken the next morning with a cup of tea.

As with the ocean liners of the day, North American railways provided such luxury because they were labor-intensive. They could afford to be — the labor pool they recruited from was cheap, non-unionized, and expendable. The origins of the flight attendant profession in North America can be traced to the railroads which relied on African Americans to care for their passengers. Treated as a simple minded and childlike, and usually addressed as "George", the "porters" (a generic term for all African American waiters, cleaners, and bartenders on the railway) were like the domestic servants of the day, invisible. "On call" throughout the journey, the hours they spent preparing the carriages while in the station were unpaid. Like much of the industrial workforce then, the porters were without paid vacation or sickness days, medical, pension or death benefits. Responsible for buying their own uniforms, they paid for their meals —

which had to be eaten either early in morning or late at night, before or after the passengers had theirs — and out of their sight. With the servitude in the transportation industry went the practice of tipping which allowed the railways to keep wages low and reinforce the dominance of the passengers — all white and mostly male — over the porters.

To mitigate contact between the porters and the white female passengers, African American maids were hired to attend to them exclusively. Being black and female, they suffered even lower wages and sexual harassment. Black women were thought to be less sensitive to pain — and no one worried about whether they could work while menstruating. Social historians will point out that racial and gender discrimination were not exclusive to the transportation industry, as women in the labor force, whatever their skin color, fared little better elsewhere.

The parallels between the porters' and flight attendants' fates are obvious but, for all of the injustices, such was the predicament of both African Americans and single white women in the Depression, that there was never a shortage of applicants for either job.[76]

British Airways can trace its origins to Aircraft Transport & Travel Ltd (AT&T), which on August 25, 1919, operated the world's first daily international service between Hounslow Heath (now Heathrow Airport) and Paris-Le Bourget. To help their charges ignore the aircraft's headache-inducing roar, nauseating fuel fumes and bumpy ride, Daimler Airways would employ slightly built teenage "cabin boys" like 14-year-old Jack Sanderson to look after them. Trained at the Savoy Hotel, London, they wore page boy uniforms — and before take-off distributed pre-packed lunch boxes filled with a selection of fruit and sandwiches. As with the passengers, pre-flight, the boys were weighed and if over seven stone (98 pounds) were fined. They were more for reassurance than any real service — to help the travellers stay calm. Sadly, five days after its first flight to Paris, on April 7, 1922, a Daimler Airways aircraft collided in the mist with a CGEA Farman Goliath and among the six killed was Sanderson, the first flight attendant to die in a plane crash. After that, the service was discontinued.

But, despite the discomfort and danger, passenger air traffic in the United States soared from 9,000 in 1927 to 400,000 in 1930. With such incentive, aircraft manufacturers like Donald Douglas and Boeing pooled resources with Pratt & Whitney, to design aircraft that would carry mail as well as passengers, and both at a profit. Boeing's first collaboration with the aero engine makers Pratt & Whitney was the Boeing 80A —a three engine, 12 passenger aircraft exclusively built for its own airline Boeing Air Transport (BAT). The cabin was cold, drafty, cramped and stank of oil, and because it was a biplane, the wire cross bracings shrieked in the wind and sometimes broke loose, leading to hysterics in the cabin.

To entice the public to pay to risk their lives, the fledgling air companies faced the Sisyphean task of "selling the sky" between crashes as a safe, comfortable place to be in. Ironically, the stewardess profession was invented not by an airline public relation "whizz kid" but by a female pilot who desperately wanted to be back in a plane. Ellen Church (opposite) had been turned down too many times for flying jobs when on February 12, 1930, she walked in the office of Boeing Air Transport (BAT) in San Francisco. As it was a holiday, Steve Stimpson the traffic manager was alone. Ebullient and ingenious, Stimpson was paid to convince people that flying his airline's unsafe shaky Boeing 80A biplanes would not be a terrifying experience, likely to end in body-crushing death. To do so he attended Rotary lunches, made rousing speeches to men's clubs and cajoled celebrities into being photographed while boarding the planes.

When Church approached him with the idea for putting nurses onboard to look after the passengers, the BAT traffic manager was in an amenable mood. He had just gotten off a company flight that had suffered from severe turbulence. As the co-pilot could not leave the cockpit to distribute the sandwiches, Stimpson had taken charge, reassuring, and feeding them. Once on the ground, he wired his superiors for permission to hire stewards to do this.

In Britain, passengers who flew Imperial Airways were pampered by Jeeves-like stewards, their first duty once the flying boat had lifted off was to uncork the clarets "so they could breathe unhurriedly before lunch." But those US airlines that had hired male cabin attendants had encountered problems. White males were found to be unsuitable as it was seen they lacked the necessary "subservience" that passengers expected of servants.

African American males were not considered at all as airlines wanted to distance themselves from the racial connotations associated with railroad porters.

Even as Church entered his office, Stimpson was considering hiring short, lightweight Filipino males as stewards. Neither African American nor white, they would "fit" into the skin colour spectrum. According to aviation lore, she reminded Stimpson that as flying induced dizziness and sheer terror in passengers (as he had just witnessed) nurses would be a better choice than any man. Used to shift work, to nausea erupting all around them and to enforcing regulations, they were already halfway to being ideal flight attendants. "Mr Stimpson," Church is supposed to have said, "if women were casually living in the air, choosing to work there, wouldn't it have a good psychological effect and help rid the public of any fear?"

The racial and class identities of the women were essential if airlines were going to convince the public that flying was safe. It wasn't Amelia Earhart, or any of the other aviatrixes that could accomplish this, but the efficient young woman handing out drinks and pillows. If she flew every day, travel by plane must be safe.

It was a stroke of genius. Of the few careers open to middle class white women then, the profession of nursing had achieved a respectability close to sainthood. Heroines since the Crimean War, nurses were accepted in society for their dedication and virtue.[77] With their strict demeanor and starched uniforms, they were regarded as nuns without the religious vocation. Commercial aviation deluded itself to be a socially advanced mode of transport — both in the cockpit and cabin — and hiring young white women and not men — either African American or white (or Cubans as Pan American Airways had done) allowed airlines to demonstrate that they were not just technologically advanced but socially as well. In the social hierarchy of the day, unmarried white women were one rung above African Americans. Their feminine presence would highlight the masculine competence of the cockpit crew, just as their white skin would distinguish air travel from the railway porters.[78] Being middle class meant that they could be counted on to be respectable (i.e., moral) and more importantly, distrustful of organized labor.

Without wedding rings, the women were vulnerable to whatever humiliation they encountered and as they would inevitably leave to marry, temporary. They would demonstrate, Church pointed out, that if the "weaker sex" could daily brave the perils of flight, so too could male passengers.

Convinced, Stimpson wrote to the BAT president that nurses would know what to do in an emergency and not panic because "the average graduate nurse is a girl with some horse sense". As he expected, management was cool to the idea. "We don't want any flappers or usherettes in pantaloons." they wrote back. Having a girl on board, they warned, would lead to sexual impropriety (on the part of the girl, not the pilots). Stimpson countered that a nurse "has seen enough of men to not to be inclined to chase them around the block at every opportunity."

Considering this an experiment with dubious results at best, Boeing's managers reluctantly agreed to a three-month trial and allowed Church, who became history's first female flight attendant, to hire seven more nurses. The first eight stewardesses were Church, Margaret Arnott, Inez Keller, Cornelia Peterman, Harriet Fry, Jessie Carter, Ellis Crawford, and Alva Johnson. Because of the Boeing 80's narrow aisle and weight limitations, Stimpson drew up some sensible restrictions for what the third crew member would be: no older than 25 years of age, up to 5'4" in height and weighing no more than 115 pounds. A hundred nurses were interviewed and on May 15, 1930, stewardess service began on BAT aircraft with Church herself looking after 14 passengers on a flight from San Francisco to Chicago. Being a stewardess, she realized, was the only way that a woman could earn a salary in aviation during the Depression.[79]

Stimpson's next innovation caught the attention of *TIME Magazine*. What kept men out of airplanes the magazine reported was fear. "Another was their wives' fear and Boeing Air Transport's West Coast manager, Stephen Stimpson, who had introduced stewardesses to the flying public, decided to do something about wives' fear." A survey revealed that 36 per cent of wives did not want their husbands to fly, according to Stimpson, primarily because they themselves had never flown; many had never visited an airport and most had never seen a plane newer than a trimotor Ford. He advertised in the California newspapers his company's "very special invitation" to wives to accompany their husbands on a complementary ticket. The promotion was so successful that soon happy, loving couples filled BAT's planes. When the airline wrote to the wives and asked how they enjoyed the experience, their reply was "What flight?"

In Britain, where Imperial Airways used stewards for their far-flung colonial routes, the only way that a woman could get a job as a stewardess was to be hired by another woman who owned the airline. The Honorable Victor Mildred Mary Bruce saw a Blackburn Bluebird in a Regent Street showroom with the ticket "Ready to go anywhere." She bought the plane and twelve weeks later, having learned to fly it, took off on September 25, 1930, for Japan. She said that her call sign G-ABDS stood for "A Bloody Daft Stunt." She arrived home on February 20, 1931, having become the first woman to circumnavigate the world — albeit crossing the oceans by ship. In May 1936, with a single aircraft, Mary Bruce set up her own airline "Air Dispatch", flying between Croydon and Paris. She had already begun a commuter air service she called the "Tube of the Air", flying from small airports that circled London. Bruce was already something of a legend — the first female in Britain to ride a motorcycle on a public road (at fifteen with her collie dog in the sidecar!) and twice appeared before the magistrates in court for doing so.[80] On the busy London-Paris route already served by Imperial Airways (which used stewards);

Bruce saw the potential in a young woman taking care of the passengers. But all the girls she hired got air sick and quit. That was when she looked at her secretary, the nineteen-year-old Daphne Kearley (said to be "an attractive blonde") from Golders Green, and supposedly said: "You're pretty and don't get air sick. How would you like to be an air hostess?"

Kearley (below) was paid £3 weekly to serve the passengers smoked salmon and caviar and somehow had the time to take dictation from the businessmen. As Britain's first air hostess, she is said to have received as many as 299 marriage proposals in her ten months service. After the Second World War, Bruce's company couldn't compete with the state airlines and went into coachbuilding.

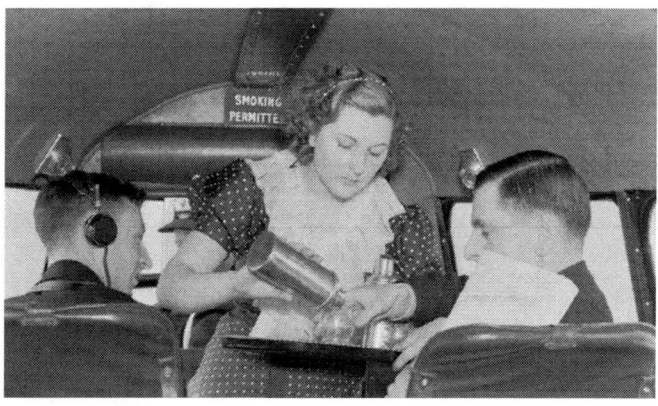

What to call the airborne Florence Nightingales presented Stimpson and later airline managers with a variety of choice — "escort" had unsavory connotations and "air maid" was too bucolic. When Boeing Air Transport became United Air Lines, management at first called the growing number of nurses hired "air conductresses." Only an ad agency could have dreamed up names like "airette" or "air aide", "page" and "skipper" were too boyish and "airess" was definitely out; giving the idea that she was a debutante doing this until the trust fund came in. "Courier" or "courierette" sounded as if she worked for the Post Office and "attendant" as if she gave out towels in hotel toilets. To promote interest in the movie *Air Hostess*, the Roxy Theatre in New York held a contest on the subject of a "quicker" name for an air hostess.[81] Ruth Nichols was on the committee to choose from suggestions. In that order, "Bellaire", "Airbelle", "Skylass" and "Skyette" were chosen. The first prize winner won a round trip by air to Hollywood, and the other three won return trips from New York to Hartford, Connecticut.

Steamship companies had long relied on stewardesses to care for female passengers — they cleaned their cabins, ran baths and were on call throughout the voyage. As the airlines had already borrowed the rank of "captain" from ships (to say nothing of the nautical uniforms that flight crews wore), "stewardess" suited, and remained until the gender-neutral 1970s.

Pre-flight, the BAT stewardess swept the cabin, adjusted the altimeter and clock on the cabin wall, tightened the screws that held each wicker chair to the floor and (because the windows on the Boeing 80 slid open,) swatted the flies that got in. As the ubiquitous air sickness bags would not be designed by Gilmore Tilmen Schjeldahl until 1949, they also emptied and washed the porcelain "erp" containers tucked under each seat and — for those passengers who had been unable to reach them in time on landing — hosed the vomit off the cabin floor. There was no formal training for stewardesses yet — it was "learn-as-you go" with advice from colleagues. Commercial aviation was so new that roles hadn't been settled yet so at small airports the stewardess also helped push the plane out, sometimes carrying cans of gasoline to it and loading the passengers' luggage. Much of what they were expected to do — serving food, cleaning the toilet, and catering to men, airline executives reasoned, was "women's work" anyway. It was what they would have done at home with a large family.

Initially, the eight stewardesses wore their own nurses' uniforms to reassure passengers. Perhaps because they were still unsure about the experiment, BAT management went in-house for the design of their uniforms. Zay Smith, one of the BAT pilots already responsible for designing the company logo is credited with this.

When the passengers boarded a BAT plane, they were no longer greeted by a co-pilot who looked too young to be flying but by an efficient young woman in a dark green uniform with matching cape and 'shower cap' tam, (the last because of the wind) who knew their name. On board, the young woman relieved the passengers of their tickets, hats, coats and especially their shoes — exchanging them for slippers. The businessmen must have assumed that this last was part of the service. More critically, the slippers were used because of the aircraft's instability and centre of gravity. Even with the pilot's judicious use of the trim tab wheel, airliners then were dangerously sensitive to anyone moving about, especially to the toilet in the rear, and particularly if they were heavy businessmen.

In flight, the BAT stewardess used the closet-sized toilet to change into a white uniform, chosen because it was reminiscent of a hospital. Where the stewardesses sat when not moving about the cabin was of little regard to management and the women referred to the mail bags that they sat on at the back as the 13th seat. Later, a fold down seat would be attached to the toilet door. The planes had steam hampers and, no matter the time of day, the passengers were served coffee or tea, fruit cocktail, fried chicken, and rolls. In between, the stewardess made conversation to alleviate the passenger's fears and distributed sedatives, blankets, magazines, playing cards, chewing gum or aspirin as necessary. To (unsuccessfully) counter the headache-inducing drone from the Boeing's three engines, the passengers gratefully accepted from her wads of cotton wool.

Before inflight entertainment, the stewardess was required to be familiar with the weather and topography they were flying over — passengers wanted to know the names of the cities, towns, and rivers underneath them and what that factory made — and were dismissive when she couldn't answer them. Before landing, once more in her green uniform, she reversed the process, handing passengers their hats, coats, and shoes that she somehow found time to polish inflight, wishing them farewell again by name. For 100 hours work she earned $100 a month and was entitled to a free pass on the airline.

That was how it was supposed to work in theory. Inez Keller was one of the 8 original BAT stewardesses, and her memories were quite different — and illuminating. "We had to carry the luggage on board and join a bucket brigade to help fuel the aircraft." Inez worked on the Oakland, CA to Cheyenne, WY route of 950 miles and 5 refueling stops. The complete flight was supposed to take 18 hours but because of bad weather (the Boeing flew at 2,000 feet) it was usually 24 hours. When the weather was bad, they would land in a farmer's field and wait for it to clear, after which she had to assist in removing the farmer's fences, so the aircraft could take off.

Against all odds, she had never been in a crash, but Inez remembered "some pretty close calls." On one occasion, the stabilizer broke and the plane, "quivering like a bird," made an emergency landing on the shores of Salt Lake. Another time, the plane ran out of gas and the pilot made an emergency landing in a wheat field near Cherokee, WY. "People from the surrounding area came in wagons and on horseback to see the plane," she said. "They'd never seen one before, and they wanted to touch it and to touch me. One of them called me 'the white angel from the sky."' Although the passengers took to the stewardesses immediately, Inez remembered that the cockpit crew did not. "The pilots did not want us at all." she said "They were rugged, temperamental characters who had once carried revolvers to protect the mail (this was a left over from the Pony Express days). They wouldn't even speak to us during the first couple of trips."

Worse than the pilots were their wives who began a vicious letter-writing campaign to Boeing, accusing the stewardesses of trying to steal their husbands and demanding their removal. Her funniest experience, Inez remembered, was the time when the plane was full, and the pilot couldn't get enough altitude to make it over the mountains outside Salt Lake City. "He finally flew back to the airport and dropped me off." she laughed, "Then the plane made it over the mountains." At that time, she weighed all of 120 pounds. Inez Keller quit flying after she lost hearing in one ear when the plane hit an air pocket over Reno and dropped 500 feet. Of the original eight stewardesses, three quit (including Church) within 18 months and the others soon after. According to *TIME Magazine*, they found husbands immediately after — but contrary to expectations few married pilots.

For a generation of passengers that had grown up with railways, the sliding windows on unpressurised planes were a great temptation to throw out empty Coke bottles, used cutlery and full "erp" containers — and the stewardess was on a constant look out to prevent this from happening, especially in populated areas.[82] Much to the dismay of air travelers then, the later Boeing 247 and DC-2 would end this convenience. But with the fuel tank no longer carried within or under the cabin, they did allow for smoking on board and the stewardesses carried cigarettes and lighters with them. The cabin was soon a fug akin to a night club, the cigarette smoke disguising the smell of fear and for days after, everyone's clothes stank of smoke, the lethal effects of pneumonia, emphysema, and lung cancer unknown.

Then as now, cleaning the aircraft's toilet was an unloved but essential duty. Before pneumatic vacuums sucked liquids and solids away, the original aircraft toilets were (as on trains then) of the hole-in-the-floor variety. For anyone brave enough to use one in an unpressurised aircraft like a Lockheed Electra, this made for a drafty, bumpy, freezing experience. When one lifted the cover over the "can" (and it was literally that), the user was greeted by the sight of clouds and the countryside below. For good reason, passengers were forbidden to use the toilet over towns and stewardesses warned to latch the cover on tightly as the air flow interfered with the aircraft's balance. But as bad as cleaning the toilets inflight were, the stewardesses sympathized with the poor maintenance men who had to hose down the aircraft's tail on landing - by which time all the effluent had defrosted. When chemical toilets replaced the holes-in-the-floor, they were appreciated by everyone except the company accountants as all that sewage storage added extra weight to the plane. Nicknamed "the blue room" by the stewardesses (because of the blue "Anotec" liquid used) the early chemical toilets blocked quickly and leaked constantly.

As expected in the male preserve that was aviation, Stimpson's decision to employ women wasn't popular with rival airlines. Other airline managers pressured BAT to desist after the trial period — knowing that to compete they would have to follow suit. The former air ace Eddie Rickenbacker, now president of Eastern Airlines, even flew to BAT's head office in Chicago to make them change their minds. With the Depression, he argued, every woman hired took a man's job from him. As a breadwinner, he had a family to feed and the stewardess (it was thought) spent her pay on female "frivolities." Besides, it was a "given" that respectable women did not work outside the home.

But it was too late to put the genie back in the bottle and other airlines began hiring women as stewardesses — Eastern Airlines in 1931, American Airlines in 1933, Western Air Lines and Trans World Airlines in 1935. When American Airlines bought a Curtiss Condor, a twin-engine biplane airliner that could carry up to 15 passengers, it advertised for stewardesses. From the flood of applicants, an apprehensive four were selected. The maximum height allowed was 5 feet as even an inch taller meant that the poor girl had to spend the entire flight in a crouched position to avoid the Condor's low ceiling. No one at American Airlines knew what their training was to be — the only employee knowledgeable about inflight hospitality was the co-pilot, formerly the disgruntled sandwich-passer. The four women were given a tour of the Curtiss aircraft factory, a glimpse of the interior of a Condor and "some rudimentary psychology to keep the passengers happy"— more than likely to distract them from the vomit-inducing roller coaster rides to come.

In May 1934, Swissair became the first European airline to copy BAT, hiring Nelly Hedwig Diener (below) as its first air hostess. Lufthansa followed, the German airline credited with realizing that as the center of attraction on any flight, the women could be walking, talking advertisements for the airline.[83] Its stewardesses were stylishly attired in white box-cut jackets and jaunty fez style hats, mid-calf-length A-line skirts with dark ties that sported the airline's motif of the flying crane (and after 1936 a swastika) on the shoulder sleeve.[84]

Captains, like mariners of old, considered a woman onboard bad luck. Flying was dangerous enough they protested, without them also having to look after the weaker sex. Piloting a ship or aircraft was a strictly gendered male occupation and they objected to a female presence in such cramped surroundings — as did their wives (who it was said, would drive to the airport to look over the women their husbands spent the day with). Initially envious of the media attention the first stewardesses were getting, when the pilots realized that they would no longer have to leave the cockpit to serve passengers coffee — or bother about their welfare at all, the idea quickly gained favor. Besides, the women did bring the pilots their meals into the cockpit! And in keeping with contemporary mores then, male dominance on board (so the pilots told themselves) would still be maintained because as former nurses the stewardesses were already trained to be deferential to the all-powerful doctors. It was of course expected that they would not question the decisions of their employers or the captains in the cockpits, and that they would just as unquestioningly stop working if they married. The pilots maintained this hierarchy with hazing, teasing, and groping which served in the words of a reporter "to keep air hostesses in their place." American Airlines even made their stewardesses stand to attention outside the aircraft door and salute the captain as he boarded.

Best of all for commercial aviation, was the free publicity gained by hiring "eye candy". Unlike the railways, the airlines realized early on that age-old marketing axiom: sex sells.[85] Audiences could not get enough of these wonder women or "sky girls" as the stewardesses were called in the movies — plucky young women braving the elements at the unimaginable height of 5,000 feet. while serving appreciative businessmen but (as in the movies) giving their hearts to the pilots. As an appreciative male passenger remarked, "She was your wife, only younger and prettier."

From the first, tipping the stewardess was forbidden. With several airlines, many stewards were tipped well into the 1970s as one would doormen and head waiters. But giving a woman money for services rendered cheapened the "hospitality experience" and besides the college-educated nurse was on the passenger's own social level. She wasn't a waitress or hostess and to emphasize this, American Airlines even designed the "sorority girl" look in uniforms for their stewardesses. Substituting for your wife, sister or daughter, the stewardess addressed you by name (surname only and prefixed by "Mister") and made polite conversation at your seat. She also personally belted each passenger in — something that given the social norms of the day, the African Americans could never do.

Rather than the servility associated with black porters and all the uncomfortable racial connotations that went with it, pre-war airlines marketed family domesticity. As few passengers had seen the inside of an airliner let alone flown in one, the aim was to convince them the experience would be as safe as being in their own living rooms. The reality was otherwise, but air travel was touted as your easy chair on wings — with your dutiful wife or daughter in attendance.

In an era when society and the media depicted single women as either femmes fatales, nymphomaniacs or sexually repressed librarian/virgins whose only ambition was to seduce men — the first stewardesses had to walk a fine line in an all-male world. With little else to look at, the eyes of a bored male audience followed her every move as she performed her duties. While in uniform, she wasn't allowed to smoke or chew gum either onboard or at the airport or linger too long in the cockpit or with any one passenger. She had to be "girl-next-door friendly" but not invite lechery, be firm but not intimidating, gracious but not fawning. She was placed on a pedestal, but not until the 1960s, was she overtly pimped. Aware of the inherent danger and discomfort that everyone on board was in, the stewardess also had to wield complete authority over her charges, all of whom were older than her. Alone and vulnerable, fending off sexual advances and marriage proposals, she had to make the work look glamorous even as it was grueling, repetitive, and socially demeaning.

With their country's social diversity, airlines in the United States scrutinized their applicants thoroughly. Family background, religion and moral character were taken into consideration at interviews. Social poise, regional accent and vocabulary were studied. Were small town girls more amenable to middle class values than their sophisticated big city cousins? No doubt it was here that the potential stewardesses' physical attributes were checked: did she have any visible scars? What were her teeth like (dental care during the Depression was minimal), her posture, her neatness, her ease at conversing? The profession of nursing had already screened much of these requirements for the airlines, and accustomed the women to uniforms, discipline and shift work.

No one, not the airline or the women, considered this a lifetime career. At best for the women, it was an adventure between homework and housework — with a chance of meeting a potential husband. Early retirement was rigidly fixed. Customers expected youth and beauty to look at — and in their eyes a 30-year-old possessed neither. Like society, the airlines deemed a woman a failure if she hadn't "caught" a husband by then. As one airline manager warned recruits, "If you haven't found a man to keep you by the time you are 28, then TWA won't want you either."[86] As in fairy tales, airlines celebrated innocence and virginity before marriage and women got one shot at romantic happiness. Looking after the passengers, the stewardesses were told, was a good rehearsal for their married lives to come — the ultimate goal of every single woman then.

In 1936, in preparation for its new fleet of DC-3s, American Airlines began a stewardess training course at a Chicago hotel. On their first day, it was drilled into the applicants that marriage — even the hint of an engagement — during their employment, led to instant dismissal.[87] "Supervisors combed through wedding announcements in local newspapers looking for evidence of rule breaking." Gail Collins, author of *When Everything Changed: The Amazing Journey of American Women* wrote. "They discovered one stewardess was secretly married while she was on a cross country flight — when she landed in Denver, a supervisor met the flight and made sure she didn't catch the returning one back home".[88]

In ancient Rome, the vestal virgins vowed to chastity were fundamental to the Empire's prosperity and longevity. If they strayed — wars, plagues, even erupting volcanoes were sure to follow. As an embodiment of Roman society, they belonged to no one — and everyone. So too was a stewardess to her airline. Catering to male fantasy, even while being ogled, she had to appear "untouched". Well into the 1970s, besides the written and oral exams, airlines subjected applicants to a thorough physical one that included a pelvic examination — to make sure they weren't pregnant or had given birth. In short, as a stewardess you had to be desirable but (in theory at least) unavailable. Being widowed or divorced was out — somehow management (all male of course) reasoned that it was impossible for the women to appear virginal after either experience.

By social convention, a married woman's place was in her home and the airlines reasoned that were she a wife or mother, the stewardess's focus would be on her husband

and children rather than the passengers she was being paid to serve. With marriage, their very identities were subsumed into their husband's. As religious orders had discovered centuries before, for complete concentration on her duties, the novice had to be wed only to the vocation, to be "a bride of the airline." Performing as men required of them, social historians will point out, was what all women did then — as wives, daughters, secretaries, actresses or waitresses.

Injected into an all-male environment, there is no doubt that the early female pilots and stewardesses suffered sexual harassment and like their sisters since, endured it for practical reasons — to avoid the career-destroying labels of "whiner" or "troublemaker" or because during the Depression, they couldn't afford to lose a job. Human beings cocooned in a metal tube from the outside world, said a former flight attendant, think that the rules no longer apply. Even the original eight stewardesses hired in 1930 endured sexual advances. Decades later, Harriet Fry Iden recalled, "Men tried to get fresh. That was an occupational hazard. We could handle that." She slapped a professor when he chased her around the cabin. Her supervisor supported her, saying that the man "must've had it coming."

Why didn't the early stewardesses report sexual harassment to their employers? (This is a rhetorical question like "Why didn't actresses, female recruits in the military and police, shop assistants, secretaries, waitresses, or nurses?") As late as 2018, only 7 per cent of flight attendants who have been victims of harassment or abuse say they have reported it to their employers. "And what that tells us," said Sara Nelson, the president of the Association of Flight Attendants union, "is that flight attendants don't believe that they have the backing of the airlines, nor that if they reported this, anyone would do anything about it."[89]

In Canada with its sparse population and overbuilt railway system, until 1938 there was only bush flying — and it was very much "a man's world". As one contemporary bush pilot remarked, the bush was hard enough for men, let alone white women. Pilots were recruited from the Royal Canadian Air Force (RCAF) and the maintenance staff from technical schools and auto garages. The only females who regularly flew as passengers in Canada were prostitutes and, for obvious reasons, the government and press did not acknowledge this. Because of the hundreds of lonely men in isolated mining communities, bush pilots made a profitable living by ferrying in bootleg alcohol and prostitutes from the outside world. Accompanied by their madam, the women were customarily flown to the mining camps on payday — and considerably wealthier, flown out the following week. Sometimes they shared the aircraft with the regional parish priest also doing his rounds. "In Red Lake, Manitoba" remembered the bush pilot Herb Seagrim, a future vice president of Air Canada, "a nice balance was maintained between praying and sinning."[90]

Canadians had heard of the uniformed young women who tended passengers inflight but never seen one. In 1938, Trans Canada Airlines (TCA) barely a year old had a single revenue flight, the Vancouver-Seattle run. On this route, passengers were flocking to TCA's rival, United Air Lines (UAL), because its Boeing 247D had a stewardess. As tiny as TCA's Lockheed 10 Electras were — five seats on either side of the aisle — they did allow for a toilet at the rear and other airlines had attached a folding seat to its door for the stewardess's use — without a seat belt. Billy Wells, the TCA Vancouver office manager was told to hire two women as stewardesses for the Seattle flight. With Vancouver-Montreal passenger flights to begin the following year, this would be a rehearsal for more stewardesses.

He interviewed Lucille Garner and Pat Eccleston, two nurses who had never been to an airport, let alone flown in a plane. Neither knew what stewardesses did, never having seen one at work. But for Garner, the job was a unique opportunity and a chance for adventure. "Oh, to be a stewardess was something." she remembered. "Nurses didn't make that much money. It was an adventure; everything was new about it; it was a brand-new life for women."

Adolf Hitler had annexed Austria and the Japanese were committing mass atrocities in China, but more germane for Canadians was surviving the Depression, then in its eighth year. For a woman to be employed at all was to be more fortunate than 40 per cent of the country's workforce. Garner and Eccleston were put on the company payroll on July 1, 1938, and have the distinction of being not only the first Canadian stewardesses but also TCA's first female employees. Told to get uniforms for the job, the pair went to the local Hudson's Bay Company store. There "the staff came up with what appeared to be an appropriate cap and uniform." Management recognized the beige gabardine uniforms as those worn by female elevator operators. "So, we went with navy blue and started again." Garner said, choosing a single-breasted navy-blue serge suit.

The passengers treated the two nurses as maids (which many must have had then) but as stewardesses the pair were paid $125 a month — without emptying bed pans — as opposed to the $100 that they got in a hospital. It wasn't enough to put down on a mortgage or even a car loan — but in an era when banks did not allow single women to open bank accounts without a male relative co-signing, neither would have been contemplated.

In Australia, Victor and Ivan Holyman used a pair of DH.84 airliners for their Melbourne-Sydney flights until 1936 when they got the ban lifted on the purchase of

American aircraft and bought a fourteen-passenger DC-2. Holyman's Airways flew between Hobart, Launceston, Flinders Island, King Island, Melbourne, Cootamundra, Canberra, and Sydney. Blanche Due and Marguerite Grueber were the first Australian air hostesses to be hired. Both were working towards their pilot's licenses and Blanche had been a nurse for seven months. They underwent a six-week training course conducted by the Hostess Service Superintendent, Capt Holyman's wife, Hazel. On graduation, the pair designed their own navy-blue uniforms and had them tailor-made in Melbourne.

Before departure, Blanche and Marguerite would check the passenger list, put the coffee and sandwiches onboard — and answer all questions. Unique to Australia, one of their duties was to fix the straps around each of the passenger's legs before take-off and remove them inflight. Coffee was served in wax cups until it was noticed that the wax melted and stuck to passenger's lips. With the DC-2, passengers were allowed cigarettes but not pipes. The first scheduled flight with stewardesses was on May 2, 1936, from Melbourne to Sydney with a number of VIPs onboard. Holyman's Airways would merge with West Australia Airways on July 1, 1936, to form Australian National Airways (ANA).

The opportunities that the airlines afforded stewardesses everywhere were incalculable, they had joined a male world that they were now the physical and social center of. As teachers, they would have seen only snotty nosed children, as nurses it would have been the demanding sick and elderly, as telephone operators or hairdressers, their clientele would have been other women. Now they were surrounded by men — captains of industry, movie stars, playboys, or the dashing young pilots they daily worked with. The opportunities of upward mobility to marry someone that they would have never met in a typing pool, library or Woolworth's were an added bonus. In the 1930s when few women traveled outside their hometowns — and those that did were not respectable, the first stewardesses took pride in that unlike their earthbound sisters, they were part of a mode of transport that was closer to Buck Rogers than Jane Austen. That they flew every day mysteriously made them more attractive to the opposite sex — as one stewardess discovered when she visited her hometown, "and all the Lotharios now came out of the woodwork."

Although they had no training to do either, comic books and girl's novels had stewardesses thwarting hijackers (called air bandits then) and rescuing their passengers (invariably handsome young unmarried executives) after an air crash. When the last actually happened, it only reinforced the super woman mystique. On April 7, 1936, a TWA DC-2 hit a Pennsylvania mountain, and Nellie Granger the 5' 2" air hostess was thrown unhurt from the burning fuselage. She returned to the aircraft, pulled passengers out of it, and then walked many miles in darkness for help.

Helen Wells authored the Cherry Ames series of mysteries for teenage girls in the 1940s, similar to the Nancy Drew stories. Cherry Ames and Vicki Barr both solved mysteries while pursuing careers as a nurse and a stewardess. In *Silver Wings for Vicki*, even while coping with passengers that she categorizes as "Mr Bore" and "Mr Wolf", Vicki alerts the G-men that the heavy jowled, swarthy foreigner (of course) onboard is a jewel smuggler. As amazing as that was, after serving a

steak dinner to each passenger, Vicki hands them an envelope containing a mint and a cigarette!

Flying in the sexist world that aviation was, working for employers who ranged from condescending to misogynistic, having to live by male-designed restrictions on their weight, grooming, sexual mores and social lives, the pioneers could not afford to be overtly feminist — gender equity like racial inclusivity, was fifty years in the future.

In 1938, the Civil Aeronautics Act began to regulate ticket prices and routes for airlines, leaving them few opportunities to compete. Pandering to businessmen, the airlines would begin using stewardesses as their basis of competition. Marketing cast the stewardesses as performing what women did naturally — providing charm and comfort. But going about their work professionally was one thing — thinking it to be a profession was another.

8: MARKHAM: LOUCHE AND LYRICAL

Four-year-old Mary Price never forgot the turquoise plane with silver wings, its engine sputtering. The fishermen in her village of Little Lorraine on the tip of Cape Breton Island, Nova Scotia "knew it was in trouble." The engine let out a final cough, the propeller froze, and the pilot aimed for a patch of level ground near Baleine Cove. The plane lurched to a halt and its nose buried itself ostrich-like in the mud of a bog. "To see a plane coming low," Mary remembered of that September afternoon in 1936, "at that time was quite a thing."

A tall figure with a mop of wavy blonde hair stumbled out of the cockpit, bleeding from a cut where her forehead had struck the instrument panel (overleaf). Vincent William Burke was the first villager to reach her as she struggled out of knee-deep mud.[91] They shook hands, he recalled years later, and the exhausted flier asked two questions: "Do you have a cigarette?" and "Where am I?" Beryl Markham had become the first woman to fly East-West across the Atlantic.

She was born on October 26, 1902, at Westfield House, Ashwell in the East Midlands. Her father Charles Clutterbuck having been "removed from the army" (shorthand for fast women, slow horses, and unpaid bar bills) struck out with the family for British East Africa. In 1904, he purchased 1,000 acres at Njoro, Kenya to farm. Even at four years old, life in Africa so suited Beryl that when her mother returned home two years later (she

had scarpered with a colonel), she took only elder son Richard with her.

Beryl spent her childhood with her contemporaries, the children of the farm's migrant workers. From them, she learned Swahili and to hunt pig barefoot with a spear or bow and arrow. Throughout her life if she hunted, it was for the pot, not the trophy wall. Africa, she would later write, was the breath and life of her childhood. A natural rider, she accompanied her father to the races in Nairobi for which they both trained racehorses. He treated her as a son and gave her a racehorse called *Pegasus* — a horse with wings. She hero-worshipped him — so that all through her life, she never found a man who measured up to him.

In 1919, Beryl was married off to Jock Purves, a neighboring farmer and also one of her father's biggest creditors. The gossip at the Muthaiga Country Club in Nairobi was that Jock, who was in his thirties, agreed to forget the debt if Clutterbuck would allow him to marry the tall sixteen-year-old.[92] Beryl's promiscuity, even in a society known for the decadence of the "Happy Valley" set, was well known. The novelist Martha Gellhorn thought she was an African Circe who turned men into pigs. She had a complete disregard for fidelity or finance and lived off the generosity of friends and lovers. With her sandy hair, blue eyes, and colt-like legs, she was never short of either. Typical of "expat" communities, the Kenya colonials thrived on scandal, and she was remembered as being feckless and amoral. For a young woman to succeed in a man's world of horse racing — women in Britain were still forbidden to train horses — she displayed an intuitive professionalism that later she brought to aviation.

Through her friendship with Tania (Karen) Blixen of *Out of Africa* fame, she would meet her ex-husband, Baron Bror Frederick von Blixen. A charming adventurer and womanizer, he would shape the child-woman in Beryl. Bror would later marry the celebrated Swedish aviatrix Eva Dickson, the third woman to get a pilot's license in Sweden.

It was all too much for the helpless Jock who gave Beryl her divorce and in 1927, the opportunity to marry Mansfield Markham, heir to a coal mining fortune. In her two years of formal schooling, Beryl might have read Thackeray's novel *Vanity Fair*, for she played the character of social climbing Becky Sharp well. On honeymoon in England with Markham, she met the two princes — The Prince of Wales (the future Edward VIII), and Prince Henry, the Duke of Gloucester and somehow, Beryl managed to be presented to the King Emperor George V and Queen Mary.[93] When both princes came out to Kenya for "the season", Markham, like all of Nairobi, had good cause to be suspicious of his wife's relationship with Prince Henry while the pair were on safari. Beryl liked His Royal Highness who won races — the other riders courteously holding back so he could — and on safari, rationed himself to shooting only two of each species — unlike his brother the Prince of Wales who took random pot shots at elephant herds from the air.

When the royal pair were recalled to England as the king was dying, Beryl followed them, reportedly running barefoot down the corridors of Buckingham Palace, and hiding from Queen Mary in a closet. She had learned how to use her sexuality as a weapon without fully considering the carnage left in its wake. She gave birth to a son and devoid of maternal feelings — having had a childhood without a mother — gave the baby up to the Markham family. Uncertain as to who the father was, Mansfield would bring an action for divorce against her, threatening to name His Royal Highness in the proceedings. Divorce still carried the social stigma of disgrace and Prince Henry was third in line to the throne. Queen Mary made it clear to the Markham family that one did not cite a Prince of the Blood in a divorce petition. Beryl and Mansfield separated and in return for her to stay away from Prince Henry, the Queen bought Beryl off with a small annuity of £750, payable until her death. She returned to Kenya in 1930 to take Denys Finch Hatton as her lover. In the movie *Out of Africa*, Finch Hatton was played by the actor Robert Redford who failed to capture his languid magnetism — or looks — Denys was as bald as a billiard ball. Years later, Beryl would say that he was the only man that competed for her affections with her father.

Finch Hatton refused to teach her how to fly — being too new at it himself, so she turned to Tom Campbell Black, the managing director of Wilson Airways, Nairobi. Tom's pioneering flights from Nairobi to England had been financed by the recently widowed fifty-year-old Florrie Wilson. Beryl proved an apt pupil, soloing after eight hours of dual instruction and purchased a blue and silver Avro Avian. She would write of it. "The ship would rather hunt the wind … she has a derelict quality in her character; she toys with freedom and hunts at liberation but yields to her own desires gently."

Denys's Gipsy Moth crashed on May 14, 1931, killing him and a passenger. Contemplating suicide, Beryl was consoled by Tom and became his lover. Throughout her life, her insecurity only came alive when she had a strong personality to soothe it. Tom helped her get a commercial license, the first for a woman in Kenya, and both discussed wanting to emulate the record-breaking flights of Amy Johnson and Jim Mollison. Partly to escape the Muthaiga Club gossip that he had exploited his romantic relationship with the widow Wilson, Tom moved to England in March 1932. With just 127 hours in her logbook, as she had with the two princes, Beryl was determined to follow, flying her Avian from Nairobi to London. She was held up in the Sudan with a broken piston but otherwise made the Mediterranean crossing via Tripoli and Malta to Naples, Rome, Pisa, Marseilles, Lyon, and Paris. That it was done in an open cockpit aircraft without a radio or direction-finding equipment was a feat that the British media applauded. Tom was surprised and not a little embarrassed to see her, as he was now enamored with the actress Florence Desmond.

Beryl returned to Kenya, bought a DH Leopard Moth, and began an air taxi service, safari spotting from the air, and delivering medical supplies to Kakamega, a gold mining community near Lake Victoria with its pocket handkerchief-size airfield. She scouted for Bror Blixen's big game celebrity hunters like Ernest Hemingway (who would make Bror the model for Robert Wilson in his *The Short Happy Life of Francis Macomber)*; "Freddie" and Amy Phipps Guest and Alfred Vanderbilt. When she read that Tom had won the 1934 Mildenhall to Melbourne Air Race with Charles Scott — and proposed to Desmond who had paid for the Comet DH.88 he flew, it was hard to know what must have hurt Beryl more — the forthcoming marriage or the record breaking that she could have been part of.

Now thirty-three years old, Beryl was determined to show Tom and the world that she too could set records. Women had flown the London-Cape Town and London-

Australia routes but London-New York was still an unpicked plum. Somehow, she clung to the fantasy that if she succeeded, Tom, now married to Florence, would return to her. In March 1936, Markham sold the Avian, and set out for England in her DH Leopard Moth with Bror for company. She describes the flight in *West with the Night*, the autobiography that has immortalized her. It is here rather than her transatlantic flight, that her lyricism shines. She writes of clouds: "They lay on the earth like sadness come to rest; they clung to people like burial clothes, white and premature." In Cairo they overnighted at Shepherd's Hotel and a fortune teller prophesized that Beryl would fly over "a great water to a strange country, and that she would fly alone."

Libya was then an Italian colony and flying across it meant enduring the rubber-stamped bureaucracy of heavily bemedaled officials "with three lira worth of authority." To satisfy them, Beryl and Bror had to circle each of the newly built Italian forts three times. She noted that "the sons of Rome" were making "grandiose preparations. Their forts and their chests extended outward far beyond their usual confines." At Benghazi, an Arab driver who had lain in wait to ambush them outside the airport, dropped them off at a brothel for the night. With its crone of a mistress and patrolling cockroaches, the contrast with Shepherd's Hotel was inescapable, but neither mentioned it. They crossed the Mediterranean at an altitude of 100 feet and "saw the sea snatch at the wind with white, frustrated hands." France was soon on the horizon and then Paris and the next day Blix, Beryl and Tom sat at the Mayfair Hotel, London where they drank a toast to Africa "because we knew that Africa was gone."

Those who knew Beryl said that she hoped to win Tom back by attempting the Atlantic but without an aircraft, this was a dream. Then at a dinner party, the Anglo-Irish peer John Carberry offered his Percival Vega Gull for the crossing and use of it for a national tour after. Known to be a thoroughly unpleasant character, Carberry must have been hoping that she would refuse. The only woman who had flown the ocean solo West to East ("the easy way") was Amelia Earhart. The fates of Princess Anne Lowenstien-Wertheim and Elsie MacKay when they flew against the prevailing winds were too recent to ignore. But Beryl accepted, no doubt with alacrity, and as the other dinner guests were witnesses, Carberry could not back down.

The Gull, christened *The Messenger,* was ready by September 1. For her flying gas tank, she chose as her launch point RAF Abingdon, a bomber base with its mile long runway. The media headlined Beryl as a "a daredevil society woman", "the blonde huntress", "a young mother" and not knowing that she and Mansfield had separated, "Her Broken Heart is Not Mended"— all of which she thought flippant.[94] But she hired Harry Bruno, a press agent in New York in anticipation of success and the money she would make. Jim Mollison (whom Tom detested) had flown from Ireland to New Brunswick in 1932 and he offered advice on her route. On September 4, the adverse weather reports did not discourage her from taking off at 4:50 pm. What did, was Tom's absence at the airfield. Mollison was there and made a big show of

MRS BERYL MARKHAM — PERCIVAL GULL

giving her his watch. When she took off, he shrugged and said "Well, that the last we'll see of her."

Of the flight, Beryl would write: "Being alone in an airplane for even so short a time as a night and a day, irrevocably alone, with nothing to observe but your instruments and your own hands in semi darkness, nothing to contemplate but the size of your own small courage, nothing to wonder about but the beliefs, the faces, and the hopes rooted in your mind — such an experience can be as startling as the first awareness of a stranger walking by your side at night. You are the stranger."[95]

Twenty-two hours later with accurate navigation and a few anxious swigs of brandy, she landed nose down at Baleine Cove, a few miles from Sydney Airport, Nova Scotia. Later it was discovered that *The Messenger* had fuel enough for a further three hundred miles, but ice had blocked the air intake of the tank, causing the engine to cut out and Beryl to think she was out of fuel. She was flown to New York but, alas, with Fiorello La Guardia as mayor, there was no ticker tape parade. When reporters asked those who knew her to comment on her flight, their replies are revealing. From Mansfield ("our son clapped his hands at the news"), Mollison ("delighted at her success because she went on my advice"), her father ("our Beryl's a grand girl!"), Amelia Earhart ("she did a splendid job"), Tom Campbell Black ("I thought she'd do it") and later, Mrs Kirkpatrick ("my daughter has always been extremely self-confident since she was a tiny tot.")

Envious of the attention she got, Carberry true to form, reneged on his promise to allow her use of the Gull for a national tour — which dampened her financial prospects. When Beryl heard that Tom was killed on September 19 when another aircraft ran into his plane on the runway at Liverpool airfield, she caught the *Queen Mary* home. Having lost the two men she loved, she was grief-stricken and moved in with Florence Desmond — the two having Tom in common. Inevitably, Beryl, who all her life had used friends with an incredible ruthlessness, was soon asked to leave for running up unpaid bills with Florence's dressmakers.

Alone and nearly penniless, she returned to the United States to unsuccessfully lobby the Hollywood studios for a movie about her life.[96] Giving Markham his divorce, she married Raoul Schumacher, an alcoholic and mediocre script writer. In 1940, Beryl met the pilot poet Antoine de St Exupéry who encouraged her to write of her own flying experiences.[97] Financial problems forced her to vacate California without Schumacher and move to the Bahamas. Here she could sponge off the former Prince of Wales, now the Duke of Windsor, who had been exiled to the colony by his brother. (Oh, to have been a fly on the wall when Beryl and the former Wallis Simpson chatted.)

There she began *West with the Night*, giving credit to Schumacher. Published in 1942, the book was lost in the fog of war but reissued in 1983, it was on the New York Times bestseller list for forty weeks. With the exception of Saint-Exupéry's *Wind, Sand and Stars*, nothing comes close to projecting the romance and isolation of flying at night as she does. Hemingway recommended it with "She has written so well, and marvelously well, that I was completely ashamed of myself as a writer." This did not prevent his machismo from later undermining Markham as a "high-grade bitch" and "very unpleasant."

Beryl divorced Schumacher in 1960 and lived out her last years in Nairobi, where she dominated the racing circuit until poverty and old age sentenced her to obscurity. She never recovered from a home invasion in which she was savagely beaten. Beryl Markham died on August 4, 1986, almost fifty years since her famous flight. If feminism at its core is about choice, Beryl Markham exploited her sexuality to achieve her ambitions. To quote Hemingway — she lived life all the way up.

8: AMELIA EARHART: COURAGE IS THE PRICE

F ew American icons have provoked so much fascination as Amelia Mary Earhart, best known today for her disappearance while attempting to circumnavigate the world. A few might be aware of her solo flight across the Atlantic, when everyone should know of her insatiable desire to get women the recognition, she felt they deserved.

Born on July 24, 1897, in Atchison, Kansas, in a white two-story Gothic Revival house overlooking the Missouri river, Amelia had a tomboy childhood, surpassed in the paean of American culture only by Huckleberry Finn's. In reality, her early life was closer to that of a Jane Austen heroine. Growing up in a loving family beset with genteel poverty, she coped with an absent alcoholic father and struggled to maintain her identity, especially after marriage to the overpowering George P. Putnam.

That her first airplane ride on December 28, 1920, was with Frank Hawks, later to be the legendary "Speed King", was fate. Enraptured by the experience, she recalled, "By the time I had got two or three hundred feet off the ground, I knew I had to fly." Amelia learned to fly at Kinner Airport, Los Angeles and was taught by Anita Snook, one of the first women to give flight instruction. "I'll never forget the day she and her father came to the field," recalled Snook, "I liked the way she stated her objective. 'I want to fly. Will you teach me?'"

AMELIA EARHART: COURAGE IS THE PRICE

She soloed in 1921 and bought her first plane, a sporty Kinner Airster, and on May 16, 1923 was granted an FAI flying certificate (No 6017), the sixteenth woman to do so. Not a "natural" pilot like Louise Thaden and Laura Ingalls, she was bright and enthusiastic. The first thing she did after a crash in the Airster, Snook remembered, was powder her nose, saying "We have to look nice when the reporters come." When the photo of her in her new leather flying coat appeared in the newspapers, her family were unimpressed. "The only time a lady's name should appear in print," fumed one uncle, "is at her birth, her marriage and her funeral." The most famous aviatrix of them all, Earhart was destined to appear in the media for decades after.

As an adult, Amelia lived with her mother and sister in Medford, MA, then a picturesque town where after watching a sleigh ride, James Pierpoint would go home and write the music and lyrics for *Jingle Bells*. It was through her courtship by chemical engineer Sam Chapman that Amelia must have seen her first destitute immigrants and marginalized women. Realizing that she had a strong social conscience, he took her to Industrial Workers of the World (IWW) meetings — the "Wobblies" as they were called, who organized strikes by longshoremen, fruit pickers, textile workers, actors, and lumberjacks. It was these illegal meetings for which she wore what she called her "slumming clothes", that introduced Amelia to the inequalities that women suffered and that she would use her later fame to bring attention to.

Engaged to Chapman in 1923, she refused to wear his engagement ring and put off marrying him, fearing that he would keep her from flying. Marriage was a "cage" she said that she was determined not to be trapped in, as her mother and sister were. Witnessing her parent's unhappy experience of such a union gave her, as she wrote, "no heart to look ahead." In reality, even before her first Atlantic crossing in 1928, she had outgrown domesticity and Chapman.

Amelia disliked being pigeonholed as a feminist. The word was associated with pre-Nineteenth Amendment suffragist picketing, parading, and behaving disgracefully (for women) in public. In the 1930s, mass feminist movements had coalesced into the celebration of the achievements of individual women — Margaret Bourke White, Eleanor Roosevelt, Freda Kahlo, Margaret Sanger, Katharine Hepburn, Francis Perkins, Margaret Mead and Earhart herself. Amelia was the equal of any man and the two men she loved — Chapman and Putnam — accepted this.

As the female ferry pilots would discover during the Second World War, by inhabiting and attempting to compete in a man's world, wearing slacks and leather jackets or uniforms made them sexually 'suggestive' as lesbians. Earhart (unlike Elder or Klingensmith) was never presented to the media as a sex object but like Greta Garbo and Katharine Hepburn, she was accepted as a woman who possessed "manliness in a feminine presence."[98]

She was the embodiment of the post-suffrage era's individualistic attitude towards feminism. When she became the first woman to conquer the Atlantic solo in 1932, newspaper headlines proclaimed, "Mrs Putnam Flew the Atlantic". Amelia vigorously objected to this. She flew under her own name she said — her husband George had not been in the cockpit, and he did not mind that she had done so solo — quite to the contrary. She hoped her influence would help combat the negative stereotypes about her sex. In her speeches to women's groups, Earhart emphasized the need for women to "break out of their platitudinous sphere", asserting that unlike the prisoner at the bar who is innocent until proven guilty, the woman is guilty until she proves that she can do the things men do. When asked her opinion of the roles of husbands and wives in the home, she answered, "I don't even think this is mere 'modern thinking' or 'feminism' or anything of that kind, but just good common sense".

Even in fashion, women were disadvantaged in aviation. From earliest times, they couldn't have loose clothing billowing in open cockpit planes. To the public, the dresses and hats they wore in the 1930s suggested frivolity and helplessness. Male pilot's clothing as aviator Roscoe Turner wore — slacks, leather jackets and riding boots, displayed rugged power and military authority, making air race promoters and aircraft manufacturers confident in the wearer's abilities. But when the women wore the same for flying, the radio host Will Rogers joined with the public, in making a moral judgment on them, suggesting they were somehow "unwholesome". It was Earhart who designed the first practical aviation suit for females. She shied away from femininity by putting emphasis on male practicality with loose trousers, large pockets, zipper tops and long shirt tails. "I made up my mind," she said, "that if the wearers of the shirts I designed for any reason took time out to stand on their heads, there would still be enough shirt to still stay tucked in!"[99]

Her career in aviation was inextricably conjoined with that of Lindbergh's. Unashamedly isolationist, racist and an anti-Semite, Lindbergh, to use that Alan Bennet phrase, "pissed in our soup and we drank it." In self-imposed exile first in Britain and later France, Lindbergh's honeymoon with the American public had been short lived. But "Lady Lindy" (she hated the name) showed herself to be an example of what women might achieve. Unlike Lindbergh, she had a generosity, an interest in people and an instinctive embrace of all women in her achievements. Jackie Cochran, who would warn Amelia about the circumnavigation flight, would speak for all at her memorial. "To know her was to love her." Cochran said.

Perhaps naively, Earhart believed that if her sex proved themselves competent in aviation — and by extension in all aspects of modern life — prejudices would fade and barriers would fall. Her work at Dennison House made her aware of social and sexual inequality and she spoke against it. Although friendly with Franklin and Eleanor Roosevelt, Earhart espoused no political affiliations, belonging only to the Ninety Nines. As a guest speaker at a conference of three thousand members of the Daughters of the American Revolution, she castigated them for lobbying for rearmament without doing anything to foster equality for women in the military.

Unmarried female pilots were considered 'suspect' and socially less acceptable in society. If they flaunted their sexuality as "Pancho" Barnes and Beryl Markham did, they were stigmatized, and sponsors dropped them. The media fawned on married couples setting aviation records — the domesticity, false though it was, of Jim and Amy Mollison ("the Flying Lovers") and Anne and Charles Lindbergh ("The Lone Eagle and His Mate") were ideal fodder to fill newspapers. Earhart (unlike Elder or Klingensmith) was never presented to the media as a sex object but with Greta Garbo and Katharine Hepburn, she was accepted as a woman who possessed "manliness in a feminine presence."[100]

Amelia and George Putnam became lovers soon after the "Friendship" flight — his wife Dorothy having had an affair with their son's tutor, divorced George in 1929. He proposed marriage seven times before his protégé accepted and they were quietly married on February 7, 1931. For a life that has been painstakingly documented, the privacy with which Amelia guarded her thoughts in a few scraps of poetry makes one feel a voyeur. Yet she would pen the most free-thinking public approach to marriage of her generation — that sexual freedom for both parties be implicit in the arrangement. "I want you to understand I shall not hold you to any medieval code of faithfulness to me, nor should I consider myself bound to you similarly." Conceding that she was a "loner", she wrote that she "could not guarantee to endure at all times the confinement of even an attractive cage." Her success in aviation had allowed her an independence and financial security that other women could only dream of, and she was not willing to lose either in marriage.

There are always those who claim that a woman needed a man, preferably wealthy, if they were going to succeed in aviation — Jackie Cochran and Floyd Odlum, Earhart and Putnam were prime examples. If it wasn't for Putnam, Earhart's critics asserted, Amelia would have lived out her life as a drudge at Dennison House. "Probably saved her from becoming an old maid." said one. But she was never Trilby the artist's model to George's Svengali. In his *Soaring Wings: A Biography of Amelia Earhart* in 1939, he would acknowledge: "She felt that no human being of normal intelligence should be 'managed' by anyone else. She had a healthy distaste for the implication of being led around by the hand."

In the short space of time, between the "Friendship" flight and her disappearance (1928–1937), besides a solo record crossing of the Atlantic and an autogiro transcontinental flight, Amelia wrote three books (the last published posthumously), gave hundreds of speeches for the Putnam publicity machine, designed a clothing line for women, wrote for *Cosmopolitan* magazine, entered the first Santa Monica-to-Cleveland Powder Puff Derby — placing third — founded the Ninety Nines and was its first president, set seven women's speed and distance aviation records, was Assistant General Manager for Transcontinental and Western Air, a member of the Guggenheim Committee for Aeronautical Education in schools, a technical advisor to the Department of Aeronautics and served as a faculty advisor at Purdue University. One might ask, had she lived to be 80 years of age, what else would the tomboy from Kansas have done? The whole mythology of her dying young and in unknown circumstances has blinded us as to what her short life meant.

Hollywood was quick to capitalize on Amelia Earhart, the female Sex and Death theme always lucrative, with a television mini-series and movies — the last was Mira Nair's *Amelia* in 2009. The first in 1933, was RKO Pictures' *Christopher Strong* directed by Dorothy Arzner, the only female director of the decade. A married politician has an affair with a headstrong young aviatrix, played by Katharine Hepburn (below) in her second starring role. When she discovers that she is pregnant, both lovers realize that getting married would hurt his career and family and her ambition to fly around the world. They call it off after which Hepburn's character commits suicide by removing her oxygen mask at altitude. The movie not only joined the powerful feminist personalities of Earhart and Hepburn, but also that of Arzner. A hidden lesbian in the old boys club that Hollywood was, Dorothy Arzner made the movie her own and not just for the memorable lamé 'silver moth' costume that Hepburn

wore. Feminists saw in the aviatrix's fate the gender inequality of the day — the male returning to his loving wife, (played by Billie Burke soon to be Glinda the Good Witch in *The Wizard of Oz*) with the female paying the ultimate price for his infidelity.[101]

If anything proved Earhart's single-mindedness, it was her determination to fly the Atlantic solo. Her own severest critic, she knew that she owed her fame as America's best-known female flier for imitating a "sack of potatoes" on the 1928 flight, and it annoyed her. Now she had the ideal aircraft, a red Lockheed Vega, for such a flight. On May 31, 1932, after flying 2,026 miles from Harbour Grace, Newfoundland in fourteen hours and fifty-four minutes, Amelia bumped down on a farm pasture in Culmore, Northern Ireland. With poor frontal visibility, the Lockheed Vega was always difficult to land. In her memoir, Elinor Smith would write that it had "all the glide potential of a boulder falling off a mountain". The first woman and only the second person to fly the Atlantic solo, Amelia had also established a record for the longest non-stop distance flown by a woman. Courage, she famously said, is the price that one pays for peace.

But the euphoria that had overwhelmed Lindbergh five years earlier had faded. As a female flier, she had flown too close to the sun and was now criticized for being a

"publicity hound." Had she killed any cows on landing on the farm? she was asked by the press. No, she replied, she hadn't. "Only an average flyer (sic)," another critic groused, "she has pushed herself to the front by following the tactics of feminists

… Using a man-made perfect machine, tuned by men mechanics, and a course laid out by a man, by a lucky break she has made the hop." Less fortunate was another female transatlantic pilot, four months later that year, when Edna Newcomer's Bellanca disappeared without a trace somewhere near the Azores.

On January 12, 1935, after an 18-hour solo flight from Honolulu, Amelia Earhart would land at Oakland Airport, becoming the first woman to cross the Pacific. Rather ominously, radio stations tuning in to her broadcasts heard her say "I am feeling so tired." With the triumph of her solo flights came notoriety — her supposed affair with aviator Paul Mantz — and academia. To increase female enrolment, Purdue University President Edward C Elliott invited Amelia to serve as a consultant in the Department of Careers for Women. While there, she lectured on topics as diverse as aerial navigation to partnership in marriage.

Both she and Putnam were very aware that by 1936 the public were bored with record flights and that at almost forty years of age, Amelia's "boyish" image that the media had once fetishized over, was now dated. Besides, with the introduction of stewardesses and female air racers, women were no longer the oddities in aviation they had been. Nor were aircraft regarded as the mechanical messiahs of peace and prosperity as in the previous decade. With Italian bombers dropping poison gas in Abyssinia, Japanese aircraft strafing helpless Chinese and the German Condor Legion setting Madrid on fire with incendiaries, the newsreels revealed the darker side of technology.

Round-the-world flights began with the four Douglas World Cruisers in 1924 and continued with Jimmie Mattern's two failed attempts 1932 and 1933, Wiley Post's success in 1931, and death with Will Rogers in 1935. Circumnavigating the Pacific Ocean via the stepping stones of Alaska, Siberia, and Korea — as the men had done, was dangerous enough — Mattern's crashes were proof of that — but Earhart now chose to fly the longest distance possible on the planet — west around the world as close to the Equator as she could. "I am undertaking this one," she told President Roosevelt, "solely because I want to, and because I feel that women, now and then, have to do things to show what women can do."

When her ambition became public, the Purdue Research Foundation bought her a Lockheed 10E Electra to use as a "flying laboratory" for the trip. She took delivery of the Electra on her birthday, July 24, 1936. This was to be, she said, her final gesture.[102]

The sequence of events that led to her disappearance began at Luke Field, Honolulu on March 20, 1937. In posing for the media, Amelia ground looped the Electra. Harry Manning, the navigator, was adamant that it was because of her inability as a pilot. To be remembered as the woman who had failed to fly around the world — her pride in rebuilding her reputation as a pilot would not allow it. She was now going to fly east.

The news reels of June 1 at Miami Airport captured Amelia's affection for George, showing (as Hepburn had played in the movie), a female pilot torn between love and ambition. One month, 22,000 miles and 146 flying hours later, the photos of her and Fred Noonan at Lae, Papua New Guinea, depict both as almost zombie-like. The boyish smile apart, Amelia looks haggard, with sunken cheeks and an emaciated look. But she had told George, from Bandoeing, Dutch East Indies, that there was no cause for alarm and he continued booking engagements for her return. Entrapped in the celebrity cycle of photo-ops and dinners wherever they landed, her last message to the *Herald Tribune* begins with Hamlet's "Denmark's a prison." The next day, July 2,1937, the pair flew into history — and immortality.

Noonan's hangover, the chronometers, the radio

traffic, the part that the USCGC *Itasca* played, have all been minutely debated. George believed that Amelia had run out of fuel somewhere near Howland Island and died during an emergency landing at sea.[103] On July 18, after 10 days, the use of 48 aircraft scouring 250,000 square miles of ocean, the US Navy called the search off. Amelia had once said if she had her choice of time and place to leave the world, it would be in the middle of one of her long flights.

The conspiracy theories of secret government involvement began in 1943. Also produced by RKO studios was *Flight for Freedom,* released while the Battle of Midway was raging. With a screenplay supposedly written by Putnam, the movie is based on Earhart's last flight. It claimed that she had been shot down while spying on the Japanese at the request of President Roosevelt. The answer may never be known.

A model of women's achievements, few today are aware that Amelia Earhart was an outspoken feminist. That she is remembered primarily for her disappearance is indicative of our culture's inattention to female accomplishments, then and now.

10: WHAT DID YOU DO IN THE WAR, MUMMY?

Diana Barnato Walker, Lidiya Litvyak, Melitta von Stauffenberg and Betty Huyler Gillies all did the same thing. In different air arms, they proved that in a war, women were equal in flying to men. The most destructive in history, the Second World War was also the greatest social leveler in all things, especially aviation. If females had been forbidden to fly in the previous war, they were the wonder women in this one.

The very real possibility of invasion in 1940 brought about the feminist dilemma in Britain of whether women should be armed. Ingrained in Western culture was the idea that the female sex was to be protected by men and the symbolism of a gun (or a fighter aircraft) was the key descriptor between the sexes. Although many British women hunted, or were members of gun clubs, the physical and moral attributes of their sex using a gun to kill an enemy soldier were questioned. The War Office ordered that weapons and ammunition in charge of the Army and Home Guard units were not to be given to or used for instruction of women. Not allowed to join the Home Guard (until 1943), to defend their homes against the expected German panzers, the women were instead supplied with hockey sticks and pitchforks. The reasons given by the War Office were that the weight and recoil of a rifle was unsuited to female physiology and secondly the firing position of being flat on the stomach, with legs wide apart was unsuited to female dignity and decorum.

There were a few exceptions — the female agents in the elite Special Operations Executive were armed — clandestinely. The idiocy of not arming the women of the Auxiliary Territorial Services (ATS) who manned searchlights, anti-aircraft batteries and radar stations even penetrated a sexist bureaucracy. It was decided that in case of invasion, the women should at least be trained to use weapons — the results were sometimes humorous, dangerously so.[104] In key positions, a few ATS women were issued with revolvers. Thinking they were to defend themselves with them, the women did target practice — only to be told that the real reason for the revolvers was to shoot themselves and prevent torture by the Germans and the revealing of radar secrets. The exclusion of women from combat roles ensured male supremacy.

Guernica's annihilation by the Luftwaffe in April 1937, gave the British sufficient reason to be concerned of aerial attack and a year later, the Minister for Air, Sir Kingsley Wood began the Civil Air Guard (CAG). A civilian organization, it was visualized as a kind of Territorial Air Force. Subsidized pilot training was offered to men and women aged 18 to 50 who could pass the 'A' license medical examination. Once affordable by only a wealthy few, the scheme put flying within reach of many, especially women. When the Germans invaded Poland on September 1, 1939, 83 of them had taken advantage of the scheme to earn pilot's licenses.

Gerard d'Erlanger, the director of the pre-war British Airways, believed that civilian pilots who, because of age, disabilities or being female, were unfit to fly for the RAF were an untapped resource that could be put to good use in wartime. He wrote to the Director-General of Civil Aviation, Sir Francis Shelmerdine, in May, 1938 with a plan to make use of them. Shelmerdine agreed and put d'Erlanger in charge of setting it up. The Air Transport Auxiliary (ATA) originally came into being to fly medical supplies, patients, VIPs and mail in war. What would save it from bureaucratic blunder was that because its pilots were ineligible for service with the RAF, it could not be militarized. It was to be run by the new airline British Overseas Airways Corporation (BOAC) which provided a chief instructor, A R O Macmillan, and an Avro Anson for "taxi" service.[105]

The Air Ministry tentatively gave d'Erlanger permission to recruit thirty male private pilots who because of advanced age and/or disabilities were not in the air force — at one time there were three single arm pilots all of whom flew aircraft quite successfully — and d'Erlanger joked that ATA stood for "Ancient Tattered Airmen". The ferrying of aircraft from factories and maintenance units to active squadrons had always been done by the RAF Reserve Command but with the severe losses suffered in France, it was overwhelmed in trying to keep up with deliveries. From February 1940 onward, the ATA took over all ferrying of aircraft and in doing so, released RAF pilots for combat duties.

When First World War air ace Harold Balfour, the Under Secretary of State for Air, proposed that the ATA allow female pilots to join, the RAF vehemently objected. Flying was a man's job Air Chief Marshal Sir Trafford Leigh-Mallory said, and all female pilots should be absorbed into the non-flying Women's Auxiliary Air Force (WAAF). C G Grey, editor of *The Aeroplane,* harrumphed, "The menace is the woman who thinks that she ought to be flying in a high-speed bomber when she really has not the intelligence to scrub the floor of a hospital properly." The old arguments were resurrected — the "Sky Menaces" were taking men's jobs away from them, handling complex fighters like Spitfires was beyond a woman's physical and psychological capabilities and finally, what would happen if they were menstruating?

It was a case of cometh the hour, cometh the woman. On December 14, 1939, twenty-nine-year-old Pauline Gower (below) was appointed Senior Commander of the ATA's women's section at Hatfield. A civil defense commissioner in the CAG, with her political contacts and powers of persuasion, Gower was the ideal choice. She said, "Women are not born with wings, neither are men. Wings are won by hard work, just as proficiency is won in any profession." Basing her on Gower, Capt W E Johns, the creator of Biggles, would also create the less well-known character of Flying Officer Joan Worralson (opposite).

Initially allowed to hire eight women and realizing they would be scruti-

nized by the RAF and exposed to photo-ops by media, Gower chose them carefully. Each female pilot had to have a minimum of 250 flying hours — later when the need for pilots was greater, this was lowered to 150 hours. Winnifred Crossley had been a stunt flier and towed banners for an advertising company. Margaret Cunninson was an instructor. Gower's Deputy Commander Marion Wilberforce had ferried farm animals about in her DH Cirrus Moth, avoiding taxes as the aircraft was then a farm implement. The Rt Hon Margaret Fairweather had flown her own Puss Moth since 1937. Mona Friedlander was an international ice hockey star. Joan Hughes got her license at seventeen, the youngest in Britain, and at 5ft 2", had to stuff her shoes with newspapers to make the 5 feet 4" height restriction. She used to

take a cushion with her when she flew so that she could see over the top of the instrument panel.

In 1935, Gabrielle Patterson, an ardent feminist, was the first British woman to get an instructor's license. A former ballet dancer and acrobat, Rosemary Rees also had her instructor's license. The "First Eight" had on average 600 hours each and Gower had logged over 2,000 hours herself.

"Eight Girls Show the RAF", headlined the first photo-op article, making the government uneasy about the publicity — the Luftwaffe might think that Britain was running out of male pilots and was forced to use women.

The ferrying of fighter aircraft was initially for the ATA male pilots only as they had to cross the Channel to pick them up in France. The women were only allowed to deliver light trainers like Tiger Moths to freezing Scotland which if/or when they 'broke' them, could be easily fixed. "It's assumed," Pauline remarked caustically, "that the hand that rocked the cradle wrecked the crate." And after delivering an aircraft, no matter the hour, the female pilot had to find her own way back to Hatfield by train. The official logic was that it would be socially disruptive if the women overnighted at all-male stations.

Thanks to "Pops" d'Erlanger's business experience of running an airline, the ATA worked like a well-oiled machine. Headquartered at White Waltham, Berkshire, and spread across the country, at its height, it included pilots, flight engineers (one of whom was Freddie Laker), instructors, operations officers, meteorological officers, administration staff and Air Cadets. In all, there would be 4,000 ATA employees of which 1,152 were male pilots and 168 female. The pilots would be assigned to ferry pools near aircraft plants, some of which like Hamble, Cosford, and Hatfield (later moved to Luton) were all-women ferry pools. Others were "mixed," with men and women pilots working side-by-side. On July 2, 1941, for greater efficiency, the ATA would be placed under the control of Lord Beaverbrook's Ministry of Aircraft Production.[106]

Throughout the war, Gower was inundated by letters from women who wanted to join the ATA. They all wanted as Mary Ellis wrote, to fight for England and to fly. Irene Arckless was the daughter of a Carlisle organ-builder and known as "the flying school-girl." She made her first solo flight when she was 21. Until 1940, Eleanor "Susan" Slade had managed the restaurant at Heston Aerodrome. But before the war, she had flown her own DH Puss Moth across Europe, once landing at Berchtesgaden — Hitler was not there but the surprised staff gave her a tour of the place. A domestic science teacher, Janice Harrington applied to join in April 1943 as a pilot. But at 5 feet 3½, she was rejected as the minimum height for pilots was 5 feet 5. Instead, she became one of four female Flight Engineers in the ATA, soon commended for her work on the Halifax bomber. Leslie Murray had done 6 hours solo under the CAG scheme and pestered the ATA about joining. Accepted in 1943, she ferried aircraft until killed when the Hudson she was flying crashed on April 20, 1945. Before the war, Grace Brown flew for Air Dispatch between Croydon and Le Bourget. When the British Expeditionary Force were retreating in France, she filled her Tiger Moth with medical supplies and flew to their field hospitals. Margaret Gore had been an osteopath and would become the first female pilot to fly the Halifax and the Lancaster. Honor Pitman Salmon's grandfather Sir Isaac Pitman invented the Pitman shorthand system. She joined the ATA in March 1941, where her instructors thought her overconfident. Diana Barnato Walker, the daughter of Woolf Barnato one of the "Bentley Boys" who raced at Le Mans, had been presented at court in 1936. By the war's end she had flown 80 types of aircraft and delivered 260 Spitfires — she proudly said, "without a scratch." When Lettice Curtis was a child, "Meccano" not dolls, was her favorite toy. A triple blue at Oxford, she captained the tennis team and was named an "Isis doll" by the male students.

All the female ATA pilots began as Cadets, they were made Second Officers when qualified to fly light aircraft and First Officers when they flew twin-engine aircraft. The women were paid £230 annually with an extra £8 each month for flight pay. That it was 20 per cent less than the male pilots was corrected in 1943.

If the RAF fighter pilots were the "Brylcream Boys", the female ATA pilots were "The Glamour Girls" of the war, forever memorialized by the photo on the front cover of *Picture Post* of Argentinian-born Maureen Dunlop (then aged 24) alighting from the Fairey Barracuda she had just brought in (overleaf). What would make them the envy of the WASPs, was that the ATA pilots were protected by insurance and, from the start, wore a distinctive uniform made to measure by the local tailor in the high street. It was a very dark blue, single-breasted jacket with four patch pockets and a blue cloth belt, followed by dark blue versions of WAAF officer skirts with black stockings and flat black shoes. Trousers identical to the design of WAAF officer trousers but in the ATA colour were to be used 'on base only'. All qualified ATA pilots were issued with a set of golden wings which were worn above the left breast pocket, like RAF wings.

THE STORY OF THE A.T.A.
(See inside)

HULTON'S NATIONAL WEEKLY   *In this issue :*   CHURCHILL IN ITALY   4D

SEPTEMBER 16, 1944   Vol. 24   No. 12

The ATA motto "Aetheris Avidi" translated as "Eager for the Air" but more appropriate was the nickname "Foreign Legion of the Air", as pilots of all nationalities were accepted. Besides the Dominions and Empire, there were pilots from China, Chile, Siam, Russia, Eire, and Argentina. Forbidden to fly for their own country, the women came to Britain to be part of female history.[107]

Each had a story of how they had got to the ATA headquarters at White Waltham. Seventeen Poles including three women had escaped through the Balkans and France. One was Anna Leska who in June 1939, qualified as a pilot of the parasol-winged Polish RWD-8 and in September, managed to snatch one from an airfield guarded by the Germans and fly it to Rumania. Not allowed to fly for the air force at home, five New Zealand women paid their own way to Britain. Betty Black had flown with the Otago Aero Club, June (Judy) Howden would fly 22 different types of aircraft in the ATA, Trevor Balfour Hunter, (named Trevor because her mother was convinced she was going to be a boy) soloed at age 16 and Edith Marie Furkett who, although a pilot, joined BOAC's clerical staff. Engaged to New Zealand Pilot Officer Angus Carr Mackenzie in the RAF, Jane Winstone joined to be near him in England. He would be killed in action on June 9, 1942, and tragically Jane would also die when the Spitfire she was ferrying on February 10, 1944 suffered an engine failure and crashed.

Four Canadians flew for the ATA — Violet Milstead and Marion Orr had been turned down by the RCAF as instructors, Elspeth Russel lied about her age (she was not yet 21) to join up and Helen Harrison, the only Canadian woman to ferry a B-25 Mitchell across the Atlantic. Wanting to fly for the Free French, 19-year-old Margot Duhalde from Santiago, Chile spoke no English and on joining the ATA was sent to learn the language from the maintenance engineers — predictably a lot of her initial language was of swear words. Edith Foltz, the first female to get a pilot's license in Oregon, would join the ATA rather than the WASPs because she said the British judged her by her flying skills and not her gender. She was once chased by a German aircraft and had to dive into clouds to lose it. Another time, she was mistaken for a V1 "buzz bomb" and almost shot down by friendly fire.

Born Veronica May Innes, Veronica married Flt Lt A Volkersz of the Netherlands Navy. She qualified as a pilot in the CAG and joined the ATA in March 1941, having spent the previous 15 months as a driver for the London Ambulance Service in the Blitz. She remained with the service until it was wound up in November 1945, finishing as a Flight Captain. In her post-war military contract, Veronica became the first woman anywhere in the world to pilot an operational jet fighter, delivering a Meteor III from the Gloster factory to 124 Squadron at RAF Molesworth in September 1945.

In early 1942, at the request of the British, to help with the ferrying, Jackie Cochran brought over 25 female pilots — none of whom had travelled abroad or been in a war zone. Joining their ATA colleagues, the Americans flew all types of aircraft, six days a week, in British weather, all the while dodging barrage balloons and the Luftwaffe. The first time the women heard air raid sirens, they hid under their beds. Food was scarce due to rationing and to American palates, inedible. Accommodation was either damp or freezing as heating fuel was in short supply.

The British on the other hand, didn't appreciate Cochran (who did not fly) being made an honorary officer, or arriving at the airfield wearing a mink stole and in a Rolls Royce. It was a case of overpaid, over dressed and over here.

Helen Richey replaced Cochran as commander of the American pilots when she hurried home. Whether it was her mother's illness, homesickness, or a nervous breakdown, after four crashes, Richey too wanted to return home. In early 1943, suffering considerable mental strain, she underwent a nervous breakdown and was sent home to earn her wings with the WASPs at Sweetwater, Texas.[108]

Nicknamed "Atta girls" and sometimes "Always Terrified Airwomen", the women knew that as the only members of their sex who flew, they were being scrutinised — by the air force, the media and every male who watched them take a plane up.[109] "We had this appalling responsibility weighing on our shoulders, you see," one said, "if a man took [an airplane] up and broke it, it's just too bad ... but if we'd broken one immediately, they'd say, 'you see, we said they couldn't do it! And they can't!' so we had to be twice as careful as everybody else..."

With the RAF on the offensive in 1941, hundreds of aircraft were waiting to be ferried and to cope with the backlog, the ATA women would be admitted for the first time to the RAF Central Flying School in Upavon. As Lettice Curtis (below) remembered of those days, "They didn't care if you were a man, woman or monkey." The boast of ATA men and women was that every plane that the RAF flew, they had already flown twice — once to

the maintenance unit and then to the squadron. The RAF pilots had only to learn to fly a single aircraft — while they had 151 types to figure out before take-off. Besides their versatility, the ATA pilots had three key assets — the Conversion School where they trained to fly various aircraft, the air taxi Anson that delivered the pilots to their day's starting destinations and picked them up to take them home, and the Ferry Pilot's Notes. These were 4x6 cards on two rings, that had everything a pilot needed to know about flying that particular aircraft — usually all on just one card, front and back. Settings and speeds, take-off, climbing, cruising, landing and stalling speed. Richey remembered, "Sometimes, we would hurriedly skim through the pilot's operating manual to find out how to take-off, then keep reading the book while in flight to find out how to land the damned thing."

The myriad types of aircraft were organized into six categories:

Class 1: Single-engined light aircraft

Class 2: Single-engined operational aircraft (fighters like Hurricanes, Spitfires and P-51 Mustangs)

Class 3: Twin-engined light aircraft

Class 4: Twin-engined operational aircraft (like Hudsons, Mosquitos and B-25 Mitchells)

Class 5: Four-engined aircraft (heavy bombers, such as Lancasters, Stirlings, B-17 Flying Fortresses, and B-24 Liberators)

Class 6: Flying boats (PBY Catalinas and Sunderlands)

Only the men were allowed to ferry flying boats as it meant they would be overnighting at the all-male stations.

To the cheers of the watching women, on July 19, 1941, Winnie Crossley became the first to be checked out on a Hurricane. On June 24, 1942, Lettice Curtis was the first woman to fly the difficult Typhoon fighter. Class 4 pilots had to be capable of flying 138 different types and 82 women pilots attained that ranking. Twelve women attained a Class 5 Ranking. They were then expected, at a moment's notice, to fly any of 147 types of aircraft. "You never knew, "one said "what aircraft or number of aircraft you were going to fly that day. It was terribly exciting!"

With all radio channels reserved for the RAF, the ATA pilots flew without radio, instrument instruction or maps (in case they fell into enemy hands) of where the barrage balloons and anti-aircraft guns were.[110] Not allowed to exceed 2,000 feet or fly through clouds, they followed roads and railway lines. By 1944, the women's fame was such that when faced with a new aircraft that their pilots were nervous to fly, a favorite tactic of RAF commanding officers was to request that it be delivered by a young female pilot. They could then say to the assembled squadron: "If a woman can fly that Typhoon, so can you." At one RAF base, the ground crew refused to believe that Mary Ellis was the pilot of the Wellington bomber she had just brought in. "They actually went inside the airplane and searched it" she recalled. By war's end, ATA rightly stood for "Anything To Anywhere".

One hundred and seventy-three ATA members were killed in service and 20 of those were women.[111] The year 1943 was a particularly black one for the ATA. On January 3, Irene Arckless's Airspeed Oxford experienced engine failure over Cambridge Airport. Attempting to avoid hitting a house, she was killed, one day short of her 28th birthday. On April 19, Honor Pitman Salmon was ferrying an Airspeed Oxford in company with a Spitfire. When the visibility deteriorated, the other pilot turned back but Honor continued — until she hit high ground at Roundway Hill, Wiltshire and was killed. Susan Slade was killed on July 13, when the Wellington bomber she was flying crashed on take-off at Little Rissington. "We lost so many friends; you see." Ellis would write, "The next morning their name would be scrubbed off the chalk board in the office, and the place would be horribly quiet."[112]

When her pilots died, Pauline Gower had the poignant task of informing their families. On March 2, 1944, when Janice Harrington was killed with Dora Lang in a Mosquito on approach to Lasham, she wrote: "Dear Mr Harrington, it is with the deepest regret that I have to inform you the sad news conveyed to you last night regarding the fatal accident to your daughter…"

The reply was equally heartbreaking:

Dear Miss Gower,

It is most kind of you to send a personal note to us about dear little Janice. I can assure you we are proud indeed to be the parents of a girl who gave up her safe profession as a domestic science teacher for the dangerous one and only regret she was not spared longer to serve the noble cause you represent.[113]

By war's end, the ATA pilots had delivered over 300,000 aircraft of 151 different types. Lettice Curtis alone delivered 222 Halifaxes, 109 Stirlings; part of a total of 1,500 aircraft. Four female pilots, Pauline Gower, Margot Gore, Joan Hughes, and Rosemary Rees were awarded MBEs (Members of the British Empire). It had been, many of the women said, the best years of their lives.

After the war, Elspeth Russell married Gerry Burnett, a fellow ATA pilot. They settled in Matane, Quebec where they began Matane Air Services. Gabrielle Patterson became involved with the Women's Junior Air corps. She died of cancer in October 1968, at the age of 63, and her ashes were scattered from the air over White Waltham airfield. In 1946, Margot Duhalde realized her dream and served in the French Air Force, becoming France's first female combat pilot. She was appointed a Chevalier of the *Légion d'Honneur*. But none of that helped her get a job flying for LAN Chile which did not hire female pilots. Michelle Bachelet, the first female president of Chile, described Margot as a pioneer who "demonstrated in a world of men that nothing is impossible for women".

Joan Hughes (below) became a movie stunt flier, flying in *The Blue Max* and *Those Magnificent Men In Their Flying Machines*. She flew her Tiger Moth under a bridge as Lady Penelope's stunt double in the 1968 *Thunderbirds* movie. Marion Orr would run a flying club, fly helicopters, and become the first Canadian woman licensed to operate an airport. Mary Ellis became the manager of Sandown Airport on the Isle of Wight in the 1950s and hired a former ATA colleague, Vera Strodl, as chief flying instructor. Violet Milstead suffered with secretarial work in a Toronto office "after her parents urged her to go out and find a real job." Returning to instructing, she married fellow instructor Arnold Warren and in 1947, began flying for Nickel Belt Airways, Sudbury. "Vi was an inspiration to any young woman because of her ability to fit into a male world and retain a sort of femininity," said novelist Jane Urquhart, a neighbor and distant relation of Mrs Milstead Warren. "She never paused for a moment to think that she couldn't do it." Edith Foltz became a real

estate agent in Portland Oregon, the only one to have been awarded the King's Medal for Courage in the Cause of Freedom. Diana Barnato Walker would pilot an RAF English Electric Lightning on August 26, 1963, to Mach 1.6 (1,262 mph or 2,031 km/h), becoming the first British woman to break the sound barrier. Sadly, Pauline Gower, the heart of the women's ATA, died on March 2, 1947, giving birth to twin sons, who survived.

The British have never idolized militarism, priding themselves as a nation which somehow always muddles through — the "little ships" in the Dunkirk evacuation a good example. On a par with *Dad's Army* (the Home Guard), the female ATA pilots are held with great affection. In understated heroism, for the remainder of their lives, the women would protest that they were just 'doing their bit'. *The Times* of London described them as "the pluckiest sisterhood in military history." They are memorialized on a tablet in St Paul's Cathedral, London, the citation ending with:

Remember Then, That Also We
In A Moon's Course Are History.

◊◊◊

There was one other British woman who flew — inadvertently — but deserves recognition. Margaret Horton was a WAAF flight mechanic at RAF Hibaldstow. On February 9, 1945, there was a flight order for one of the ground staff to sit on the tail of each Spitfire as it taxied from the dispersal to the runway in rough weather, to prevent the wind from tipping the machine over on its nose. Margaret's pilot, Flight Lt Neill Cox, did not receive the order "Rough Weather Procedure," which was issued from flying control, and hadn't seen her jump on the tailplane of "T for Trouble" while the other mechanics were removing the chocks. The severely increased rate at which they were tax-iing told Margaret something was wrong. She flung herself across the fuselage and grabbed the elevator in an attempt to attract the pilot's attention. Having got to the runway, the standard procedure was for the aircraft to pause for the mechanic to drop off. This didn't happen and as the Spitfire became airborne, Margaret held on to the tail assembly for her life. Another WAAF who'd seen what happened, ran to the control tower, who ordered Cox's Spitfire to make a tight circuit and land immediately, but he was not advised why. Thanks to the noticeable tail-heaviness of his aircraft, he had already figured that something wasn't quite right, but due to the aircraft design, he couldn't see his airplane's empennage. After a successful recovery, and relieved to be back on the ground, Margaret had a cup of tea and a ciga-rette, then was back to work!

◊◊◊

In Canada, as in the other Dominions, the women pilots who volunteered their services were summarily reject-ed by their governments. Even "The Flying Seven", the female aerobatic team, were rebuffed when they volun-teered to serve as instructors in the Commonwealth Air Training Plan.[114] In Australia, the only woman to fly for the military was Nancy Lyle who in May 1933, had been the first woman to fly to Tasmania. She used her Hornet Moth to train ground forces in anti-aircraft practice.

The most visible change in Canada with the war was that the TCA stewardesses were no longer the only young women in uniform. The Canadian government lagged behind the other Dominions to mobilize women, with good reason. It would rather they joined the munitions industry than the military — the shortage of women in uniform was not as desperate as the shortage of shells. It was the RAF who forced Ottawa's hand when it indicated that Canadian airwomen would be welcome to serve in Britain. This, combined with the tidal wave of female patriotism, coerced the government to create the Royal Canadian Air Force Women's Division (RCAF WD) on July 2, 1941. A recruitment campaign was begun, appealing for women "to free a man to fight." As in Britain and the other Dominions, the women who enlisted accepted that they would never be near an aircraft. The RCAF(WD)'s very motto said it all: "To Serve That Men Might Fly". The closest they came to aircraft were as Link trainer operators (but never actually sitting in the trainer itself) and much later as aircraft engine mechanics.

The recruits, confined to clerical jobs or as fabric workers, drivers, switchboard operators, "batwomen" to officers, cooks, and laundry helpers, were paid two thirds of a man's salary doing the same work. The official reasoning was that it took two women to do a man's job. In all fairness, the RCAF were entirely unprepared for "a species that until then had only pushed prams around," and was now dropped into a completely male environment. It wasn't just that the uniforms didn't fit or that the messes were for men only and the hastily put up spartan barracks for the women were woefully inadequate in prairie winters. It was the mind-set, as the recruits were told in Basic Training. "If you are one of those women who need to take off one or two days every time you menstruate, you may as well pack it in now. We don't want you to be running to the medical officer every time you have cramps." It was ignorance as much as indifference. For an all-male military, there were no guidelines regarding menstruation or pregnancy. The latter meant instant discharge, the unfortunate woman put on a train home to her relatives — who, given the times, had to be persuaded to take her.

The few women who were commissioned as officers

in the RCAF(WD) had to defer to men of equal rank and most galling of all — lower male ranks saluted them only as a courtesy, if at all. When Willa Walker was made commanding officer of the WD in February 1943, she discovered that at all air force bases and training depots, the officers' messes were for men only. Fed up with this regulation, one day Willa ordered her female driver to park in front of the officers' mess. In sub-zero temperatures, she sat inside the vehicle during a snowstorm, eating her cold lunch, until the male officers were so ashamed that they invited her in. "Across the country, women officers let out a cheer, as they were never again prevented from entering the officers' mess!"[115]

Despite the patriotic appeal, the public whether Canadian, American, or Australian, never quite accepted service women, barely tolerating them for the duration. In 1943, a survey revealed that only 7 per cent of the Canadian population thought women should be in uniform at all. Entering an all-male bastion (it was thought), a woman assumed a masculine identity, and this 'deviant' feminism became associated with lesbianism. The National Film Board quickly put out two movies to counter this: *Proudly She Marches* and *Wings On Her*

Shoulders, both of which emphasized (in a male voice-over) that joining the ranks was definitely not "unfeminine".

Like the stewardesses, service women were also held to a stricter moral code than their male counterparts. Off duty, they were refused access to canteens and clubs where alcohol was served, forced to attend "chastity" lectures and unlike their male colleagues, not issued contraceptives as they might encourage rampant immorality.

Having disrupted the gendered stereotypes in a conservative country, the WDs suffered censure from the public — especially shopkeepers, bus drivers, boyfriends and landladies, an attitude that was virulent in rural communities. In the Catholic province of Quebec, where women had just been granted the vote in 1940, in some parishes the message from the pulpit was that those who had enlisted would not be allowed to receive the sacraments. Widespread rumors didn't help recruitment — that the government had recruited ladies of easy virtue in Toronto, that there was a building in every city where illegitimate babies were dropped off and that women in uniform "drank like Indians". Thought of as promiscuous "husband hunters" who enticed lonely soldiers far from home with sex, the women were said to be spreading venereal disease, intent on destroying the fabric of a postwar society.

In the United States, the press trivialized and sexualized the servicewomen by focusing on their underwear, makeup, or dating patterns. Major General Jeanne Holm enlisted in the US military in July 1942 and retired as the first woman to reach the rank of a two-star general. She wrote of the "vicious" and pernicious "slander campaign", involving "dirty jokes, snide remarks, obscenities, and cartoons" against servicewomen in wartime that almost ended the recruitment effort. Certain that this was the act of enemy saboteurs, President Roosevelt launched FBI and Army Intelligence investigations, only to find that the military's own officers and enlisted men were responsible. Despite the numerous accomplishments of women in the military, the legacy of the "scandal campaign" from the Second World War, Holm would write, has lingered into the 21st century, and many women who enlist continue to be stigmatized as "whores or lesbians" as a result of their service.[116]

Media scrutiny into sexual assault and harassment was decades away and sexual harassment in the RCAF (WD) — as in all wartime militaries — was commonplace because, as author Spencer Dunmore wrote, "Canadians in the main preferred to believe that it didn't exist. Society then had an indulgent 'boys will be boys' attitude to the behavior of servicemen in wartime, and unless outright rape was involved, complaints seldom received much consideration."[117] Besides, if the posters were to be believed, rape was what the enemy did, not the boy next door. One former WD member who later joined TCA remembered that the smartest thing to do was to get a "protector", preferably an officer. And it didn't matter if he was married… If in the 2020s, military commanders continue to sweep cases of sexual assault under the rug, side with the perpetrators and intimidate the survivors, one can only imagine what it must have been like 80 years before. But taking a leaf from the airline playbook, the military prided itself on training women during the war who, as they would be used to hardships and taking orders from men, would be "perfect post-war wives".

"We knew when the war was over, they'd tell us about it" remembered one former RCAF (WD), "and we could all go home." She and 17,037 other Canadian women had allowed men to fly. She only hoped that "From now on, it was all going to be different." The RCAF (WD) was disbanded in 1946 and in 1951 when the service was scrambling to meet its Cold War commitments, women were permitted to rejoin the RCAF.

Both Stalin and Hitler saw in their women pilots ideal subjects with which to paper over the mass atrocities they committed. The NSDAP, or the National Socialist German Workers Party, ruled that a woman should stay home and fulfill her domestic duties by rearing children and keep the house ready for their husband's return. The two women did not were Hanna Reitsch (below), who played Hades to Melitta Schiller's Persephone. Both carved out careers in the male world that was Nazi aviation. Born in Poland and with Jewish ancestry, Melitta Schiller was officially a "half-blood." With her blond hair and blue eyes, Hanna Reitsch was the poster girl of an Aryan goddess. Born in Hirschberg, Silesia, Reitsch began her

flight training in 1932, excelled in the glider competition in the 1936 Olympics, and never forgot meeting Charles Lindbergh, her admiration for him second only to her fanaticism for Hitler. Both women were awarded the honorary title of Flugkapitan, and as military test pilots, both were sometimes at Rechlin, the German equivalent of Farnborough. They avoided each other there, with Reitsch suspecting that Melitta was a British spy because of her "racial burden." Reitsch would the first woman to fly a helicopter and later a rocket-powered plane, the Me163. In 1941 she received the Iron Cross, Second Class, from Hitler himself.

Melitta would marry Alexander von Stauffenberg thus becoming a "half-Aryan" and as an aeronautical engineer worked on bomb aiming devices and dive sights for Stukas, flying the aircraft in tests herself. Chosen by the Luftwaffe to represent her country, in 1938, she flew to England for the opening of Chigwell Aerodrome and met with other female pilots. She secretly wrote that she felt loyalty to Germany but did not agree with the National Socialist ideals. Melitta wholeheartedly supported her brother-in-law, Claus von Stauffenberg, in his plot to kill Hitler in 1944 and by doing so, lost her family to Buchenwald concentration camp. But such was her value in stress testing aircraft that she was tolerated, and even allowed to borrow a Fiesler Storch to fly over the camp and look for her husband. On April 8, 1945, she was flying a Bestmann trainer aircraft to rescue her husband when she was shot down by an American fighter aircraft and killed.

In the *Götterdämmerung* of the Reich, with Field Marshal Robert Ritter von Greim as a passenger, Reitsch flew a Storch through Russian artillery fire to rescue Hitler from the Führer bunker. She crashed it at the Brandenburg Gate, just behind the Victory column. Preparing to marry Eva Braun, Hitler refused to leave.

Hanna then offered to fly the Goebbels children out but their mother Magda Goebbels refused as well. She and von Greim, whom Hitler had made head of the Luftwaffe, then took off in a two-seater Arado, escaping the fire of Russian shock troops who thought Hitler was escaping. Hanna Reitsch was later captured by the Americans and interrogated by US military intelligence.

In 1941 when the Soviet Union was invaded by Germany, Marina Raskova, its most famous female pilot (known as the Russian Amelia Earhart) persuaded Josef Stalin to let women fight in the Voenno Vozdushnye Sily (VVS), the Military Air Force. Under Communism, women had been allowed to join since 1935 but unofficially male chauvinism prevented them from doing so. Stalin agreed on the proviso that the female pilots would never allow themselves to be captured and if they ever retreated, their families would suffer the consequences. Completely staffed by women — pilots, mechanics, armorers, and support — Raskova's three regiments were deployed to the frontlines. At first, they were supplied with ancient, open cockpit biplanes that exploded like bombs when hit by antiaircraft fire. The women, all volunteers — some in their teens (if you survived to 23 years of age you were considered an "old woman") flew thousands of bombing missions at night — earning the German nickname "Nachthexen" or "The Night Witches."[118] Aware of the propaganda that the female pilots' victories attracted — and to the resentment of the all-male regiments — Stalin later ensured they were given the latest Yak fighter planes. The three female regiments fought on to the fall of Berlin and were promoted to becoming Guards Units, the highest honor awarded a Soviet regiment.[119]

When Raskova died in an air crash in 1943, her ashes were interred in the historic Kremlin Wall, the first female pilot to be accorded that honor. She would have been pleased to know that one day a volcanic crater on the planet Venus would be named for her.

The most famous Soviet female pilot was Lidiya "Lilya"

Vladimirovna Litvyak. Her father had been purged as a traitor and the family shamed but that did not prevent the teenager from single-mindedly pursuing a career in aviation from 1937. It was Stalin's fascination of the heroic Soviet aviators called "Stalin's Falcons" that saved Lilya from following her father and millions like him to execution. The Great Patriotic War began with the decimation of the VVS which forced Stalin to draft women into the military and Lilya to be accepted in the 586th Fighter Aviation Regiment. She became history's first female air ace by shooting down five German aircraft over Stalingrad, earning the name "The White Rose of Stalingrad".[120] She then went on score a dozen more documented victories as the front moved over Kursk. On August 1, 1943, in a dogfight with a Me 109, Lilya's Yak was hit by a cannon shell. Her comrades saw the aircraft explode and there was no parachute.

The small female pilot who used to fill her cockpit with wildflowers disappeared without a trace. It was recommended she be awarded a posthumous "Hero of the Soviet Union" award but, because there were no remains, there was no proof she had actually died.[121] The paranoid regime of Stalin that had imprisoned thousands of its own solders as traitors believed that she had been captured and turned against the Motherland. For their own safety, her family changed their surname so as not to be associated with her. As with Amelia Earhart and Amy Johnson, there were theories and sightings of her over the years. In March 1986, the Orwellian Soviet bureaucracy removed Lilya Litvyak from the "missing" list to declare her officially "killed in action." As part of the 45th commemoration of the end of The Great Patriotic War, on May 5, 1990, Mikhail Gorbachev, in one of the last acts of the Soviet regime, awarded Lilya Litvyak "The White Rose of Stalingrad", a posthumous "Hero of the Soviet Union" medal.

As early as 1930, the War Department in Washington

had considered using female pilots in the military. Unfortunately, the Chief of the Army Air Corps condemned the idea as "utterly unfeasible", stating that women were "too highly strung" to fly a plane. With the military's attitude and Congress's isolationist stance, when the CAA's Robert H Hinckley planned the Civilian Pilot Training Program (CPTP) that would teach young men and women to fly, he buried it within the Aeronautics Act of 1938, as a stimulus for the aviation industry during the Depression. The CPTP only allotted three per cent of the available slots to women, but it allowed the National Airmen's Association of America to get black women admitted to it at the same ratio as whites — 1 per 10 males. Hinckley's radical vision was phenomenally successful. The number of women pilots in the United States rose from 675 in 1939 to 3,000 by 1941 and included 42 per cent of those who would fly for the WASPs. But after Pearl Harbor, trainees had to enlist in the military on graduation — and this automatically excluded women.

With the fall of France, Nancy Harkness Love, who as a thirteen-year-old had seen Lindbergh land at Le Bourget, knew that thousands of pilots would soon be needed by the US military. She contacted the Army Air Corps, suggesting that if the United States went to war, female pilots could release aviation personnel for service. But Major General Henry H Arnold, the Chief of the Air Corps firmly refused to consider this. Public sentiment and Congress were against women serving as military pilots. An alternative for them was the Civil Air Patrol (CAP). Organized six days before Pearl Harbor by the Office of Civilian Defense to patrol forests and shorelines, it was desperate for pilots — males and females, white and black — who wanted to defend their country. Willa Brown would be active in CAP as an officer, the first African American female to attain the rank. Females were welcome but they

were not allowed to fly coastal patrols where enemy submarines might lurk.

Nancy (left) wasn't the only one who thought women pilots should play a part in the coming war. The indomitable, irascible Jackie Cochran (below) had been on a roll since 1937, setting speed records, entering the MacRobertson race, winning the Bendix race for women, and serving on the Collier Trophy Committee where she first met General

Arnold. Still mourning the loss of Amelia Earhart, Eleanor Roosevelt presented Cochran with her first Harmon
Trophy on April 4, 1938. With this, she had won the Ely-
sian prize for female aviators of those times — access to
the White House. The First Lady's newspaper column *My
Day* was read by millions and never one to miss leveraging an opportunity, Jackie would write to her in September 1939, about the use of female pilots in case of war. She
knew that her letter would find its way to the President
and to the Secretary of War.

The two women differed on their plans for female
pilots in non-combat missions. It was Nancy's Long
Island Country Club elegance versus Jackie's poor white
hardscrabble upbringing. Nancy wanted an elite group of
women with all the rights and responsibilities of Army
Air Force pilots. Cochran, like Arnold, wanted them to
be integrated into the Army Air Force — with her as
its commanding officer. She wanted the women in the
military for the purposes of discipline so she could have
more control over them.[122] As Shakespeare warned: two
women placed together makes for cold weather — and
their rivalry was just that.

Love's good fortune was that she got a civil service job in
Baltimore, next to the office of Air Transport Command's
Col William H Tunner. He would soon organize large
scale military airlifts — over "The Hump" to China and,
post-war, the Berlin Airlift. In 1941, Tunner was at that
very moment looking for pilots to ferry aircraft. Love's
enthusiasm and plans suited him.

General Arnold did not want to risk Eleanor
Roosevelt's disfavor and sent Cochran off to Britain
to consult with Pauline Gower and her ATA women.
With the Lend Lease aircraft being delivered through
Canada to Britain, Jackie flew a bomber across the
Atlantic, becoming the first woman to do so.[123]
Newspaper articles of the period gave her credit for her

flight but did not hesitate to mention her outfit or her lavish collection of undergarments she brought along with her, seemingly belittling the fact that she had just broken a barrier for women. One article described her as a "32-year-old brown haired little aviatrix" and another as "slim fair-haired Jacqueline Cochran."[124]

She returned home with ideas to begin an operation similar to the ATA in the United States. In early 1942, at the request of the British government, Cochran accompanied 25 American women pilots to Britain to fly for the ATA. It would keep her in the spotlight and demonstrate that women pilots could do the same at home. But, while there, Jackie heard that Nancy Love had been made the director of all female ferry pilots in the United States.

On September 10, 1942, Tunner organized the Women's Pilot Group of Ferry Command to be run by Nancy from Wilmington Airport, Del. Civilian female fliers would ferry aircraft from factories to Army airfields.[125] Arnold maneuvered around the limitations of the women's reserve legislation and even suggested the name "Women's Auxiliary Ferrying Squadron (WAFS)". Congress was about to hold hearings on militarizing the Women's Army Auxiliary Corps (WAAC) to make it the Women's Army Corps (WAC). The women pilots were led to believe that they too would be formally adopted by the military with all the benefits that went with it — like insurance and burial in Arlington National Cemetery when they died.

Between 21 and 35 years of age, applicants for the WAFS had to hold a commercial license, a 200-hp rating and have 500 hours flight time. Earning $250 a month on a 90-day renewable contract, the women paid for their own room and board and their uniform. Designed by Nancy, this was a gray jacket with skirt or slacks and khaki overalls to fly in. The irrepressible

Betty Huyler Gillies was made Love's executive officer.

With the Army Air Corps still uncertain about the women flying fighter aircraft, the first WAFS ferried six Piper Cubs from their Lock Haven factory on October 2, 1942, to historic Mitchell Field, NY. They were restricted to cross country flying only in daylight hours and without radio. Navigation was as the barnstormers would have known it — by rivers, roads, and railways — all made more difficult now as the 1930s air markings on roofs of barns and railway stations had been covered up because of the war. Not until Gillies would solo in a P-47 Thunderbolt "Jug" — an 8-ton monster (she had to put blocks over the rudders to reach the controls) would the women be allowed to fly more advanced aircraft, culminating with the B-17 Flying Fortress.[126]

With thousands of aircraft being turned out by 1943, pilot shortages were inevitable and base commanders were happy for anyone — male or female — to deliver them. There were now enough trained WAFS to be sent to ferrying commands at Love airfield, Dallas, Romulus, MI and Long Beach, CA. At the last two commands, it was the wives of ferry pilots who caused a fuss, fearing that sharing a cockpit with the women would lead to impropriety — on the part of the WAFS of course, not their husbands. To avoid potential scandal, the base commanders restricted female pilots to single-seater aircraft (which would prevent them from advancement), flying only on alternate days and in opposite directions to the men. Using the WAFS spotless flight record as ammunition, Nancy went to Tunner's boss, General C R Smith, the Army Air Forces chief of staff. Smith, the former and future president of American Airlines, was astute enough to see that ferrying war planes by whatever sex was a small but vital cog in a global transportation system. He wrote to the Ferrying Division that the WAFS should be allowed to fly any aircraft they were capable of flying.

Jackie's wrath on her return from Britain must have been somewhat mollified when Arnold allowed her to organize a civilian training program for women called the Women's Flying Training Detachment (WFTD). With female pilots no longer allowed in the CPTP, the WFTD would make use of them. Arnold wanted the women militarized but to be independent of the WAAC. It would demonstrate to the War Department that the new Army Air Force (AAF) needed its own women's corps.

To catch up with Nancy Love, Jackie used the business drive she had developed running her cosmetics company. She began by sending telegrams to all of the 2,733 licensed female pilots that the CAA had records of. Those chosen reported to Houston airport, where they discovered that the military was ill-prepared to accommodate females. They were issued men's surplus mechanics' overalls — in sizes 44 and up — which the women dubbed "zoot suits." As the airfield had no facilities for them, to eat or use the toilet they had to walk a mile to the municipal airport. Jackie soon found them Avenger Field in Sweetwater, West Texas, the town so named because it was an oasis amid bitter-tasting gypsum streams. The only tenant at its airfield then was a flying school contracted by the Canadian government as part of the Commonwealth Air Training Pan to train British and Canadian pilots.

In February 1943, Avenger Field became an all-female installation, except for a few male instructors and other officers. Ever aware of publicity, Jackie ensured that the media covered the first graduation on April 24, 1943, with the women having their silver wings (bought by Jackie and Floyd), pinned on them. Nancy Love had been invited but did not attend. *Life* magazine and the newsreels wanted the women to sunbathe to show that they were just "ordinary girls who flew planes". Avenger Field was suddenly a popular "emergency landing" stopover for male pilots who wanted to see the women actually flying. Aware that even the hint of a scandal would have the program shut down, Jackie kept her women to strict military standards, so much so that Sweetwater was called "Cochran's Convent."

The town of Sweetwater, which depended on the RAF and RCAF trainees spending their money and flirtations on local girls, was not pleased. With the female pilots on the base, the men didn't have to travel far to socialize. The poor reputation that women in the military had didn't help, and the townspeople were quick to believe that all the female pilots were either prostitutes or lesbians.[127] To forestall a mob wielding pitchforks and torches, Jackie put on a charm offensive, inviting the townspeople to the graduation ceremonies, and serving alcohol.

On July 5, 1943, General Arnold succumbed to giving Jackie what she wanted — complete control over all WAFS and WFTDs, the women to be brought together on August 5, as the Women Air Force Service Pilots (WASPS). Nancy Harkness Love was made an executive of women pilots in the Air Transport Command Ferrying Division. The press sensed a catfight behind doors and the headline was "Coup for Cochran". But, at least in public, the two women agreed that this made sense.

The mascot for the WASPs was Fifinella, a female gremlin from Roald Dahl's first book *The Gremlins*. Dahl had been flying Hurricanes with the RAF but with injuries after a crash in Libya, was posted to Washington as an intelligence officer. In 1942, he wrote about the gremlins sabotaging RAF aircraft as revenge for their forest home being razed for an aircraft factory. The

Walt Disney studios reworked the story to warn about the hazards of combat flying and granted the WASPs the right to use the image. At a time when everyone seemed to be in uniform and covered in badges, the women took Fifinella as their own, adding a large bomb for the well-proportioned gremlin to ride on.

Promoted to brigadier general, Tunner no longer had control over the women pilots in Ferry Command. But to demonstrate what the Wilmington women ferry pilots could do, on 15 August 1943, he sent Love and Gillies for training to fly the mighty B-17 Flying Fortress. Thirty-one hours of training later, the pair became the first females to qualify as pilots of the bombers. Later that month, they almost made it across the Atlantic before General Arnold got wind of it and stopped them at Gander from entering a war zone.

Sometimes it was felt that their male colleagues and not the Nazis and Japanese were the enemy. Besides sexual harassment, acts of sabotage designed to demonstrate the incompetence of female pilots were common. Engines wouldn't start because sugar or grass had been put in them. Cochran herself discovered sugar in the gas tank of a crashed plane that had killed a colleague, Betty Davis. Fuel lines were found filled with rags, acid in parachutes, and plane's tires slashed. The women feared that if they reported these acts of sabotage, they would lose their jobs.

When the United States began sending aircraft to the Soviet Union, the WASPs came into their own. The women would pick up the aircraft from factories in Texas, New York or California and ferry them to Great Falls, Montana. There men would take over, flying the planes through Canada to Alaska for the Russian crews to continue on to the Eastern Front. The WASPs were restricted to domestic flights only because of the lack of segregated accommodation on bases in the Canadian and Alaskan wilderness. There was the added fear that as women they wouldn't survive a crash in the harsh winter conditions.

In September 1943, California representative John Costello submitted House Resolution 3358 that would give the women the same rights as male pilots in the Army Air Force and remain independent of the WAC. With the war winding down in 1944, hundreds of male ferry pilots and instructors would soon be unemployed and losing their draft-deferred status. The men organized and, with the assistance of the American Legion, lobbied hard against the militarization bill, and opposition grew in Congress. Women were now painted as taking away men's jobs and with so many male pilots available, they should return home to their families. Why was the government paying the women when there was the likelihood that men would soon be cleaning windscreens at gas stations? *TIME* Magazine asked if the WASPs were "Unnecessary and Undesirable?" The media even accused poor Arnold of being smitten with Jackie's "shapely figure." The militarization bill was defeated in Congress in June 1944, and on December 20, 1944, the WASP organization was disbanded — the women having to pay their own way home. The "experiment" had lasted for twenty-six months.

Jackie was awarded the Distinguished Service Medal in 1945, presented to her at the Pentagon by her old friend General Arnold. Her biggest fan, Floyd, bought a commanding share in Canadair to further his wife's aviation exploration. The company had no choice but to allow Cochran to pilot a Canadair F-86 on a 12-pylon course at Edwards Air Force Base, California. Her good friend Major Chuck Yeager, the first pilot to fly faster than the speed of sound, trained her by flying alongside, radioing instructions. On May 18, 1953, the pair flew side by side faster than the speed of sound. Cochran was timed at 652.337 miles per hour, making her the first woman in history to break the sound barrier.

With the end of the Second World War, women in aviation were pressured out of jobs which were given to the returning service men. Helen Richey went to New York, looking for work as an instructor, but was unsuccessful. On January 8, 1947, she was found dead in her one room apartment, the toxicology tests revealing that she had died from an excessive amount of sleeping pills. She was 37 years old.

Thirty-eight WASPs had been killed in service but as civilians, they received no benefits and had no right to a military funeral — not even a flag for the coffin. Their groundbreaking, patriotic work swept into the footnotes of history, left many of them embittered. It would take 33 years for the WASPs to be granted veteran status through an Act of Congress. On November 23, 1977, President Jimmy Carter signed Public Law 95—202 that added "Title IV — Women Airforce Service Pilots, Section 401", which stated the WASP service during the war was "active duty" (as defined in 38 USC 106) for the purposes of programs administered by the Veterans Administration. In 2009, President Barack Obama would award the WASPs the Congressional Gold Medal for Service.

In the Soviet Union, although the "Night Witches" had proven themselves better than their male colleagues in combat and the accuracy of their bombing, they were never commended with monuments, lauded in official history books, movies or folk tales. Instead, rumors were circulated that while at the front they had prostituted themselves and spread venereal disease. The Soviet government was well aware that if their devastated country was to be rebuilt, returning soldiers needed faithful wives and compliant girlfriends waiting to welcome them home, not battle-hardened Amazons who killed — and were killed.

Everywhere, the war's end returned both sexes to their traditional roles — the women to motherhood, nursing, and teaching — and the men to building and flying planes. Having had their "adventure" to tell their grandchildren one day, unsung and largely unknown, the women went back to their pre-war lives, married, and raised families. Surveys in the 1950s and 1960s indicated that some would have liked to return to work, this time on equal terms with men. But maternity leave, wage parity and day care were years away.

Perhaps, for the daughters of the Greatest Generation, their mother's contribution to the war effort was one of the catalysts in the rethinking of women's work that led to the second wave of Feminism in the 1960s.

11: MEN GROW COLD AS WOMEN GROW OLD

With the war's end, the aviation industry returned to the pre-war status quo, with management making it clear that female "hires" would be replaced by the returning veterans. But, having fought fascism (at least on the home front), women had gained enough self-confidence to refuse to endure the inequities of the labor market as it had been. The war years had brought increased opportunity, and rising expectations, which would help fuel the civil rights and feminist movements. Female roles would transform post-war — with the exception of stewardesses: they remained in a strange no-woman's land — smiling, servile symbols of male fantasy, brides to the airlines while their peers were at home, bringing up families.

This came about, in part, because of the ubiquitous DC-3, the most widely used airliner in commercial aviation. Like the Boeing 747 thirty years later, it changed the whole concept of air travel. Able to carry 21 passengers, in comfort and safety when compared with its predecessors, the DC-3 made commercial aviation (for the first time in its history) profitable, especially during the war when the airlines benefited from lucrative government contracts. Now able to walk upright through the cabin, soon to heat meals in the Maxson oven, the stewardess could better attend to passenger needs.[128]

As the post-war generation of passengers did not have the fear of flying that the previous one did, the women dealt with a vastly increased workload. The number of revenue passenger miles on US domestic airlines increased 220 per cent from 1,052 million in 1940 to 3,362 million in 1945. With the pressurized cabins, smoking, meals (and soon free alcohol) went an attractive, attentive hostess who, as the customer base was 90 per cent male, dared not complain if she was overworked, underpaid, and demeaned. It was, remembered a stewardess retiree, what happened in all other jobs available to women anyway.

They had contributed to victory as much as any Rosie the Riveter and the stewardesses knew that no one had done more to sell airplane travel to "first time fliers" than them. But the airlines saw no need to pass their wartime good fortune down to the women who had not had a pay increase for years. With an inexhaustible supply of amenable young applicants, airline executives had little interest in their well-being. The saying was "Use them 'til their smiles wear out; then get a new bunch." At United Airlines, the stewardess's base pay in 1942 was $125 per month. During a second year of employment, her pay rose to $150 per month. It would be increased annually by $5 per month until a maximum of $170 was reached, by which time the woman had long escaped to marriage.

Ada Brown, who joined United Airlines in 1940 recalled, "We were always promised things from the company, but nothing was ever done — except to throw parties for the stewardesses." The airlines relied on the women's patriotism, and the lifestyle the job promised. What the women did wasn't a "real" job anyway. Pilots, usually ex-military, had been licensed as professionals for decades because, working with machinery, their expertise was quantifiable. But alone, with unpredictable passengers, a stewardess's skills were intangible to measure. They did what her sex did at home as babysitters, wives, and mothers

— and no specialized knowledge or training was required for any of that. Without professional certification, the stewardesses had no leverage in negotiations for security or job improvement.

The efficiency that allowed American industry to churn out a Liberator bomber every 63 minutes at Willow Run, was put to good use by the airlines in preparing young women to be stewardesses-in-the making. Both American and United Airlines invested in large training facilities to teach them socializing, figure improvement and poise — "charm farms" the women called them. Weigh-ins, girdle checks, the no-marriage rule and age ceilings were how the airlines recouped their investment. It was dunned into the women that they were being sculpted — at great expense — to be obedient wives and caring mothers. "Training in the Sky makes her an Angel of a Wife" explained an airline's press release. With "homemaking" the destiny of all females, the women were grateful to be "finished" in what was euphemistically called "brides' school". In the 1950s, when marriage meant social and financial security, only a third of American women were still single at age

24; some years, it was said that more teenage girls walked down the aisle than attended their prom.

"What we are doing" said Bill Borden, the TWA manager of hostess training in 1962, "is to recruit brides for the nation's bachelors. By the time a girl's finished her six-week course and has been flying for a year, she's a combination mother, teacher, nurse, confidante, comforter, cook and companion. She knows when to talk, when to listen, how to entertain and be gracious. What more could a man want?"[129] The national average then was supposedly one divorce for every four marriages — but apparently (because she had been trained to please her husband) only one out of forty-seven stewardess's marriages ended in divorce. Into the late 1960s, an airline advertisement promised, "Every passenger gets warmth, friendliness and extra care. And someone may get a wife."

Hollywood played its part with films that revered domesticity. Movies like *Courage of Lassie* portrayed wholesome eligible females as played by a young Elizabeth Taylor or heroic wives and mothers who kept the family together in *Best Years of Our Lives*. In what was the ultimate product placement, in 1951, American Airlines cooperated fully with MGM to produce *Three Guys Named Mike*. It traced the career of spunky stewardess Marcy Lewis (played by Jane Wyman, recently divorced from Ronald Reagan) who loves her job and inevitably attracts the affections of three suitors, all named Mike. Spurning the attentions of two of them — a pilot and an advertising executive — Marcy chooses to settle down with the "Mike" who is a small-town science teacher, trading her glamorous life for the quiet domesticity of the suburbs.[130]

As to the women who strayed from the traditional role of faithful wife, in movies like *Brief Encounter* and *The Postman Always Rings Twice* — they rightly suffered for their self-indulgence and after some torrid

scenes (Sex and Death again), paid the requisite *femme fatale* price.

In 1944, Ada Brown now United's Chief Stewardess, saw that her and her colleagues' low earnings had not increased, (and in some cases even decreased), from the 'original eight' BAT stewardesses' pay in 1930. Frustrated and looking to secure better wages and greater job protection, Brown decided to start some sort of "movement" to give her fellow stewardesses a collective voice. Under the provision of the Railway Labor Act of 1926, she set up a labor union. "Girls that had tried to form an association," Brown said, "were fired or threatened."

Her colleagues approved of the goals that she suggested, but the idea of a "union" was repugnant. No longer required to be nurses (which meant they had lost their professional status), they believed that what they did was "hostessing" and a "union" downgraded their job prestige. This mindset would retard feminism for decades as it was "unfeminine" for women and especially glamorous stewardesses, to strike and picket. Men were disproportionally active in aviation unions because they remained on the job longer than the women. It was also because they were the family's breadwinners, that society held labor organizing was a masculine endeavor. Brown agreed with her co-workers and the organization was named the Air Line Stewardess Association (ALSA).

She doggedly signed up 75 per cent of United's stewardess and was elected president, with Frances Hall as vice president. At first, United failed to take their demands seriously, especially any reduction in the number of hours flown each month. Continuing to fly while negotiating, with no experience in labor negotiations, the women were up against the airline's high-priced lawyers. Ida ambitiously hoped to include the stewardesses from all other airlines as well but, with a shoestring budget, nationwide communication was not possible. In March 1946, after a seven-month battle, ALSA's executives went to the National Mediation Board which gave them a positive ruling. On April 25, 1946, Brown, Frances Hall, Sally Thornetz and Edith Lauterbach signed the first contractual agreement with United. The Magna Carta of all future cabin crew contracts, it forced United to recognize the Association as a union — the first formal recognition of any flight attendant organization.[131]

It not only legitimized the stewardess's work — it wasn't yet considered a profession — but that first contract raised the starting salary from $125 to $155 per month, the first increase since 1930. A uniform allowance was provided, a grievance procedure set up and mandatory rest periods created. Flight time was limited to 85 hours per month with a maximum of 255 hours "within any three consecutive calendar months." Further, flying time was limited to eight hours a day and the women were entitled to a rest period of two hours for every flight hour.

It was a victory that United's president, David Behncke, (who had helped create the Air Line Pilots Association [ALPA] in 1931), was willing to concede — the critical no-marriage and age ceiling battles were far in the future. Threatened by the women's independence, that year the pilots began the Air Line Stewards and Stewardesses Association (ALSSA) that it could control. Given ALPA's money and muscle, three years later, ALSA sold its soul and merged with it.

Recognition of flight attendants as more than flying waitresses came as early as 1952 when, to facilitate cabin evacuations, the Civil Aeronautics Authority (CAA) required their presence on all aircraft carrying 10 passengers or more. The CAA's successor, the Federal Aviation Administration (FAA) began the first passenger/flight attendant ratio in 1962 based on "seats fitted". The minimum number of flight attendants on an aircraft was calculated according to the following formula: one for planes with 10-44 passenger seats; two for 45-99; three for 100-149; and four for more than 149.

Sexism, stewardess Lucille Chase, author of "Skirts Aloft", wrote in the 1950s, was always a problem. The power dynamics of omnipotence in the air (and on layovers) meant that the male flight crew felt themselves entitled to "hazing", sexist jokes, impromptu girdle checking and sexual harassment. For the airlines, trading on their vulnerability and sexual allure, the stewardesses' plight was in character with those of their sex who were pictured on the lurid Mickey Spillane paperbacks of the 1950s. Sometimes, Life imitated Art with headlines like: "JILTED STEWARDESS PUMPS SIX SLUGS INTO AIRLINE ROMEO."[132]

When Sara Nelson, the future Association of Flight Attendants (AFA) President joined United Airlines in 1996, she remembered a flight attendant pulling her aside after she had had a "tussle" in the office with the supervisor. "Here I was a brand-new flight attendant and she said, 'Listen, I've spent thirty-five years on the job.' It was 1996, so think about when she started. She said, 'Management thinks of us as their wives or their mistresses, and in either case they hold us in contempt. Your only place of worth is with your fellow flying partners. And, if we stick together, there's nothing we can't accomplish.' That was a lot to take for a 23-year-old fresh out of company training. But it's the thing that sticks with me the most."

Post-war, airlines everywhere were spoilt for choice of aircrew, with hundreds of either seconded or unemployed air force pilots, navigators, and flight engineers available. Recruiters for British Overseas Airways Corporation (BOAC) and British European Airways (BEA) which came into being at Northolt on August 1, 1946, made it clear that no matter how many flying hours an ex-ATA female applicant had, piloting was strictly limited to men. Both airlines defended their actions with: 'We don't employ girl pilots because we don't think they do the job as well as men and many people would not be prepared to get on a plane if they knew a woman was at the controls.'[133] Not until 1987 would British Airways (created in 1974 by the merger of BOAC and BEA) hire Lynn Barton as its first female pilot.

In Britain and Australia, both BOAC and Qantas had inherited the crusty old flying boat stewards as cabin crew. If women were hired, it was as a wartime expedient. This began in November 1943, for BOAC's feeder service from Whitchurch Airport, Bristol to Rineanna, Shannon by DH Albatross to connect with the flying boats at Foynes. The airline advertised for "young ladies with poise and an educated voice" and among the first employed were Helen Wigmore, Peggy Kyte, Jeanne Cox, Rosamond Gilmour, Viva Barker, Janet Huntley, Mary Cowper, and Felicity Farquharson. All were British, white, unmarried and did not speak with a pronounced regional accent. Most had been nurses, or in the military, and were used to working long hours in the company of men, sacrificing their personal lives for little reward.

To the chagrin of the stewards, BOAC not only retained the women but hired more. The sun hadn't yet set on the Empire and with a substantial number of British military and civil personnel overseas, the airline needed motherly nurses to look after their wives and children enroute. In competition with Pan American Airways on the North Atlantic, BOAC also hired stewardesses (still purely on 'an experimental basis ') to serve on its 049 Constellations.

"Cabin crew" was very much a male occupation in Britain — the women were female stewards and not stewardesses. They wore a dark blue, military style uniform, similar to that worn by the males. Both wore collars and ties; the only difference was that the female uniform included a skirt rather than trousers. To avoid a 'tarty' appearance, the stewardesses uniform hem lengths were strictly controlled and kept to well below the knee, close to ankle-length. Blouses had an extra-long shirttail to tuck into skirts so that when stewardess had to bend for any reason she wouldn't expose 'any enticing flesh'. [134]As the ambassadors of an austere Labour Britain, the women projected the image of prefects at Cheltenham Ladies College.

The same generation as Princess Elizabeth who, in 1947, declared in a radio broadcast on her 21st birthday that all her life she was going "to serve", the first British stewardesses had a strong sense of occupational identity. They valiantly coped with working on the Solent flying boats from Southampton to Johannesburg, the British South American Airways (BSAA) Lancastrians to Buenos Aires and the Dakota flights (DC-3s) from Croydon to Lisbon and Lagos.[135] Until BEA got Dakotas, it's poor stewardesses suffered the interim Vickers Vikings with 36 passengers sardined into them.

South African born Yvonne Pope Sintes — nee van den Hoek — grew up near Croydon Airport where she fell in love with aviation (image overleaf). Her hero was

"Cats Eyes" Cunningham and she devoured W E John's "Biggles" adventures in class, hidden under her geometry text. In 1950, the only aviation job the twenty-year-old could get was as a BOAC stewardess. When Yvonne got her commercial license in 1958, she wrote, "I also had the strange feeling I was walking towards my destiny". She tried to join the RAF "but they weren't interested in teaching women to fly". While working as a flight instructor, she and Frankie O'Kane were accepted by the Ministry of Aviation as the first women to train as Air Traffic Controllers, a male bastion that she described as "one of the least enjoyable periods of my life". In 1960, she was awarded the Brabazon Cup for her work as an instructor and in 1965, the International Aircraft Owners and Pilots Association award for best air traffic controller in Europe. On February 14, 1970, Yvonne Pope Sintes became Britain's first female jet airline pilot, co-piloting a DH Comet IVB for Dan-Air and later an HS 748 as captain.

In contrast with those in the United States, both British airlines played down any hint of glamour in their stewardess's job. The nation was enduring its bleak midwinter with food and heating fuel rationed even more severely than in wartime, and the public faces of the state airlines reflected it. It was a case of "No Sex Please, We're British" — the advertisements for BOAC stewardesses warned that "Glamour girls need not apply". The airline wanted what it called hard working "plain Janes, preferably lightweight," and aged between 23 to 30 years. They had to have "a good education, patience, a pleasant, charming manner, poise and tact" and a "neatly proportioned figure". As with all other airlines, the women had to remain single during their mandatory ten-year employment and could never expect to be promoted to be in charge of cabin crew.

At their interview among the questions asked by the BOAC panel (which always included a senior stewardess), were:

Have you any objection to waiting upon colored people?

What would you do if an amorous captain tried to seduce you under romantic tropical skies?

Having provided the "right" answers, the interviewee was asked to parade the length of the room, a practice that airlines continued well into the 1990s. They felt one said, like prize cows — it was a nerve-wracking and demeaning experience that they hoped never to repeat.[136] The quote by an airline spokesman that when applicants for the position of stewardess were interviewed, he started with their legs and worked up to their faces, rang true at all airline interviews then.

The starry-eyed trainees soon discovered that not only

was their intelligence and labor undervalued but sexual harassment on the job was commonplace — by the flight deck, stewards, bosses, and passengers. And it would only get worse. Even before the mini skirt became part of the BOAC uniform (causing male passengers to constantly ask the women to reach up and open the luggage rack opposite), by 1960, to be considered at all, a recent photograph, school examination results, measurements of height, waist, bust, and hip were demanded.[137]

The successful BOAC applicants were sent on a ten-week training course at the airline's Catering Training School symbolically held at a former convent near Heathrow Airport, where they learnt the "duties required of them as waitresses and elementary first aid". Given the global reach of the company's routes, they also learned some unique survival skills — like how to cope if they landed on a desert island, to watch what the monkeys ate and how to collect water by the condensation overnight on the aircraft wings. Although there were no limitations on flying time — sometimes the crew was away from home for three weeks — and the age ceiling and no-marriage rules were strictly enforced, and it would be decades before there was never any thought of labor activism.

The years immediately after the war were a poor time to be a feminist in Britain. Despite the strides that women had made, there was a backlash against them brought on by domesticity and the welfare state. Jobs and careers were strictly segregated by gender and marriage, engagement or pregnancy meant instant dismissal. Until the female sewing machinists strike in 1968 at the Ford Dagenham plant led to the passing of the Equal Pay Act in 1970, women continued to be paid less than men in the same jobs.

That the stewardesses had been taken on because many BOAC stewards had been fired in the "gold rush", i.e. smuggling gold into India, didn't help them. The resentment by the ex-flying boat stewards to the female invasion was memorable. To the young women, most were either lazy alcoholics or 'little Hitlers'. A few were "old queens" who groped the new young stewards who begged the women not to leave them alone with them.[138] Resentful of female cabin crew, the stewards were known to be venomous in their reports. The women were warned in training that it was inadvisable to get on their wrong

side as the men wielded considerable power on and off flights, belonging as they did to the Transport and General Workers Union (TGWU). The TGWU wanted all cabin crew to become members and its stewards intimidated the women until many succumbed. Eventually, cabin crew would be part of the British Airlines Stewards and Stewardesses Association (BASSA).

When Marilyn Monroe sang *Men grow cold as girls grow old* in the 1953 movie *Gentleman Prefer Blondes*, stewardesses understood that truth too well. Age ceilings, like weight limitations, were an accepted (though unwritten) policy throughout the industry. Airlines counted on marriage (or sheer exhaustion) to make their stewardesses quit within 12 to 18 months. A United Airlines executive confessed, "If a flight attendant was still on the job after three years ... I'd know we were getting the wrong kind of girl. She's not getting married." United even ran an ad campaign that featured a close-up of a pretty young woman. "Old Maid" the tag line shouted, pointing out that this woman had been flying for two years without getting a single marriage proposal! The public shaming of unmarried women who, even with all the airline's investment, hadn't "caught" a man made them the Hester Prynne of the day.

Male flight attendants, on the other hand, were allowed — indeed, encouraged — to work until 60 years of age, especially on overseas flights. Allowed to wear eyeglasses (unlike the stewardesses), they usually served in First Class, where it was thought their silver hair and Cary Grant urbanity conveyed a sense of continuity, facilitating a "gentleman's club" atmosphere. In many airlines, stewards were also the only cabin crew that passengers could tip — if one wanted a second choice slice of Chateaubriand.

While the no-marriage rule was in effect, airlines were fierce about enforcing it. Stewardesses who concealed their marriages not only had to eschew wedding rings, but also maintain two phones, one of which would never be answered by a man and put their maiden name on the mailbox. Wedding announcements in newspapers were scrupulously checked by the airline. A steward recalled that there was no need to do that as the women, wanting to move up in seniority, told on each other.

What alarmed American Airlines in November 1954, was that 10 of their 1,500 stewardesses were approaching the age of 32 and had no intention of quitting. The airline instituted the first written age restrictions on their continuing employment. It called for female cabin crew to retire from service upon reaching their 32nd birthday. Told that being a stewardess was "a younger girl's job" an American Airlines flight attendant (happy to give her statistics to the media as 36-24-38) asked, "So at 35, do I look like an old bag?" When ALSSA protested, the company limited the policy application to new hires only, setting a precedent of "grandmother rights" for stewardesses employed before age ceilings were introduced. This was not only for marketing "eye candy", but it also ensured that the airline could cap their salaries and not pay out on pensions or health plans. A married stewardess was also dangerous. Unlike her single colleagues who lived from paycheck to paycheck, from a two salaried household, she could afford to strike.

Beginning in 1955, United Airlines, Pan American Airways and American Airlines no longer hired stewards for their domestic routes, relegating the ones they had to galley duty, i.e. no passenger contact. It wasn't only because they had promised a floor show on the aisle, but like male nurses, in the McCarthy era, stewards were regarded by passengers and pilots as gay — just as all pilots were thought to be heterosexual.[139] The balance of power in the cabin had shifted and the gender injustice that had prevented female pilots from flying commercially, now deemed the steward (because he was a male), incapable of providing the emotional support required onboard. Not until 1971, when family man Celio Diaz Jr sued Pan American for the right to be hired as a flight attendant, did the Equal Employment Opportunity Commission force the airlines to change their hiring practices with regard to male flight attendants.

Qantas employed their first air hostesses in 1948 to serve on the new 049 Constellation service from Australia to Britain. When more were recruited the following year, newspaper headlines read: "Air Hostesses Sheilas Steal All Our Glory, Say Stewards." Because "they were no longer in the limelight", the former flying boat stewards went on a four-day strike, thinking it would ground the airline. The country, then grappling with a national coal miners' strike, the stewards expected a receptive audience and took their case to the Conciliation Commission. But Qantas declared that all their flights would continue to depart on schedule, the work being done solely by the air hostesses and, realizing that they could soon be superfluous, the chastened men returned to work.

"Glamour Air Girls Form A Union", the Melbourne newspaper *Argus.* reported on September 26,1955. "Forty shapely and vivacious members lent glamour to the occasion of the formation of Australia's most photogenic trade union". No mention was made that this was a response to the excessive hours, low pay, and poor conditions the women experienced. While government Air Navigation Orders (ANOs) prescribed the pilots' maximum hours, cabin crew could work indefinitely. Elaine Smith, a Trans Australia Airlines (TAA) hostess recalled a tour of duty of 27 hours where the pilots were replaced under the ANOs but the "hostesses crewed back to base, then picked up [their] normal roster ... No thought of relief for the cabin crew". This was the birth of the Airline Hostesses' Association (AHA). A management committee of nine

Melbourne-based hostesses was elected, three each from Australian National Airways (ANA), Ansett Australia and TAA. The AHA was unique as being the only union in Australia with an entirely female membership — none of the three domestic airlines employed stewards.

The Qantas hostesses began a seven-day strike on July 1, 1970, over working conditions and two years later, its success would lift the marriage bar in all Australian airlines. Both TAA and Ansett vehemently opposed the change, arguing that hostesses would lose their sex appeal if male passengers knew they were married. This was deflated when many hostesses revealed that they were already secretly married, some for years.

What would become the anthem for female empowerment worldwide had just been written and sung by an Australian singer. When asked what her inspiration for *I Am Woman* had been, Helen Reddy said, "I couldn't find any songs that said what I thought being a woman was about. I thought about all these strong women in my family who had gotten through the Depression and world wars and drunken, abusive husbands. But there was nothing in music that reflected that."

When the AHA supported a two-day strike in 1975 for better pay, the opportunity to fly until they were three-months pregnant and an increase in the retirement age to 45, Sir Reginald Ansett, the scrappy founder of Ansett Australia called their executive a "batch of old boilers" — they were aged between 28 and 35 years then. For most of his life, "Reg" had been fighting someone — bus companies, all levels of government, airline rivals and his own son over airport car rentals. In his airline's handbook *Demeanor in Uniform*, the hostesses had already been warned about smoking in uniform on the tarmac, chewing gum and knitting in front of passengers. When the AHA convened a safety awareness seminar for hostesses in October 1980, it attracted less attention than Ansett's full page national advertising campaign depicting a "hostess" barely wrapped in a galley curtain with the question: "If the hostess was out of uniform would you know which airline you were flying with?"

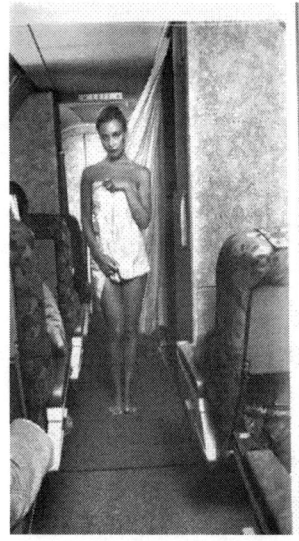

If the hostess was out of uniform would you know which airline you were flying with?

Flight instructor Deborah Lawrie first applied to Ansett Airlines in 1976 and kept sending applications for two years. During that time, 10 of her fellow male flying instructors were accepted into the Ansett pilot training program. She was finally interviewed in 1978 but was rejected solely on gender. "Your earrings are going to be an issue" she was told, "if you ever have to try and get out of an airplane." Deborah took the case to the newly opened Victorian Equal Opportunity Board and under the discrimination provisions of the Victoria Equal Opportunity Act 1977, challenged Ansett. Having married days before the case began, she chose to use her married name "Wardley". The case of Wardley vs Ansett Transport Industries (Operations) Pty Ltd, would be the first sex discrimination employment case contested before the Equal Opportunity Board.

Predictably, the Australian airline's objections to the employment of women as pilots were "that women's menstrual cycles made them unsuitable, and that pregnancy and childbirth would disrupt a woman's career to the point where it would jeopardize safety and incur extra costs for the company."

Reg Ansett's personal opposition to the recruitment of female pilots should have ended with the High Court decision in 1979 ordering him to employ Deborah Wardley as a trainee. However, the protracted legal battles continued and almost four years later (Sir Reginald having died in 1981) Wardley was finally offered employment. Symbolic of the trauma and triumph of women in aviation, the landmark victory against sex discrimination had been made possible by the media attention given to the case, the involvement of women's groups, the delaying tactics adopted by Ansett and the tenacity of Mrs Wardley herself.

Outside the Philadelphia Airport Fire Station, there is a memorial to Stewardess Mary Francis Housley. On January 14, 1951, when a National Airlines DC-4 skidded off the runway and caught fire, passengers credited the twenty-four-year-old with leading them to safety at the cost of her own life. Airline safety training for flight attendants then was grossly inadequate — more time was spent in training them to make a good Martini than evacuating the aircraft. Inevitably, their "ignorance" turned potentially survivable air crashes into fatal disasters. On October 19, 1962, the two stewardesses on an Allegheny Airlines Convair 580 noticed the aircraft's rear door "flapping." On the first officer's advice, they stuffed pillowcases around it and returned to their duties. Soon after, it blew open, sucking one stewardess out to her death — the other escaping her fate only because she was in the toilet at the time. Bizarrely, after this, Allegheny Airlines got an exemption from having to put two stewardesses on its Convairs. On June 7, 1971, when one of its aircraft crashed, killing 27 on board, passengers died of toxic fumes while trying to open the door. The National Transportation Safety Board (NTSB) cited lack of emergency exit lighting and insufficient cabin crew to assist the lone stewardess in the evacuation.[140] The union would lobby to maintain the number of cabin attendants per aircraft and for the airlines to add floor level exit lighting.

Airlines hardly advertised the dangers of flying and at a time when aircraft were unreliable, the pilots, with their military and flight school training, were responsible for passenger safety. A stewardess's knowledge of safety procedures in an emergency was deemed unnecessary as passengers were unlikely to obey a pretty young woman anyway. She had been chosen for her charm and docility — not her ability to command panicking passengers and operate emergency equipment. How could she be taken seriously when in 1955, Barbara Cameron, a United Air Lines stewardess posed in *Playboy* magazine as Miss December?

The sex-versus-safety image that the stewardesses fought came to the forefront in the late 1960s with the spate of hijackings. Barbers, real estate agents and beauticians — indeed anyone who dealt with the public's welfare was licensed and, as cabin safety experts, flight attendants asked, why weren't they? Their skills undervalued, sometimes all the women had was their courage.[141] Now it wasn't only lecherous businessmen that the women had to deal with. This with the complexity of pressurized aircraft — especially operating the doors, the administering of oxygen at higher altitudes, the use of escape chutes and water drills, all would eventually be used by the women to justify their professional status.

Soliciting the opinion of a stewardess in an air-crash investigation was unheard of. Pilots, accident investigators, and company personnel were paternalistic, feeling that some of the grisly crash scenes were too gut-wrenching for her to see. Newspaper reports of an air crash sometimes didn't even identify the deceased flight attendants, and pre-1960, few accident reports mentioned cabin conditions before, during, and after the crash. The continued insistence by airlines that the role of flight attendants was more service than safety, leaving the aircraft's operation to the pilots, was never more flagrant than what occurred on January 8, 1989, when a British Midlands Boeing 737 crashed near the village of Kegworth, UK, killing 47 on board because the pilots had shut down the wrong engine. In the cabin, the flight attendants had been aware of this but because of the prevailing cockpit-centric culture, could not communicate it to the pilots.

Where cabin crew sat was an afterthought for aircraft designers. When such statistics began to be kept, the NTSB noted that between 1964 and 1970, 43 per cent of the flight attendants in the United States involved in survivable accidents on take-off were either killed or severely injured, and 48 per cent were killed or severely injured on the landing phase. The primary cause of these injuries and deaths the NTSB noted, was their seating arrangement on board.

To take up the minimum amount of space, post-war airliners had a fold-down rearward facing seat bolted either to the toilet or cockpit door for the stewardess. In larger aircraft, the seats were attached to the bulkheads, which meant that the occupant was exposed to the same acceleration forces as the air frame of the aircraft. When the AFA investigated this, Candace K Kolander, its Coordinator for Air Safety, Health and Security discovered, "There were flight attendant seats that literally fell off the wall with little or no impact on them — even in normal flight. There were flight attendant seats tucked in corners, attached to cockpit doors, side facing, or tucked into storage areas. In fact, most flight attendant seats did not have shoulder harnesses, nor did they have padding for the head."[142]

On some aircraft, there were not even fold down seats. Former stewardess Judy Wittman remembered a flight on a DC-6B when the seats for stewardesses were tied down with ropes "... and beside the door there was radio equipment and then there was the exit door .... and this is where we had to sit." "On our 707 aircraft," recalled another, "one flight attendant was required to sit in the rear lavatory, facing a large glass mirror on take-off and landing. Our senior vice president of operations had calculated what it would cost over a period of a year to place a flight attendant in the cabin, displacing a passenger, and it would have cost the company thousands of dollars. We had flight attendants who were verbally reprimanded for not sitting in the lavatory during take-off and landing; this was their designated emergency seat." When she had to sit inside the aft lavatory — not only was her seat side-facing but it had no shoulder harness.[143] "We thought it unsanitary because we didn't want to get splashed," a stewardess said, "but this was a very desirable job ... so you didn't complain too much about things."

The onset of the Jet Age brought little encouragement for the women. With the introduction of the "wide bodies" on some airlines, on take-off and landing, flight attendants were seated on the beltless sofas in the lounge areas. On some airlines' DC-8s, the flight attendants' fold down seats were tucked away in the coat closet! Too many cabin crew were injured because of slippery galley floors, the restrictions of their tight uniforms or loose galley equipment. Not until February 1980, did the FAA mandate improved safer seating for flight attendants. From then on their seats were to be equipped with combination seat belts and safety harnesses, and the seats themselves had to have energy-absorbing backs.[144]

Second only to December 17, 1903, (the Wright Brother's first flight) is the month of October, 1958, in commercial aviation. On October 4, BOAC's DH Comet IV became the first commercial jet to fly across the Atlantic, from Idlewild Airport, New York to London in a record-breaking six hours and 11 minutes. The first stewardess to usher in the Jet Age is recorded simply as T Mullis. On the 26th, a Pan American Airways Boeing 707 with 111 passengers and 11 crew onboard took off from Idlewild Airport and landed in Paris 8 hours, 41 minutes later with a refueling stop at Gander, Nfld. Hope Ryden, a stewardess on that flight recalled: "Then jets were associated with fighter planes. None of the cabin crew had ever flown on a jet. We had many, many more passengers than we had ever seen and half the time to serve the meals."

With the advent of the jet aircraft, ALSSA's Phyllis Young presciently noted: "The stewardess is no longer a hostess anymore — she's an airborne waitress." For the women who had joined the airlines to escape the drudgery of jobs on the ground, the jets brought disappointment. An Eastern Airlines stewardess described her life to *Newsweek* in 1968 as "food under your fingernails, sore feet, complaints and insults."

The Boeing 707 and DC-8 reshaped the world beyond all expectations. Economies and trade, politics and culture, fashion and society would never be the same. The pair were the vanguard of the Swinging Sixties — the sexiness of the Kennedy Administration, of the Beatles, James Bond, the Mini Cooper and Carnaby Street in London. Not only did they offer a quieter, smoother, faster, safer ride — You'll be able to stand a half-dollar on edge! — promised the Pan American ads, but they touched off the hyper-sexualization of the stewardess image.

The two jet airliners made air travel boringly safe to a mass market — for which competition was cutthroat, especially across the Atlantic. To passengers, it made little difference if they were in an aircraft made by Boeing or Douglas — the metal tubes they were in looked the same. With commercial aviation so tightly regulated in routes and airfares, an airline's distinguishing brand were the women in the aisle serving the drinks — their age, weight, uniform, and sexuality. No longer motherly nurses, the "stews" were now bait for men (still most of the passenger load) to ogle. A male passenger, the airlines hinted, could affirm his masculinity by mentally undressing the beautiful young woman in the aisle.

Oscar Wilde observed, "Everything in the world is about sex except sex. Sex is about power." In aviation (as in all industries then), that power was exclusively male. Thousands of feet in the sky, hundreds of miles from management's supervision, this institutionalized control over clothing, hair and grooming ensured that there would be no personal variation across the airline's far-flung network. Religious orders, the military, hotels, and hospitals had used this technique for centuries. As MGM's Louis B Mayer did with his starlets, by overseeing the women's clothing, grooming and social/sexual norms, he controlled their behavior on and offscreen. What today would be condemned as sexual harassment, to prevent the "jiggles", a girdle was mandatory for stewardesses, no matter how slim they were. Patricia Ireland was the president of the National Organization for Women (NOW) from 1991 to 2001, but in the late 1960s she had been a flight attendant for Pan American. One of the seeds of her subsequent activism was, "I thought there was no better prescription for varicose veins than to go in a pressurized cabin with the equivalent of rubber bands around your thighs".[145]

The Playtex company made special girdles for stewardesses — tighter and shapelier — and to ensure they wore them, the "check stewardess" on their flight would pinch their bottoms to feel it.[146] Several US airlines also employed male "check supervisors" on what was called "girdle check patrol." Called "undergarment enforcers", they were paid to put their hands onto the stewardess's buttocks, feeling for girdles. While some enforcers only slid their hands across the women's buttocks, others squeezed hard enough to leave a bruise.

The fabled Golden Age of Flying was largely racist as mainly white people flew. Racial prejudice aside, the reason was economic. In 1950, the median income for an African American male was $1,471 annually. The average white male was paid nearly twice as much, and as air travel was a luxury, few minorities could afford it. If one saw a black or brown person at the airport, chances were he was the janitor. Although airlines in the United States fought to keep their crews — cockpit and cabin — white, the affluence caused by the booming post-war economy and the civil rights struggle made them reluctantly reconsider. While this was never shown in magazine ads or on television, by the early 1960s, non-whites were visibly filling aircraft seats.

African American males did not enter the commercial cockpit until 1963. Perry Young had been an instructor at the famed Tuskegee Army Airfield where he trained the "Tuskegee Airmen" during the war. After years of flying outside the United States as a commercial pilot, on December 17, 1956, Young was hired to fly for New York Airways, a small helicopter company that shuttled passengers and luggage between La Guardia and Idlewild (later Kennedy) Airports and Newark's Metropolitan Airport. He had broken through aviation's colour barrier by becoming the first African American pilot to be hired by a scheduled US airline. Former US Air Force pilot Marlon Green applied to multiple airlines in 1957 without getting a response. On his application to Continental Airlines, he decided to leave the "race" box unchecked and did not supply a picture. Because of this, he made it to the final round of interviews with four other pilots, all white, and all with only a third of his flight hours. Continental chose the four white pilots and rejected Green's application. Rather than accept his fate, Green took his case to the US Supreme Court, and in 1963 won a decision against Continental Airlines. Only after this did major airlines start hiring black pilots.

The first black flight attendant was Léopoldine Doualla-Bell Smith, a princess of the Cameroon royal family. She was hired in 1957 by Union de Transports Aériens (UTA) as a *hôtesse de l'air* for its African routes. Inflight, she was treated as a prostitute, encountering passengers who offered her money to sleep with them. She also suffered racial discrimination — the most bizarre in South Africa during the apartheid regime when she was not allowed to walk off the plane with the crew or stay at the same hotel. To prevent being arrested, she would be covered with a blanket and taken to a home of a black employee.

In the United States and Europe, "hostessing" was still a white, college-educated, middle-class occupation and if non-whites were hired at all, they were Asian, Hispanic, or Hawaiian to serve on the airlines routes to the Orient, Hawaii, or Latin America. In Britain, BOAC hired its first Caribbean stewardesses (below) because they were considered "jolly." Skin colour was not an issue in 1950s Canada and a stewardess who was not white was romanticized. "Eskimo Stewardess Is Realizing Her Dream" reported the *Globe & Mail* newspaper in 1958.[147] Trained as a nurse, petite, and pretty Ann

Witalkuk, which readers were told meant "Big Eyes" in her language, was said to be the world's first Eskimo stewardesses. Was she born in an igloo? Can she harpoon a whale? Eat blubber? Ann was said to parry all such queries from passengers with a shy smile and shake of her head that could have meant yes or no. Her family still lived on tiny Cape Hope island in Hudson Bay where her father traded furs for groceries. Ann spoke English, French, Cree and Eskimo — although the reporter cautioned, "... she doesn't give her phone number in any language."

Airlines in the United States, especially Delta, feared that their white stewardesses (to say nothing of their passengers), would refuse to condone "Negro girls" in the cabin, and that allowing the "help" to invade their workplace would downgrade a prestigious occupation. Reluctant to open that can of worms while fighting sexism, ALSSA and other cabin crew unions, were, as the WASPs had been in wartime, leery of addressing racism.

Told she wasn't hired because she was "a Negro", in 1956, Patricia Banks filed a discrimination lawsuit against Mohawk Airlines, TWA and Capital Airlines, the three airlines she had applied to. It took Banks four years until she won her case with the help of Adam Clayton Powell who represented Harlem in the House of Representatives, and in 1960, Capital Airlines hired her as its first African American stewardess. By that time, Ruth Carol Taylor (below) had joined Mohawk Airlines in 1958 to become the first black woman to be hired as a flight attendant.

Marlene White Ahimaz applied to the airlines in 1957, hoping to get a job as a flight attendant to help pay for college. Being fair skinned, she could have been hired immediately if she had pretended to be something other than black, but she refused to lie. "When I went to the final interview at Eastern, they said, 'You speak Spanish, don`t you?' and I answered, 'Yes.' And they said, 'You're Cuban, are`t you?' I said, 'No, I'm a black American.' They said, 'Tell us you`re Cuban, and you`re hired'. And I said, 'Sorry, I'm a black American.' And that ended the interview." Marlene chose to fight and won. Her lawsuit against Northwest Airlines in 1962 further opened the door for black women to be hired as flight attendants in the United States.

Although state commissions against discrimination in gender and colour took up their cause, the instrument for change came from an unlikely source — the Soviet Union. The United States with other Western countries was diplomatically trying to prove it was an egalitarian society, especially to potential African and Asian allies. When the Communist newspaper *Pravda* pointed out that capitalist bigotry "barred Negro girls from one of the most coveted careers open to women", the hypocrisy of the world's leading democracy having been pointed out, embarrassed Washington. Pressured by the federal government, the airlines backed down. But even then, at interviews for cabin crew, African Americans were subjected to what was called the "paper bag" test. Besides having the usual requirements like perfect teeth and figure — to be chosen, black stewardesses had to be no darker than a paper bag.

Discrimination by skin colour wasn't restricted to the airlines. Casey Grant, an early black flight attendant and author of *Stars in the Sky: Stories of the First African American Flight Attendants* would write of Eugene Harmond, the first black male flight attendant for Delta Airlines, who was hired in 1966. Once in New York City, the crew was checking in to the layover hotel and when it was his turn to sign in, the clerk informed Harmond that there weren't any more rooms. "Eugene rode around in a cab for several hours trying to find a place to stay." wrote Grant. "After being refused by all the hotels, he returned to the original hotel. By then it was time for the morning pick-up so he never got to sleep that night. Delta had paid for a room for him and one was available, but the desk clerk had refused to give it to him."

The airlines worked out a system to deal with cabin integration, knowing which pilots would not allow black flight attendants to enter the cockpit to serve their meals and adapted their schedules accordingly. There were always passengers who spat on, insulted, or refused contact with them. To keep them safe, the black stewardesses were confined to "special routes", none of which were in the southern United States. Although racial discrimination was more institutionalized, it proved easier to overcome in commercial aviation than the gender kind.

As part of his "New Frontier" program, in 1961, President John F Kennedy established the Presidential

Committee on the Status of Women. To chair the committee, he astutely appointed the historic champion of women's rights, former First Lady Eleanor Roosevelt. The Committee's revelations about nationwide pay discrimination led to the passing of the Equal Pay Act of 1963 which required equal pay for equal work. The second important law was Title VII of the 1964 Civil Rights Act. It prohibited discrimination on the basis of sex for any reason in determining employee compensation. Both gave stewardesses hope that, like race, restrictions on marriage, weight and age would now be lifted. Although US airlines were federally regulated, they hid behind state labor laws that categorized certain jobs as "women's work" and little changed. Judges ruled that as the marriage restriction was between single and married women, it wasn't quite "sex" discrimination. Every airline's defense was that "single women are better stewardesses than married women for ... passenger acceptance, changing flight schedules easier and the less likelihood of pregnancy." As encouraging as the Civil Rights Act was, it would take more to fracture centuries of gender inequity.

What garnered more publicity about the status of women than any legislation were two books in 1963–1964, which became best sellers. Working her way up from the typing pool to running *Cosmopolitan* magazine, Helen Gurley Brown wrote *Sex and the Single Girl*. Her message was that every woman should have the right to decide for herself what she wanted to accomplish in her life. Non-white women had no such choices, but that wasn't the labor pool that airlines wanted to recruit stewardesses from.

Betty Friedan's *The Feminine Mystique* also caught the frustrations of a generation of women who wanted equality in the workplace (the author had lost her job as a reporter when she got pregnant.) Her premise might have been written for/by stewardesses i.e. that women should refuse to play the stereotypical role of sex doll/ cook/maid and whose lives were incomplete until they had "trapped" a husband. Brown and Friedan's books did not begin the Second Wave of Feminism, but they made stewardesses question their lives. To conform to what men expected of them: remain unmarried, diet to remain thin and wear provocative uniforms that encouraged sexual harassment, they became magically invisible at 32 years of age. Their "profession" was a blatant example of all that was wrong with society's expectations of working women.

Many flight attendant retirees remain embittered of the hostile and patronizing attitude that prominent feminists had towards them as "mindless, Boobie-girl" symbols. The gender norms that flight attendants upheld were similar to beauty pageants, which radical feminists considered degrading to women. One who knew that their grievances were synonymous with the feminist movement was Gloria Steinem. She once witnessed a pilot kick a black stewardess off the plane because he saw her reading a book by the political activist Eldridge Cleaver. Recognizable in her cool aviator glasses, waist-long blonde hair, and miniskirts, Steinem became "a celestial bartender" for flight attendants eager to tell her their issues. As she didn't drive (she used to say neither did Jack Kerouac) she spent more than half her life "on the road" and much of that in planes. "Stewardesses" she wrote, "were hired as decorative waitresses with geisha-like instructions. The goal of airline executives seemed to be to hire smart and ornamental young women, to use them as advertising come-ons, to work them hard, and to age them out soon." As to those who claimed that women relied on their sexuality to further their careers, Steinem said: "If women could sleep their way to the top, there would be a lot more women at the top."

As to female pilots flying commercially or in the military, airlines and air forces clung to that old chestnut — the retention factor i.e. there was no point in hiring and training women because they would leave as soon they married and became pregnant — to say nothing of premenstrual tension syndrome symptoms.[148] In 1965, Pan American Airways cited two more reasons why they couldn't employ women as pilots: they couldn't share a room with a male pilot and the added expense of booking two single rooms instead of a double would be prohibitive. A bigger problem the airline predicted was crew discipline. No male pilot, flight engineer or purser would take orders from a female captain — and there was the likelihood that the stewardesses would resent doing so as well. Besides, the effect on passengers (especially men) when they heard a female voice making announcements from the cockpit would cause them "to drop their drinks"! The public wasn't ready for women in the cockpit.

For Jerrie Cobb who had been flying her father's 1936 Waco since she was 12, the glass ceiling would extend far into Space. She encountered her first sexism when she went to Florida for a job as a DC-3 co-pilot — only to be rejected when the airline discovered that "Jerrie Cobb" was not a man. Instead, she was given a job at the maintenance shop — as a typist and file clerk. Cobb eventually flew for an international aircraft ferry service and spent the next three years delivering B-17 bombers around the world.

Goaded by the Soviet launch of Sputnik 2, on November 3, 1957, the US Congress moved quickly to close the Space gap. Dr W Randolph Lovelace who specialized in aerospace medicine at the National Aeronautics and Space Administration (NASA) and former flight surgeon Brig General Donald Flickinger, both believed that women would make excellent astronauts. They weighed less than men and were shorter, so they would need less oxygen, food, and water. They were more resistant to radiation, less prone to heart attacks and better suited to handling heat and cold and (as women), were more used to pain and loneliness.

At 28 years of age, with 7,000 hours of flight time, Cobb (below) held the FAI records for speed, altitude, and distance. In 1959, she was one of only nine women selected by *Life* magazine as one of the "100 Most Important Young People in the US". Many in the aviation community predicted that Cobb would be the next Jackie Cochran. Monitored by Lovelace, she and twelve other elite female pilots underwent rigorous. physical, psychological, and mental tests, identical to those used to test the Mercury astronauts like John Glenn and Alan Shepard, with the addition of gynecological examinations.

Twenty-two-year-old Mary Wallace "Wally" Funk was the youngest of the group. As a child, she had practiced flying by jumping off her family's barn wearing a Superman cape. Giving themselves the title "Fellow Lady Astronaut Trainees" (FLATs), Cobb, Funk and the other women consistently outperformed the men in tests. Although these were privately funded by Jackie Cochran and NASA had no connection with them, the media seized on Lovelace's women as "The Mercury 13". They captured the attention of the pub-

lic. At a time when women were not allowed to be military or commercial pilots, the United States would be the first nation to put one in space. Then on April 12, 1961, the Soviet Union launched the first human, Yuri Gagarin, into space, beating both Alan Shepard to space and John Glenn to orbit.

Just as the FLATs seemed on the verge of becoming the world's first female astronauts, the door was slammed shut by a woman. Jackie Cochran testified at the special Congressional hearings against the idea of including them in the space program because of "women's lack of commitment and high attrition rates due to marriage and pregnancy." Officials seized on this and thanking her for her understanding, Vice President Lyndon Johnson put an end to the female initiative. In the summer of 1962, the 13 women were told that jet aircraft would not be available to them to train on — the only woman who had flown one was Cochran — and that the astronauts were to be drawn from the pool of military test pilots, which was reserved for men.

They were up against the Space Age's misogynistic masculine ethos, personified by the former fighter pilot, John Glenn. The battlefield was a hearing room on Capitol Hill that year, where members of Congress were considering whether women could be astronauts. "We women pilots" Ms. Cobb testified, "who want to be part of the research and participation in space exploration are not trying to join a battle of the sexes. We see, only, a place in our nation's space future without discrimination." John Glenn testified the next day. "The men go off and fight the wars and fly the airplanes and come back and help design and build and test them," he said. "The fact that women are not in this field is a fact of our social order." The women realized (as many of their gender have since and throughout history) that no one wanted them, there was no place for them to go- and no one was coming to their rescue.

Timing had been against them. Just months before the hearings, on February 20, 1962 Glenn had orbited the Earth and returned to a hero's welcome, and President Kennedy set the nation's sights on putting a man — not a woman — on the Moon. NASA did not want the distraction of a debate over whether women (or black men) could be astronauts. It excluded women from participating in the early space program, (despite the Soviet Union's launch of cosmonaut Valentina Tereshkova in 1963) because of concerns about "the suitability of women as potential astronauts, with emphasis on the potential for the menstrual cycle to alter performance during space flight ... it seems doubtful that women will ever be in demand for space roles in the very near future".

Despite her disappointments, Ms Cobb remained fascinated by space travel. On July 20, 1969, alone in the Amazon, where she was a missionary, she listened on the radio as Neil Armstrong and Buzz Aldrin landed on the moon. She then danced on the wings of her plane in the moonlight. One of the FLATs, however, did finally make it into space. On July 20, 2021, "Wally" Funk, now 82 years of age, accompanied Jeff Bezos, founder of Amazon and Blue Origin, on an 11-minute suborbital spaceflight.

NASA opened spaceflight up to women in 1978.[149] Five of the six women the Agency selected that year— Sally Ride, Judy Resnik, Anna Fisher, Kathy Sullivan, and Rhea Seddon — had all been Girl Scouts, part of an aviation program for girls begun in 1941. Not until 1983 — more than two decades after the FLATS had been turned down, would Sally Ride become NASA's first woman in Space and, at 32, the youngest American do to so.

Speaking to reporters before the shuttle flight on June 18, 1983, Dr Ride — chosen because she was known for keeping her cool under stress — politely endured a barrage of questions focused on her sex: Would spaceflight affect her reproductive organs? Did she plan to have children?

Would she wear a bra or makeup in space? Did she as a woman, cry on the job? Watching that shuttle flight, Gloria Steinem, then editor of *Ms.* magazine, presciently wrote, "Millions of little girls are going to sit by their television sets and see they can be astronauts, heroes, explorers and scientists."[150]

The race to the Moon was not only gender but colour coded as well, and this doomed Ed Dwight Jr, a US Air Force test pilot, who had been chosen by the Kennedy Administration to be the first African American astronaut. Having campaigned on civil rights issues, President Kennedy saw him as a symbolic display of emerging African American equality. Dwight passed all the tests given to the white astronauts and was sent to the flight test school at Edwards Air Force Base for the final step in the program. At a time of growing civil rights unrest, he was profiled in both *Life* and *Ebony* magazines and inundated with fan mail and requests for interviews. But Chuck Yeager, the head of the flight test school, and NASA thought differently. Yeager felt that Dwight had only been admitted due to preferential treatment. Of the 14 candidates selected for the continuation of the program in October, 1963, his name was noticeably absent. A month later, Kennedy was assassinated in Dallas and Dwight resigned in disgust from the air force in 1966. As aviation had been, early space exploration was reserved for white males only.

Legislative victories for stewardesses in the United States — one was termed the "Old Broads Bill" — were piecemeal until August, 1968, when ALSSA and American Airlines ended a contract dispute and the women won the right to marry without losing their jobs. The following year the courts ruled that women could no longer be penalized for being overweight, too tall, too old or wearing eyeglasses. What passengers, pilots and management found difficult to forgive was pregnancy. Bursting the fantasy that she was no longer a virgin hit hard — especially the male target market. [151]Both management and the pilots were concerned that her condition would hinder her in her duties, especially in evacuation. An Air Canada captain had even refused to fly with what he called "pregnant Susies". Dorothy Sue Cobble, author of *The Other Women's Movement: Workplace Justice and Social Rights in Modern America*, wrote "One transgressing employee had kept her infant secret for three years. Upon discovery, the airline gave her an ultimatum: either she resign (in which case she could keep her child) or put it in an orphanage."

With the ambiguity of "Title VII" in the United States, proving that pregnancy-based employment restrictions were discriminatory was a legal quagmire for feminist groups to fight. "Storks Fly, Why Can't Mothers?" and "Mothers Are Still FAA Qualified" were signs carried by militant flight attendants demanding childcare, abortion rights and workplace equality for women. Feminists had often reached to the law as an instrument of social transformation in aviation, but not until 1978, with media coverage of some high-profile legal successes with AT&T, General Motors, and General Electric, was the Pregnancy Discrimination in Employment Act passed in Congress.

Besides the age ceilings, unequal pay scales and two promotion lists for male and female cabin crew, the humiliating weigh-ins for the women were strictly enforced. In what the media captioned, "Only thin girls may fly so please don't feed the stewardesses" as late as September 1973, United Airlines would fire stewardess Sandi Hendrix for weighing 127 pounds. The airline's rule was that at five-foot-two, she could not weigh more than 118 pounds. The "weight in proportion to height" standard was universal and although the women held "Weigh My Job, Not My Body" protests, not until 1994 would airlines agree to a proficiency test ensuring that regardless of weight, flight attendants were physically fit to do their job.

The budding activism in the profession (the most significant of which was that the women chose to be called by the gender-neutral title of "flight attendants") came up against a particularly virulent strain of airline marketing. Sex has been used to sell everything from cars to toothpaste to ice cream but in commercial aviation, the airlines made a science (or a fetish?) of it. Equipping themselves with expensive, fuel-thirsty jets that had many more seats to sell, the airlines plunged deep into the red, especially the second-tier ones like Braniff, National and Continental Airlines.

Disregarding Friedan, the courts and ALSSA, to distinguish themselves from each other airlines relied on "naked opportunism" i.e., eroticizing their female employees. If it meant that to lure passengers (predominantly male) on board, they had to pimp out their flight attendants, so be it. For Madison Avenue which at the time consigned women in ads to baking, doing laundry, scrubbing floors, or discussing sanitary napkins (and men to looking befuddled at soiled diapers), this was a glittering prize and the "Mad Men" vied with one other to show the airlines how. The sex symbol stereotype that they came up with was an image of flawless youth and beauty — far removed from the harried, frumpy housewives with dishpan hands that those poor businessmen were going home to. With their strict beauty codes for flight attendants already in place, the airlines were halfway there.

Ironically, it was a woman who conceived the sexualization of the flight attendant profession. A copy writer for the New York ad agency McCann-Erickson, in 1964 Mary Wells was given the task of remaking Braniff Airways' dowdy image. She not only hired Emilio Pucci to redesign its cabin crews' uniforms in op-art colours, but she coined the immortal marketing phrases: "When a tired businessman gets on a plane, we think he ought to be allowed to look at a pretty girl" and "We won't get you where you are going any faster but it'll seem that way" and the sly "Does your wife know you're flying with us?" When Braniff was attacked by women's groups (but lauded in the mainstream media), a spokesman pointed out that since the ads appeared, business had been booming — the airline's shares went from $24 to $120 overnight.

McCann-Erickson's rivals dreamed up other provocative slogans for their clients, the most memorable were National Airline's "I'm Jo, Fly Me", American Airline's "She Only Wants What's Good for You", and Continental Airline's "We Really Move Our Tails for You." Even Delta Airlines, which operated in the Bible-belt Southern United States put their stewardesses in high above-the-knee dresses with the advertised "Come On: No Floor Show. Just A Working Girl Working". Pacific Southwest Airlines made their stewardesses wear large buttons that simply said: "Pure, Sober and Available." Eastern Airlines gave male passengers little black books to capture the women's phone numbers and the skies got a lot friendlier when United introduced the "skimmer" — a very short one-piece dress fashioned out of (passengers were so informed) "pure virgin wool". By dressing them in "Uniforms that Purr ..." (as they were faux fur, they might have), National Airlines also encouraged passengers to pet their stewardesses.

During the First World War, when naval blockades kept shipments of textiles from entering Germany, paper was cut into strips, twisted, and woven into cloth to make a variety of clothing. When fashion icon Mary Quant said that women should not dress like their mothers, taking their cue from that in 1966, the Scott Paper Company revived throw-away paper clothing. BOAC stewardesses on the Caribbean to New York route wore what only a man could dream up — a paper mini-dress — white with cerise and purple flowers and green leaves, "a huge flower over the left boob" — and a hem that ended three inches above the knee. The male passengers competed to write on the dresses, tear them shorter — the women had masking tape to repair this — and as the dresses were fire-proof, drunks "playfully" stubbed their cigarettes out on them. (It was later revealed that the uniforms' manufac-turer had long since run through its supply of non-flam-

mable paper and they weren't). The paper dresses tore easily, froze their wearers' legs in New York (but delighted the male ground crews) and, supposedly wa-terproof, dissolved in the Caribbean rain. TWA followed BOAC a year lat-er, hiring New York fashion designer Eli-sa Daggs to design its stewardesses' gold lamé outfits. "Girls today," said one paper dress survivor "would sue the airline or need counselling."

Not to be outdone, CP Air (formerly Canadian Pacific Airlines) introduced their flight attendants to uniforms so short that appreciative media described as "Thigh in the Sky". European airlines came up with slogans like Air France's, "Have You Ever Done It the French Way?" In Asia, Air India and Cathay Pacific airlines poured their flight attendants into form-hugging saris and cheongsams — both of which would have restricted movement in a cabin evacuation. If the ads were to be believed, once onboard,

"... the women were ready and raunchy, aggressive — and yet yielding." Male fantasies came out from under wraps and pleasure beckoned. Images of femininity were communicating blatantly opposing messages of freedom and sexual subordination.[152]

In vain did flight attendant unions campaign to end the airlines' degrading advertising with ads of their own. "Fantasies are fine but I am a highly trained professional," went one counter television ad, "and should an emergency situation arise, I urgently need the respect, confidence and cooperation of all my passengers." But until needed in emergencies, the flight attendants' proficiency in safety procedures was ignored, particularly of safety measures like cardio-pulmonary resuscitation techniques (CPR), as well as survival skills and terrorist coping tactics.

So entrenched was the "Barbie Doll mystique" that airlines knew they had society and the law on their side.[153] At Congressional hearings, airline lawyers argued that attractive single young women were as essential to the business as muscular men were to the construction industry, because, while stewards could lead evacuations they would never possess the charm or ability to massage a male passenger's ego. Congresswoman Martha Griffiths shot back "Are you running an airline or a whorehouse?" Invoking patriotism (the last refuge of scoundrels) the lawyers explained that American carriers were competing in a global arena against European and Asian airlines — and they certainly didn't shy away from sexual exploitation of their stewardesses.

Marketing sexual innuendo, the airlines encouraged even more pats and gropes of the women as passengers now felt they were invited and entitled to do so. Pinching incidents, and worse, were on the upswing. "We're the cat's scratching pole" is how a Braniff stewardess put it. A former BOAC stewardess remembered that harassment in the swinging sixties, was not only rife but considered normal and '... the girls put up with this, 'to see the world.' It was an accepted hazard of the job as a quote from an Air Canada employee newsletter of the day explained: "Stewardesses are taught to treat a passenger's kiss or casual caress 'with humor' but given their constant motion, opportunities for aisle-side lechery are now more fleeting." In an industry where the customer was always right, working in such a testosterone-fueled atmosphere, the flight attendants who rejected advances and complained, feared being "written up" and retaliated against by passengers, management, and society.

Despite being so rigidly controlled (or perhaps because of it) it was somehow accepted that stewardesses, more than secretaries, nurses, and librarians, were wildly promiscuous. Remade from virginal brides to swinging playmates, their purported lifestyles became staples in movies such as *Stewardess Sluts* and *Spread Eagles* where all they did was try on bras, take showers, and do yoga naked. With the best seller book *Coffee, Tea or Me?*, proposals from passengers were no longer for marriage, making them fair game for unwanted sexual attention.[154]

Given the cramped aisles they worked in, harassment was difficult to prove, and it was an imprudent (or unrealistic?) flight attendant who took her employer to court over it. Despite the knowledge that unwanted sexual advances in the workplace were a form of discrimination "on the basis of sex," and a violation of Title VII of the Civil Rights Act, the airlines' condescending attitude toward "the girls", while simultaneously promising male passengers that the women would "make them feel good all over", did not mean that there was much chance of justice. An example of what to expect was the Rico Petrocelli acquittal in 1974. The Boston Red Sox 3rd baseman was acquitted by a New York jury of a United Airlines stewardess's charge that, four years before, she had been molested, kicked, and punched by him in flight. Susanne Mondlin testified that when Petrocelli had grabbed her underneath her breasts, she had kicked him and poured a soft drink over him. Then, she said, he struck her in full view of the passengers. Too far away, her colleague was only able to partially substantiate Mondlin's claim.

The airline's lawyers had the case sufficiently delayed so that their detectives could "dig up enough dirt" on Mondlin — discovering that while employed she had been living with a man who was not her husband. That was enough for the jury to question her morals. In denying the woman's testimony under oath, Petrocelli (who his lawyer emphasized to the jury was happily married and a doting father of four) was supported by his teammates, all of whom testified that he had quite innocently been attempting to get past her in the aisle when, completely unprovoked, she had attacked him. Leaving the court a free man, Petrocelli magnanimously told reporters that he harbored no bitterness towards Mondlin, the now unemployed stewardess, and "wished her well." Given such an outcome, we can imagine the untold numbers of stewardesses whose stories of harassment, assault or misconduct were ignored by their employers or, if reported, ended like this.

Many stewardess retirees treasure their memories in scrap books of celebrity passengers — royalty and movie stars — they had fawned on. Their tantrums were tolerated and forgiven. Frank Sinatra was so afraid of flying that he took out his fear on the women. Elizabeth Taylor threw memorable scenes on board and when a drink was accidentally spilled on one of the Beatles, he did not pass it off with a *Let it be*. When the world's first people carrier, the Boeing 747, made air travel affordable for the masses, its size reducing the cost per seat so low — the average price of a ticket declined by 50 per cent — that anyone could afford to fly. The alternative universe that it cracked open was as if the contents of an inner-city bus had emptied into the Gilded Age. It could have been snobbery but the prestige that stewardesses had "borrowed" from serving the great and well-dressed was no longer there. The T-shirt and stretch pants toenail cutters that infected the "jumbos" had little sense of dress or decorum. Blame it on Freddie Laker's DC-10 "Skytrain", with its bone-crunching 345 seats, (a hundred more than the usual DC-10 at the time), blame it on smoking being banned or that the average pitch on an economy airline seat had shrunk from 35 inches to 31 inches (and in some airlines to 28 inches) — or on a global breakdown in social manners, but cabin crew could not help but notice that the caliber of their charges had changed — and not for the better. Air rage, first seen on holiday charter flights proliferated and cabin crews were now routinely threatened, hit, poked, or pushed. They had become public punching bags and the women looked to their union, employer and government for protection and compensation.

The democratization of what had once been an exclusive means of travel remade the public's image of flight attendants and this was reflected in literature. No longer the perfect wives-in-training or even the Madison Avenue "come-ons" for male business travelers, cabin crew were now psychiatrists, policewomen and zookeepers as depicted in Rene Foss's *Around the World in a Bad Mood* and Elliott Hester's *Plane Insanity: A Flight Attendant's Tales of Sex, Rage and Queasiness at 30,000 Feet*, both written by ex-cabin crew.

But by the mid-seventies, the flight attendant unions could congratulate themselves on achieving some leverage. Thanks to their efforts, gone from most airlines were the toxic fug of smoking onboard, the "Golden Handshake" after ten years' service, and the no-marriage restraints. It was now permissible to be widowed, divorced and soon, gay. The Swinging Sixties go-go boots and miniskirts had been discarded for more modest working attire that revealed less flight attendant flesh. Blue suits and neckties, Ralph Lauren midi-length skirts and sarong kebayas now covered the women, in the last instance from neck to ankle.

On January 1, 1974, ALSSA flight attendants chose self-determination and broke away from ALPA to form their own union, the Association of Flight Attendants (AFA), affiliating with Communications Workers of America in 2004. Newark-based flight attendant Jacqueline Jacquet-Williams founded the Black Flight Attendants of America in 1974 to promote Black History in Aviation and sponsor aviation career days at inner city schools. The Organization of Black Aerospace Professionals (OBAP), then called The Organization of Black Airline Pilots, was formed when Ben Thomas, a pilot with Eastern Airlines, invited thirty-seven African American pilots (half the industry total then) to a meeting on September 17, 1976.

There still remained the airline presidents who confused professionalism with paternalism. Bush pilot Max Ward began the Canadian charter airline Wardair in 1952 and, as with all "non-skeds" then, he skirted around federal control of fares and regulations. But by the 1970s, tourist traffic had made charter airlines a large-scale business. Lauded as the little guy who took on bureaucrats and the mega carriers, Ward squandered all that goodwill on how he treated his flight attendants. Not only did he cancel their annual parents' pass (which was sacred to them) but their issues ranged from extended duty days to being allowed to wear trousers in a Canadian winter — the only cabin crew not allowed to. Organized by the Canadian Air Line Flight Attendant Association (CALFAA), Wardair flight attendants struck on January 12, 1973. Said one, "None of us had any problems surviving on strike pay because none of us were making much money anyway." Nonplussed, Ward continued to operate his aircraft using office employees,

friends, relatives, and pilots' wives.[155] As a lesson to them, he also stranded the striking flight attendants in various locations across Canada, Europe and Hawaii and they were brought home at CALFAA's expense. It was only when other aviation unions threatened to come out in sympathy with the women (who had been picketing for two months in a severe winter) that Ward dictated terms of settlement, leaving CALFAA and the strikers poorer but even more militant for future strikes.[156]

Two years later, National Airlines was grounded for 127 days when its flight attendants struck to protest long hours and low pay. The action, which came a year and a half after their contract had expired, demonstrated what the media called, "cutting edge feminism." What had once been a glamorous one-year fling before marriage was now a career for many National's flight attendants, prompting activism for pay and against their sexual exploitation. They had a particular animosity towards the airline's famous "Fly Me" and faux fur advertising campaigns which had led to innumerable sexual expectations on the part of male passengers. The airline now planned for follow-up television ads that had models pose in skimpy bathing suits with the promise "We're going to fly you like you've never been flown before". Fortunately, these would be struck down by the Federal Communications Commission — not because of their offensiveness towards women but on a legal technicality that they did not actually fly the planes. But without strike pay and up against the airline's chairman L B Maytag Jr, the tough-minded washing machine scion, the flight attendants had little chance of success.[157]

In Britain, the Equal Opportunity Act in 1975 allowed stewardesses to undertake training programs to be promoted as senior cabin service officers. The sensible Hardy Amies uniforms appeared in British Airways as did more mature cabin crew with the recruitment age up to 49 years of age. Crew Resource Management, which grew out of the 1977 Tenerife Airport disaster in which two Boeing 747 aircraft collided on the runway, killing 583 people, led to the beginning of teamwork between pilots and flight attendants.

Airlines were now being grounded by imminent, unannounced work stoppages by women who once had thought labor activism was for blue collar only. When Cathay Pacific flight attendants struck in 1993, their weapon was the feminine allure they had been hired for and trained in. It was as if, wrote a surprised columnist, Snow White had told the Seven Dwarfs that she was no longer going to do their cooking and laundry. By combining femininity with feminism and picketing in their distinctive uniforms at airports, flight attendants used their visibility to not only attract the media's attention to their grievances but that of the public and politicians.

The labor solidarity demonstrated by the TWA flight attendants in a bitter strike has taken its place in feminist protest history. Led by the Independent Federation of Flight Attendants (IFFA), on March 7, 1986, the 6,000 TWA flight attendants went on strike. It began over the 22 per cent wage reduction that the airline's CEO, Carl

Icahn, had imposed on them. The sexist lines were drawn: the women were not considered the main wage earners for their families by Icahn who had negotiated less severe wage cuts with the pilots and machinists, all of whom were male. The airline also had "in the wings" 1,500 cabin crew replacements and planned to shift other TWA employees, ranging from reservation clerks to accountants, to cabin crew. The flight attendants had counted on the machinists coming out in sympathy with them, but a court order prevented that. They picketed at all TWA stations for ten weeks until IFFA unconditionally called off the strike. Their replacements now considered permanent; the strikers were left without jobs until vacancies arose. It was a pyrrhic victory both for TWA, which never recovered financially, and the women who, on returning to work, found it difficult to accept the young new hires and old friends who had crossed the picket lines.

The strikes demonstrated how the demographics of the airline industry had changed. Of the 63,496 flight attendants on U S scheduled carriers in 1985, 29 per cent were between 30 and 34 and 30 per cent from 35 to 39. The media age was 34 years. Most were married or divorced, some were gay, 43 per cent had children and 14 per cent were male. American Airlines even featured an ad with a flight attendant in a blue blazer, her hands casually crossed over the headrest of a chair so her wedding ring was apparent. Airlines might protest that they were now coping with hormonal imbalances and the "invisibility" of middle-aged women but older stewardesses, they discovered, were more mature (and if mothers, were used to dealing firmly with the childish antics of passengers) than the eye candy they had courted. Interestingly, later studies showed that the passengers were largely unaffected by these so-called "defects" in cabin crew.

In 1964, the unknown Jerrie Mock did what Amelia

Earhart couldn't — she piloted a single engine plane solo around the world. She referred to herself as just a "flying housewife," and when a magazine asked her why she had undertaken such a treacherous journey alone, Ms. Mock simply said, "It was about time a woman did it".[158]

But her sex could not breach the commercial cockpit door until April 30, 1969, when Turi Widerøe (below) became First Officer on a Scandinavian Airlines System Convair 440. Inspired in school by Saint-Exupery's *Wind, Sand and Stars*, Emily Howell Warner, began her crusade to fly for an airline. Frontier Airlines bravely hired her in 1973, as the first female commercial pilot since Helen Richey. "Airline Pilot to Fly by Seat of Her Panties" was how the media announced the revolution in the cockpit. Warner recalled that the glory of making history didn't last. On her second flight, when the captain entered the cockpit, she put out her hand to shake his. "He looked at me and said, "I don't shake hands." He only said six more words to her during the whole flight. "Don't touch anything on the airplane." It was a textbook case, wrote a psychologist of the need for men to mark off their occupational territory to assert their masculinity. The first female member of ALPA, she would make history once more, leading the first all-female flight crew in 1986.

In Canada, Transair would hire 25-year-old Rosella Bjornson as a co-pilot in July 1973, the first Canadian woman to achieve that status, the airline asking her to keep the cockpit door closed when passengers were being boarded.[159] Transair remained the only Canadian employer of a female pilot until Air Canada hired Judy Cameron in April 1978. When she was introduced to the media, a journalist gushed, "Judy Cameron, age 24, hair honey-colored and flowing almost to her waist, looks like a female version of the All-American Boy. She is the girl next door with a pilot's license and diamond and emerald studs in her ears." No mention was made of how she got there. Cameron recalled that her worst moment occurred when a female television interviewer asked her: "How do you fly when you have premenstrual tension?"

In 1978, when Jill Brown became the first black woman to fly for Texas International Air, there were 110 black pilots employed by the airlines and two barriers, gender and colour were broken. She had already been the first black woman to enter the US Navy's flight school in 1974. Of the 38,000 pilots flying for airlines in the United States that year, 50 were female. All were on regional airlines as flight engineers or second officers as they had not accumulated the hours and seniority to become captains. Two of those were Beverly Burns and Lynn Rippelmeyer who would make aviation history when they captained two 747 aircraft on July 19, 1984. Burns was the first woman to captain a 747 cross-country, and Rippelmeyer the first woman to captain a 747 on a transatlantic flight.

It was thus a sad irony that by the time women had won a measure of respect and gender equity in the aviation industry, a new era of threat and anxiety dawned. Cassandra herself could not have foreseen what would happen to air travel in the coming decades. The Airline Deregulation Act of 1978 removed government control over the commercial airline industry in the United States, surrendering airline fares and routes to the free market. With escalating energy costs and low-cost carriers including People Express snapping at their heels, the second-tier airlines like Braniff, Continental and Eastern filed for bankruptcy — it was cheaper to do so than pay out on union contracts. Flag carriers British Airways and Air Canada were privatized and reorganized with lower labor costs and employee concessions. In a twilight of the gods, Pan American stopped flying on December 4, 1991, and a gutted TWA was bought by American Airlines in 2001. With travelers using websites like Kayak, Expedia, or Orbit to find the best fares, brand advertising became less important. Price, and not what the women served or wore was what "put bums on seats." For flight attendants, the consequences of deregulation were catastrophic as union-busting and lower wages meant that thousands quit. Somewhat ironically, belated recognition for their cause came from the White House when President George W Bush proclaimed July 19, 1990, officially as Flight Attendant Safety Professional Day.

The terrorist attacks on the World Trade Center, New York, on September 11, 2001, when twenty-five flight attendants and eight pilots died, were thought to be the most tragically momentous events in aviation — until the Covid pandemic in March 2020. Of the hundreds of acts of heroism that day, those of two women — a flight attendant and a pilot, deserve recognition.

Shortly after the take-off of from Logan Airport, Boston, Los Angeles bound American Airlines Flight 11 was the first of four to be hijacked that morning. Flight Attendant Betty Ann Ong had asked to work that flight so she could join her sister in Los Angeles to vacation together in Hawaii. During the hijacking, using her phone card, she called the American Airlines reservation agents in Raleigh-Durham, NC and alerted the world to the hijacking. In her 23-minute call, she identified the seats the terrorists had occupied, enabling the FBI to learn their passport details. When the Boeing approached Manhattan, flying ever lower and tilting wildly, Ong warned that the pilots were probably no longer flying the airplane. Although knowing that she and all onboard were soon to die, she remained calm and professional, ending the call with "Pray for us. Pray for us." Seconds later, the line went dead.

Lieutenant Heather "Lucky" Penney had been the only woman in her fighter pilot training class and was now the only woman in her squadron with the District of Columbia Air National Guard, stationed at Joint Base Andrews, outside Washington. That fateful day, the orders came from Vice President Dick Cheney for her squadron to get airborne immediately and stop Flight 93 from reaching the capital. Penney and her squadron leader, Mark ("Sass") Sasseville, were to launch first. Without live missiles, they had only their aircraft as weapons.

Prepared to ram her F-16 into United Flight 93, she was going to aim for the Boeing 757's tail while Sasseville would go for the cockpit. Penney's father was a flight captain for United at the time and she was aware that he might be on the plane (he wasn't). "I've been asked what it felt like, running to the jet knowing that if my mission was successful that I would not return," she later said. "And honestly, I did not feel any fear. You don't have any time to think about it. If anything in my life mattered, it was that moment. I had to do it right." As she raced toward the airliner, all she thought was "God, don't let me fuck this up." Before the two F-16 pilots could reach them, the passengers of Flight 93 took matters into their own hands, and the Boeing crashed in Pennsylvania.

Hijackings had been occurring since the 1960s, but using packed airliners as cruise missiles to kill on such a scale was unprecedented. The 9/11 attackers had correctly worked out the weak spot in air travel — that within the domestic airline system, passengers were subject to few checks and restrictions. And, once onboard, all the terrorists had to overcome were (mainly) female flight attendants. From 9/11 onward, the relationship between a flight crew and their passengers changed in several ways. Flying was no longer an enjoyable extension of the vacation experience — but something to anxiously endure. Despite billion-dollar aid packages from governments, the main reason airlines remained flying were employee concessions and layoffs. Those airlines that survived pared onboard services to the bone.

The tragedy transformed air travel, introducing passengers to the now familiar rituals of removing their shoes and belts, placing electronics into separate bins and travel-size liquids into see-through plastic bags. Full body scanners, pat-downs, and other advanced screening tools, such as facial recognition and computed tomography scanners soon became commonplace. Gone were the steak carving knives and the Royal Doulton, and visits to the cockpit for future pilots. The number of cabin crew on flights was cut to the minimum, armed air marshals were put onboard aircraft and locked and reinforced-proof flight deck doors installed to limit access to the cockpit.

The United States created the Department of Homeland Security and the Transport Security Administration to prevent a repeat of 9/1I. In November 2003, Congress agreed that cabin crew should be issued licenses, finally recognizing the men and women as safety professionals. For the thousands of flight attendants who had lost their jobs, the recognition must have been bittersweet. Congress also mandated self-defense training and crew members learned how to physically restrain people and defend themselves, using dummies to practice eye pokes, elbow jabs and kicks to the groin. When some airlines complained of the cost, before the program could be implemented, it was changed to voluntary training conducted by air marshals.

Sara Nelson, the AFA President, said, "September 11th affects our jobs every single day. New flight attendants may be too young to have any memory of the attacks, but their training all relates back to September 11." Flight crews were trained to assess passengers as potential security risks while they boarded. Behind the welcoming smiles was the stress of profiling passengers (now called "security risks"), based on skin color or religious affiliation. Instead of having to remember how a certain frequent flier liked his Scotch, the flight attendant now made mental notes of what she could use as potential weapons if he attacked her. And if a medical emergency arose, their training addressed the potential that it was not a real health emergency but a diversion. It was no longer Ellen Church's profession.

In 2020, the effects of 9/11 on air travel were dwarfed by that of the pandemic that closed borders, grounded flights, furloughed thousands of flight crews, and once more pushed airlines to bankruptcy. Planes that flew in 2021 were deathly silent with the window shades down, full of passengers who avoided eye contact with each other. In-flight food service where passengers remove or lower their masks or touch utensils had been severely reduced as had the serving of alcohol, both safety precautions made at the behest of flight attendants, who had been hit hard by the pandemic. An estimated 4,000 flight attendants on US carriers have contracted the virus since March 2020 and 20 died. Not only were the flight crews asked to gauge whether boarding passengers were potential terrorists, but also to police mask usage. The FAA noted that most of the incidents of disruptive passenger behavior in 2021 involved disputes over the mask mandate. Reduction in flight capacity, staff furloughs and fights along with struggles on planes — all seem less an aberration than the inevitable consequences of a flying environment that has been jettisoning amenities for decades. Flying in the 2020s is to be endured, not enjoyed.

There's no real ending to this, just the place where you stop the story.

Jean Batten, aged seventy, on the flight deck of Concorde (*Evening Standard*).

12: THE PLANE DOESN'T KNOW IF YOU'RE MALE OR FEMALE

We all love a Cinderella story of transformation: about an underdog who triumphs over adversity, a scullery maid who is mocked because she didn't get an invitation to the ball — and then captures the castle. Better still is a story of affirmation in which a female succeeds in a misogynistic world while being (choose one or all) harassed, assaulted, abused, ignored, dismissed, sidelined, or forgotten. This genre is so utopian in the real world that novelists have relied on it for centuries. Their protagonists have included Daniel Defoe's Moll Flanders, Charlotte Bronte's Jane Eyre, Jane Austen's Elizabeth Bennet and (my favorite), Celie from Alice Walker's *The Color Purple*.[160] These women refused to submit to the expectations of their time, were outspoken rather than compliant, tenacious rather than accepting.

Yet, for all the hard-won affirmations of Sophie Blanchard, Harriet Quimby, Bessie Coleman, Amelia Earhart, Amy Johnson, Jerrie Cobb, and the others, theirs is a difficult legacy to celebrate. When Captain Judy Cameron disembarked after her last flight with Air Canada in 2015, only 160 of the airline's 3,100 pilots were female, or 5.1 per cent — a figure close to the North American average. In pre-pandemic 2019, the International Society of Women Airline Pilots noted that there were 7,409 female pilots flying for scheduled air carriers globally and that they accounted for barely 5.2 per cent of the workforce, with 1.33 per cent for female captains. Regional variations range from 1.55 per cent in Asia (with the exception of India, which boasts a 12.47 per cent female pilot rate) to 9.78 per cent in Africa. In Europe, it is 5.61 per cent (in Britain, 4.7 per cent and in North America 5.37 per cent, while in South America and the Middle East, the figures are 5.09 per cent and 2.05 per cent. Minorities account for an even smaller percentage of the whole pie — there are fewer than 100 African American female commercial pilots. Of the 10,964 pilots in the U S Air Force today, only 708 — just 6.5 per cent — are women and fewer than 3 per cent of them fly fighters.[161]

There are so few female pilots that they are still being mistaken for a flight attendant and asked to hang up a coat; or being told they were only in the flight deck because of affirmative action; or having passengers express shock upon seeing them in the cockpit, and then saying they would have probably got off had they known a woman was going to fly the plane.

Both Amelia Earhart and Dr Sally Ride put it down to the stereotypes that continue exist about girls and math and science — that peer pressure, especially in middle school, made them unpopular if they excelled in those subjects. Because of the efforts of both women, there are today "Amelia Earhart Girls in Engineering" programs to encourage ten-year-olds to continue STEM (Science, Technology, Engineering, Math) curriculum through middle school and high school, then pursue college degrees in engineering. Dr Ride, who wrote six science books for children, set up science programs to appeal to girls — science festivals, science camps, science clubs — to help them find mentors, role models and one another.

It goes back to that truth: you can't be what you can't see. One of the biggest hurdles in becoming a female pilot is that Catch-22: there are fewer female pilots because visibility of them is low, and because visibility of them is low, there are fewer female pilots. The highly masculine image of aviation is why women do not consider this a career, and that can be attributed to so few role models.

Once more, Hollywood is to blame, specifically the movie *Top Gun*, a direct descendant of William Wellman's 1927 *Wings*. An ill-disciplined fighter pilot nicknamed "Maverick" (Tom Cruise) joins the elite Fighter Weapons School called "Top Gun". With his rule breaking machismo, cocky grin, motorcycle, and F-14, he is the Y chromosome personified. His tenderness towards best friend "Goose" (Anthony Bradshaw) is deeper than any feeling he has for "Charlie" (Kelly McGillis), the astrophysicist and specialist in maritime air superiority who is (because this is a male fantasy) also tall, gorgeous, and blonde. Female viewers who loved Charlie because she was all brains and ambition were disappointed that she chose to become one more notch in Maverick's tally. It was yet another fictional instance when strong intelligent women bend to naughty boys.

Captain Noreen Newton, MA learned to ignore the voices saying, we never hire women or we hired a woman once, and she didn't work out, "because I knew that the sex of the pilot did not make any difference in their ability. The aircraft didn't know if you were male or female. I am in my element when the snow-capped mountains fill the windscreen, and the Gulf Islands dot the Salish Sea below, the clouds betraying the weather. As the sun rises above the mountains, and the high intensity runway lights illuminate the fog, and I can barely make out the runway, but know it is with precision and grace that the aircraft will descend and find the asphalt, the main wheels chirping in satisfaction. I was not the first woman at the flying schools and charter operations where I gained experience, and I was determined not to be the last.

"Years ago, I picked up my four-year-old son from preschool while wearing my uniform: a navy suit with gold bars, a crisp white shirt, tie, and black loafers. I embodied the image of a professional pilot. His teacher asked me, "Would

Jack like to be a pilot when he grows up?" My son stood beside me. I looked at him and asked him the question. Without hesitation he answered, 'Mom, that's a girl's job.'

"Today, the lack of role models for women persists, but is slowly changing. Despite the inherent sexism of the aviation culture, women who choose a career as a professional pilot share one common bond: the love of flying. To fit in, they have had to adapt to the cultural norms associated with the aviation industry. Speaking out and trying to change the culture to one that values their gender has cost some their careers. Others have chosen silence. The image of the masculinized pilot, the heroic, paternal male, endures. And yet, the women persist. My four-year-old son's perception of the role of the pilot as gendered is a result of the culture he experienced while growing up. Today he works at a girl's job, flying airplanes."

Work-life balance is another challenge for female pilots, particularly new mothers, as their flying schedules keep them away from home days at a time. Young pilots begin as flight instructors or crop dusters, and don't reach the major carriers until their early 30s, when they begin planning families. For the male-dominated airline management and pilot unions, women's issues are on the back burner. Airline pilot Michelle Burtch's biggest struggle was (and still is) trying to balance motherhood with a career in aviation. "The irregular schedule and time away from home is difficult to manage with kids," she said, "which is why I left aviation for almost five years when mine were little. Many women who leave to care for their families never return. I was one of the lucky ones, but it didn't come without a cost. I lost 15 years of airline seniority and had to start over as a new hire, making half as much as I previously earned without the opportunities for advancement that I previously had. This is a universal struggle for women especially. We refer to it as the "titty-tax" — the invisible penalties women pay career wise for having children, affecting career advancement, and earning potential. Nobody should have to choose between their family and the career they love."[162]

As Raymonde de Laroche knew, aviation has always expected women to enter at their own risk ... and be grateful for the privilege. It assumes that they are less intellectually capable, less ambitious, and thus they learn that the evidence of a mind is a liability and that their self-worth depends on their capacity to attract men's sexual attention. How many potential airline captains have left because they were sexually compromised by their instructors, FBO managers and formerly trusted male colleagues?

Ariane Morin, an aerial application pilot remembered, "When I was a student pilot, there were men who turned their noses up at me as though I was just a girl with a passing fancy. It was made clear that the current push for increased diversity in the flight deck was the only reason for my hiring, and not the hard-earned ink in my logbook. In a strange twist of reverse psychology, it made me resent not my male compatriots but my female colleagues. I was being painted with the "female pilot" brush and so any failure by another woman was a reflection on me. The thought of confronting any unwanted attention was terrifying because by labeling you as uptight or sensitive, it would automatically ostracize you from the brotherhood you are so desperately trying to break into. You start questioning your own logic. You get used to feeling off-balance, on the social perimeter. You are forced to laugh at breaches of your personal space. You are convinced you are being tough, but the sexism is insidious and the facade to maintain it is emotionally devastating."

For women, this is all part of breaking down that cockpit door or glass ceiling. How do you make a career work when it was designed without you in mind?

References

1   Wright, Sharon *Balloonomania Belles: Daredevil Divas Who First Took To The Sky*. Pen & Sword, 2018

2   Sage would publish her account of the flight and her portrait is on permanent display in The Linbury Gallery, Barbican, London. www.sciencemuseum.org

3   The 2019 movie *The Aeronauts* is based on the book *Falling Upwards: How We Took to the Air* by Richard Holmes. It is a fictitious account based on several female aeronauts, but Sophie Blanchard was said to be its inspiration.

4   Sophie's fame was such that the author Jules Verne would mention her in his book *Five Weeks in a Balloon*.

5   Her steering apparatuses were large wing-like hammocks on either side of the gondola, a rudder device that was connected to the rear and finally warping the edges on the platform to change airflow.

6   Jonathan Vance, *High Flight: Aviation and the Canadian Imagination*. Toronto: Penguin Canada, 2002 p.126

7   The Olympic Games held in Paris in 1900 featured ballooning as an Olympic sport — the only time that anything aeronautical has ever been contested in the Games.

8   Written in 1910, the song was for Josephine Magner Haddock who jumped from her husband's balloons at air shows. Josephine would serve as a parachute instructor during both world wars.

9   Terry Kraus, FAA Historian, *Aida De Acosta, America's First Pilot*

10   Leo Deluca, *How Ida Holdgreve's Stitches Helped the*

Wright Brothers Get Off the Ground. smithsonianmag.com. March 15, 2021

11   The Smithsonian Institution credited Samuel P Langley (1834-1906) as the inventor of the first working airplane not the Wrights, despite Langley's failure to conduct a successful test in his lifetime.

12   Henry Haskell memorialized her by having a fountain built at the southwest corner of the Allen Memorial Art Museum at Oberlin College in 1931

13   In 1915, the Coca-Cola company decided that the contoured design of the hobble skirt was so distinctive that its glass bottles should be shaped like it so that they could be grasped in the dark.

14   In 2019, the USAF got rid of a medical waiver requirement for pregnant pilots who wanted to fly late into their pregnancies. In 2021, the US Navy issued the first maternity flight suits.

15   According to the Smithsonian Institution, there is conflicting evidence regarding the exact date of Blanche Stuart Scott's first solo flight. That date was recognized by the "Early Birds" to be September 6, 1910. Unfortunately, a fire destroyed some of Ms Scott's personal memorabilia during her lifetime. Whether Blanche Stuart Scott or Bessica Raiche was America's first female aviator may never be determined.

16   Hempstead Field would be renamed Roosevelt Field in 1919 in honor of President Theodore Roosevelt's son Quentin who was killed in air combat during the war. Charles Lindbergh and Amelia Earhart would both take off from there to cross the Atlantic. Today it is a shopping mall.

17   The grandson of former slaves, Headen left the United States to escape the Jim Crow laws and settled in Camberley, England. He became a transportation authority and held patents for 11 inventions, among them anti-icing methods for aircraft.

18   Gustav Hamel was so skeptical of any woman's

chances for a successful flight over the English Channel that he gallantly offered to wear Quimby's purple satin flying suit and make the flight for her.

19   Blanche Scott had one more claim to fame. On September 6, 1948 she flew with Charles E Yeager in a TF-80C Shooting Star, becoming the first American woman to ride in a jet.

20   "Tiny" Broadwick is credited as the inventor of the first manually operated parachute and ripcord and her homemade parachutes are in the Smithsonian Institution, Washington.

21   When Amanda Gorman read *The Hill We Climb* at the Presidential Inauguration, she spoke for all the women in this chapter, especially Bessie Coleman, another "child of slaves".

22   Evelyn Adams, whose real name was Chawa Zloczower was deported by J Edgar Hoover, ironically for being "unnatural" and would end her life as Passenger 847 on Transport 63 to Auschwitz.

23   Kathleen L Brooks-Pazmany, *United States Women in Aviation 1919-1929*, Smithsonian Studies in Air and Space, Number 5 p.12

24   Jonathan Vance ibid p.129

25   Syd Love, *That Daring Young Gal on a Flying Machine: On a Wing and a Prayer, Lillian Thrilled Fans,* Los Angeles Times. Feb 19, 1989.

26   Keith O'Brien, *Fly Girls: How Five Daring Women Defied All Odds and made Aviation History.* New York: Houghton Mifflin 2018, p.164

27   Eileen F. Lebow, *Before Amelia: Woman Pilots in the Early Days of Aviation,* Washington: Brassey's Inc. 2002, P. 5.

28   Mollie Gregory, *Stunt Women: The Untold Hollywood Story,* University of Kentucky Press, 2015 p. 56

29   Well into the 1960s, "sundown" towns where blacks were arrested if outside after dark would continue to exist.

30   Barry, K. *Femininity in Flight: A History of Flight Attendants*, Duke University, 2007 ibid p.17

31   The mainstream press barely noted Coleman's death, focusing instead on Willis, who was white. The headline was: "White Man and Negress die in Plane Crash.".

32   In 1931 the Challenger Air Pilots Association, organized by John C Robinson spearheaded the construction of the Robbins, Illinois, airstrip, the first airport built for and by blacks.

33   Janet Bragg's autobiography, *Soaring Above Setbacks,* was published in 1996.

34   Katherine Sharp Landdeck, *The Women With Silver Wings,* New York: Crown, 2020, p.130

35   Barbara H. Schultz, *Endorsed by Earhart.* Little Buttes Publishing, 2016.

36   The US. Department of Commerce offered the honor of Pilot License No. 1 to Orville Wright, promising to waive the fee and examination. Wright declined because he said that he no longer flew and did not think he needed a federal license to show that he had been the first man to fly.

37   As my daughter Jade pointed out, not much had changed with the 1977 *Star Wars* movie where Princess Leia waits around to be rescued by three guys, one in a furry costume. Her sister Holly added disappointingly that there was not even a kiss here, just a wink.

38   Joseph J. Corn, *The Winged Gospel: America's Romance with Aviation,* Baltimore: Johns Hopkins University Press, 2001, 77.

39   No one had the new pilot or aerial navigator licenses that the Department of Commerce had begun issuing a few months before. Provisional licenses were granted on the spot, with Commerce inspectors handing out written exams and buzzing around Oakland on trial flights.

40   Richard A Durose, *Above & Beyond: Aunt Mildred: A*

race across the Pacific. Air & Sapce Magazine, March 2011

41   Paul F. Lambert, *Never Give Up! The Life of Pearl Carter Scott.* Chickasaw Press, 2007

42   41.202 *Cross & Cockade* International Autumn 2010

43   A memorial plaque commemorating the fateful flight and dedicated to Anne, Captain Hamilton and Colonel Minchin hangs in St Raphael's church, Kingston upon Thames.

44   The French press speculated about her marriage. Ruth was asked why she did not bring her husband with her. Said she: "Because he weighs too much in gasoline."

45   Lyle Womack would use his fifteen minutes of fame to join Commander Richard E Byrd on his first expedition to Antarctica in 1928. Here he would receive the divorce decree, on grounds of desertion, while they were at Byrd's station in "Little America", definitely a first in that continent.

46   They used the same runway that Sir Frank Whittle's E29/39 prototype jet would on May 15, 1941.

47   Emilie Gallizien, Hinchcliffe's wife received psychic messages from her late husband for years after and wrote a bestselling book about it.

48   Elsie's considerable financial legacy was left to her family to be held in trust for 50 years and then used to help pay off the National Debt. In her memory, her family installed a stained-glass window in the tiny church of Glenapp, Ballantrae, Ayrshire. Her name is spelled out in shrubs on the opposite side of the glen, flowering every summer.

49   On May 19, 2018, the inhabitants of Trepassey launched a song contest to commemorate Amelia's visit, the entries "bringing out messages of courage and a celebration of the history of gender equality." Some of those who entered the contest had grandparents who remembered the aviatrix as children.

50   Although she gave a $500 cheque to the Harbor Grace Airport Trust, Mabel Boll's name is absent from the two plaques

with names of aviators who used the airport on record flights.

51   As to the history making aircraft, *Friendship*, Donald Woodward would sell it to Jose Roget Balet of Argentina where by 1932, it was derelict and burned.

52   Like tennis star Naomi Osaka, Helen Willis refused to endure the media's prying, so they labelled her "Little Miss Poker Face."

53   Elizabeth McQueen would live long enough to see Jackie Cochran, the first female President of the FAI, elected in 1956.

54   Laura Muha, *How LI Teen Elinor Smith flew into History*. Special to Newsday, November 14, 2000

55   When Cobb was turned down by NASA despite passing all the tests to be an astronaut, in 1962, John Glenn stated at the Congressional hearing that "men go off and fight the wars and fly the airplanes", and "the fact that women are not in this field is a fact of our social order."

56   When this became a cause célèbre, the Bureau backtracked, claiming that it had just been " a suggestion."

57   When Tom Wolfe's book, *The Right Stuff*, was made into a movie, Pancho would be played by the actress Kim Stanley. Girl at Pancho's: "I just noticed that a fancy pilot like Slick over there doesn't have his picture on your wall. What do you have to do to get your picture up there anyway?" Pancho Barnes: "You have to die, sweetie."

58   Fortunately for Blanche, she wasn't flying with Dewey on December 11 1935, when his aircraft crashed in a snowstorm, killing him and his passenger.

59   In Miller and Lancaster's future was a sensational trial in a steamy Florida courtroom in 1932. They had invited a young American, Haden Clarke, into their Coral Gables home to ghostwrite Miller's memoirs. While Lancaster was away looking for work in Mexico, Miller and Clarke became lovers. Lancaster returned home, shot him, and then faked two suicide notes from Clarke. In a controversial case, the jury accepted

that Lancaster, as the very embodiment of a British gentleman would never stoop to murder, and he was acquitted. The following year, Lancaster attempted a London to Cape Town flight and vanished over the Sahara, his mummified remains were not found until 1962. His diary showed that he survived for over a week in the scorching desert, before dying of thirst, one year to the day after Haden Clarke was shot. Why hasn't this been made into a movie?

60   The twenty derby participants were: Florence L. Barnes (1901–1975), Marvel Crosson (1900–1929), Amelia Earhart (1897–1937), Ruth Elder (1903–1977), Claire Fahy (?–1930), Edith Foltz (1905–1956), Mary Haizlip (1910–1997), Opal Kunz (1896–1967), Jessie Keith–Miller (1901–1972), Ruth Nichols (1901–1960), Blanche Noyes (1900–1981), Gladys O'Donnell (1904–1973), Phoebe Omlie (1903–1975), Neva Paris (?–1930); Margaret Perry (?–1951); Thea Rasche, Germany (1899–1971); Louise Thaden (1905–1979); "Bobbi" Trout (1906–2003), Mary Von Mach (1896–1980), and Vera Walker, (1897–1978).

61   In December 1934, the Department of Commerce announced that Dr Clara Regina Gross of New York and Dr Emma Kitredge of Los Angeles had been appointed medical examiners. This was taken as an acknowledgement of the growing interest in flying among women.

62   Also begun in 1925 were two university air squadrons, one each at Oxford and Cambridge, neither of them open to women.

63   Lady Mary Heath is commemorated in her native Newcastle West, Limerick with a plaque on the wall of the building where she grew up.

64   Years later, Amy would confess that the reason she took up flying was to commit suicide. Aviation was considered so dangerous then that she thought "it would not upset her parents so much." But when she came to love it, the suicide idea dropped away.

65   *Jason*, G-AAAH, her aircraft for the historic flight

to Australia can be seen in the Science Museum in London. At Amy's suggestion (and with Lord Rothermere's influence), although the *Daily Mail* then owned *Jason*, it bought it from her for £ 300 and presented it to the nation.

66   The *Daily Mail*'s headline announced that she had set off with a "Cupboard Full of Frocks".

67   Amy received dozens of proposals for marriage from men and a few from what were said to be "perverted females".

68   Amy Johnson is the only female aviator to have a Blue Plaque in London. It was put up by English Heritage in 1987 at Vernon Court, Cricklewood, London, NW2 2PE She lived here happily in 1931 with her bull terrier "Rough" and within easy reach of friends at Stag Lane. When she met Jim Mollison and moved to Grosvenor House, her flat at Vernon Court suddenly became "dark, damp and lonely."

69   *Amy Johnson*, Constance Babington Smith, History Press Ltd. 2004. P.274

70   Sidney Cotton photographer, aviation pioneer and spy invented the Sidcot suit. His first job had been spotting seals for culling in Newfoundland. One day, he shared a meal with an eccentric fur trapper and was astonished at how his host managed to serve fresh peas. The trapper explained that he filled his baby's washbasin with salt water and peas and let the Arctic wind freeze it over. His name was Clarence Birdseye.

71   In 1932, the director Walter Summers made *Dual Control*, a short movie which had Amy Johnson and Jim Mollison descend on the Home Counties in search of fuel, meeting a gaggle of excitable schoolgirls on the way.

72   Jeffrey Quill test flew all variants of the Supermarine Spitfire. In the movie *The First of the Few*, David Niven played the part of "Geoffrey Crisp", a composite of Quill and the pilots from the Schneider Trophy.

73   Despite his heavy drinking, Mollison would complete over 1,000 flights on 62 different aircraft in the ATA. He would die in 1959 of alcoholic epilepsy.

REFERENCES

74   Jean Batten, *My Life*, London: George G. Harrap & Co, (1938) p. 252.

75   Ian Mackersey. *Batten, Jean Gardner (1909—1982).* Dictionary of New Zealand Biography. Ministry for Culture and Heritage. Retrieved 11 May 2010.

76   Because "white" unions would not allow African Americans to join, on August 25, 1925 the porters organized their own: the Brotherhood of Sleeping Car Porters (BSCP), becoming the first African American labour union. Here the discrimination was sexist. Because of the literal interpretation of "manhood rights", female African Americans were barred from participation and forced to form their own union.

77   Nurses, like the early stewardesses, were historically white as any other skin colour meant they would not be accepted by the patients. Mary Seacole, a trained Jamaican nurse was desperate to offer help during the Crimean War but Florence Nightingale, a woman of her day, refused to allow her to come to the Crimea.

78   Dominic A.Pisano, *The Airplane in American Culture*, ed. Ann Arbor: University of Michigan Press, 2003. P 149.

79   In 1932, Ellen Church suffered an automobile accident that ended her career as a stewardess. For her wartime service as a frontline nurse, Captain Church was awarded the Air Medal, the European-African-Middle Eastern Campaign Medal with seven campaign stars, and the World War II Victory Medal. While riding a horse on August 27, 1965, she fell and suffered a severe head injury. She died six hours later. The airport in her hometown of Cresco, Iowa is named in her honor.

80   When Mary Bruce was 81 years old, she performed a loop in a de Havilland Chipmunk. She used to say that going slowly always made her tired. She died in 1990, aged 94.

81   In the 1933 movie *Air Hostess* actress Evelyn Knapp played an air hostess who falls for a grandstanding pilot. The TWA Ford Trimotor used in the movie crashed soon after filming, killing all five onboard.

82   The sliding windows were more convenient for airsick passengers than locating those "erp" cups under the seat. Unfortunately, vomiting into the air stream outside meant that the airflow reintroduced it into opened rear windows.

83   Remembered in Switzerland as the Engel der Lüfte (Angel of the Skies) Nelly Hedwig Diener was killed in an air crash in June 1934, the first European stewardess to do so.

84   Lovegrove, Keith, *Airline: Style at 30,000 feet*. London: Laurence King Publishing, 2000.

85   Perhaps the best indication of success came when the U.S. railways also began hiring young white women as stewardesses to lure customers back. In 1937, the Chicago, Burlington & Quincy Railroad introduced its hostesses, calling them "Zephyrettes" after the trains.

86   Barry, *Femininity in Flight*, p.26

87   In the strange morality of the time, lovers were acceptable but not husbands, abortions were acceptable but not births.

88   One of the original eight BAT nurses was married. But when her husband kept phoning Stimpson to find out when was she coming home to make dinner, he ensured that only single women would be hired in the future.

89   Natalie Kitroeff, *The Shutdown Made Sara Nelson Into America's Most Powerful Flight Attendant*. New York Times, Feb 22, 2019.

90   Peter Pigott, *Flying Canucks II*, Toronto: The Dundurn Group, 1997 p. 115

91   As an adult, Mary Price was instrumental in having a plaque erected where Markham had landed.

92   As the legal age for marriage in Kenya was eighteen, this required some clerical subtlety.

93   As Wallace Simpson would learn in 1931, divorced women were never presented at court.

REFERENCES

94   Aware of its respectability, Beryl held on to the 'Markham' name as long as she could- it was more marketable than 'Clutterbuck.' By the time she gave it up, Gevaise was at Eton.

95   Beryl Markham, *West with the Night*, New York: North Point Press, 1942 p. 283.

96   In 1988, a television movie, *Beryl Markham: Shadow of The Sun*, would be made of her life with Stephanie Powers playing her and James Fox as Mansfield Markham.

97   On July 31, 1944, Saint-Exupéry took off from Corsica in a Lockheed Lightning P-38 reconnaissance plane, one of numerous French pilots who assisted the Allied war effort. He never returned, and as with Amelia Earhart and Amy Johnson, over the years, numerous theories arose: that he had been shot down or committed suicide.

98   Anne Herrmann, On Amelia Earhart: T*he Aviatrix as American Dandy,* Michgan Quarterly Review. Volume XXXIX, Issue 1, Winter 2000

99   The ultimate aviation fashion statement was not clothes. When closed cockpits ended the use of the flight goggles that left aviators looking like owls, Bausch & Lomb designed Ray-Bans, their reflective lenses designed to have an area two to three times the size of an eyeball. They were popularized by General Douglas MacArthur who wore them returning to the Philippines and actor Tom Cruise in *Top Gun.*

100   Herrmann, Anne "On Amelia Earhart: The Aviatrix as American Dandy" Michgan Quarterly Review, Volume XXXIX, Issue 1, Winter 2000

101   Katherine Hepburn would play a pilot once more, this time a Soviet military one in the 1956 movie *Iron Petticoat* with Bob Hope. She had agreed to do the movie, envisioning the male lead to be Cary Grant, William Holden or James Stewart. However, casting the male role proved difficult. "There was difficulty in finding a top star to play opposite Hepburn," wrote the producer Betty Box, "an example of the male chauvinistic attitude which baulks at the leading lady's part being better than

the man's." Hope agreed to play the part of her lover, which Hepburn thought made the movie into a vaudeville farce.

102   Amelia's pre-departure confession to the celebrity photographer Albert Bresnik (who had she asked in accompany her on the flight) that she was pregnant has been hotly debated but if so, it would explain her condition at Lae.

103   In 1967, Ann Pellegreno and a crew of three would successfully fly a Lockheed 10A Electra on an around the world flight, following Amelia Earhart's as closely as possible. On the 30th anniversary of Earhart's disappearance, Pellegreno dropped a wreath over Howland Island on July 2, 1967. The Electra had been one of Trans Canada Airlines' first three planes and is today displayed at the Canada Aviation and Space Museum, Ottawa. In 1997, Linda Finch would also recreate the historic flight, also dropping a wreath on Howland Island.

104   The ATS's Jessie Dunlop worked in a Cipher Room where the Permanent Staff Instructor thought that she should be able to guard the cipher. She recalled: "They brought a Sten gun for me to practice with. The [Staff Instructor] showed me how to hold it on my hip and how to put it from single shot into automatic. I watched carefully and decided to have a go. I settled it in place and pulled the trigger. It was on automatic and I couldn't stop it. I swung round to ask what to do and both sergeants vanished onto the ground behind some trees, one of them yelling, "Throw it down!" They both decided that it would be best if I used the butt end to stop intruders."

105   The legislation to create BOAC out of the merger of Imperial Airways and British Airways was given Royal Assent on November 24 1939, and BOAC came into being on April 1, 1940.

106   Their male colleagues were not above playing tricks on the female pilots — sometimes putting spiders in the cockpits to scare them.

107   Eleven American volunteer pilots on their way to the ATA were killed when the troopship *Nerissa* was sunk on April 21, 1941

REFERENCES

108   The only American female pilot to be killed was Cochran's secretary Mary Nicholson. On May 22, 1943, the plane she was ferrying developed an oil leak, causing the engine to freeze and the propeller to disengage. She was flying too low to use a parachute and attempted to land in a field. But she crashed into a stone barn and died instantly.

109   The Wrens (WRNS - Women's Royal Naval Service) who flew were attached to the Fleet Air Arm. They didn't serve as pilots but worked as air radio mechanics and had to fly to test the equipment. Sadly six Wrens died due to air crashes.

110   It wasn't until after D-Day in June 1944 that the ATA pilots were taught how to use radios.

111   Their vital war work is commemorated in the ATA Museum at Maidenhead UK (which has a "Grandma Flew Spitfires" gallery).

112   Mary Ellis, *A Spitfire Girl: One of the World's Greatest Female ATA Ferry Pilots Tells Her Story.* Frontline books, 2016. p.103

113   https://www.afleetingpeace.org/

114   Although disheartened, "The Flying Seven" would stage a "bomphlet" raid over Vancouver, dropping 100,000 "Smash-the Nazis" pamphlets. They appealed for "dimes or dollars to buy our boys more planes."

115   Elinor Florence, *Willa Walker Blazed a Trail for RCAF Airwomen,* http://www.rcaf-arc.forces.gc.ca March 7, 2019.

116   Jeanne Holm, *Women in the Military: An Unfinished Revolution,* Presidio Press, 1992. p.231

117   Spencer Dunmore, *Wings For Victory: The Remarkable Story of the British Commonwealth Air Training Plan,* Toronto: McClelland & Stewart, 1994, p. 302

118   As they flew at night and the front moved so often, their airfields could only be lit by oil lamps and car headlights. The women joked was that it would soon be by lit cigarettes.

119   Wein, Elizabeth E. *A Thousand Sisters: The Heroic*

Airwomen of the Soviet Union in World War II, Harper Collins, 2019.

120   It was actually a white lily that she had painted on the side of her Yak, which made her the target of Luftwaffe air aces who wanted to claim that they had killed her.

121   Rather ironically, the only monument erected to her is in Krasny Luch her last duty station, and now in a foreign country, Ukraine. It bears fifteen stars.

122   Katherine Sharp Landdeck, *The Women With Silver Wings,* Crown: New York:, 2020, P.135

123   Here sexism and not the Atlantic weather delayed Cochran. She couldn't fly the bomber as the male ferry pilots threatened to strike if she did. They did not want to be blamed if the Germans shot her down. Further, they felt that the presence of a woman as a trans-Atlantic pilot would demean their position. She was also taking a job away from them. A compromise was worked out between Ferry Command and its objecting pilots: Cochran would pilot the airplane in flight, but her male co-pilot would be responsible for take-off and landing.

124   Frankie Patino, *Well behaved women rarely make history: an examination of the life of Jacqueline Cochran.* California State University, San Bernardino P.63

125   There is a statue at the airport (now called New Castle National Air Guard Base) that honors the women who served here during the war.

126   As it was a single-seat aircraft, Gillies' first flight in it was also her solo.

127   A number of actual prostitutes claiming to be pilots from Avenger Field set up at Sweetwater's Blue Bonnet Hotel. Jackie sent her own women to the local churches to convince locals that they were not prostitutes and the actual ones were run out of town.

128   Long before microwave ovens were invented, William Maxson invented the forced air convention oven for

the military, its crews then subsisting on sandwiches on long flights. It allowed frozen meals to be defrosted and cooked onboard.

129   Leslie Lieber, *Training in the Sky makes an Angel of a Wife*. Pittsburgh Press, Sept. 30, 1962.

130   In contrast, when the bedroom farce *Boeing, Boeing* came out in 1965, the women were playmate dolls to be manipulated by bachelor Tony Curtis, who juggles three unwitting stewardess girlfriends, thanks to the miracle of dovetailing flight schedules, until with the new aircraft's speeds, he gets caught out and all three arrive at his apartment at the same time!

131   What gave encouragement and legitimacy to ALSA was that in 1946, the American Nursing Association also agreed to allow its members to engage in collective bargaining.

132   Who could resist a headline like that? "A verdict of justifiable homicide was returned today in the slaying of an airline official by a pretty stewardess. Twenty-seven-year-old Betty Lou Tracy, green eyed and brown hair admitted she had been "intimate" with Lawrence E Kell 43, father of three, superintendent of Ozark Air Lines where Miss Tracy is employed. Kell was found dead in his car parked outside the door of the apartment that Tracy shared with three other stewardesses. The young stewardess showed no emotion as the jury made up of six men returned with their "Not Guilty" verdict after 15 minutes deliberation." *Globe & Mail*, May 18, 1952

133   Albert James Mills, *Angels With Dirty Faces: Strategies of 'Normalization' and 'Equity' in the Immediate Post-War Era*, Saint Mary's University January 2006, p.114

134   Mills, Ibid. P.115

135   The BSAA airliners were known to be dangerous. — *Star Ariel, Star Dust* and *Star Tiger* had crashed. To stop his girlfriend, Flight Attendant Eve Huntley, from flying in them, one Edward Branson proposed marriage. Their son, Richard Branson, founded Virgin Atlantic Airways in 1984.

136   Libbie Escolme-Schmidt, *Glamour in the Skies: The Golden Age of the Air Stewardess.* The History Press, 2009. P.25

137   This should be taken in the context of the times. In 1967, when 24-year-old student Jocelyn Bell at Cambridge discovered pulsars, the media were only concerned with her hair style, if she had boyfriends and her bust measurement. Women were not astrophysicists and instead of Bell, her advisor Anthony Hewish was awarded the Nobel Prize for the discovery.

138   Ibid. Libbie Escolme-Schmidt P.130

139   After William Simpson an Eastern Airlines steward, was murdered in 1954 by two homophobic male prostitutes, the press called for greater vigilance against the corrupting influence of "sex deviates" (by which they meant Simpson, not his teenage murderers), causing airlines to stop hiring stewards. The jury in the trial, never seriously contemplated a conviction for first degree murder. Instead, they handed down a verdict of manslaughter to both perpetrators.

140   On April 8, 1968, 22-year-old flight attendant Barbara Jane Harrison was onboard a BOAC 707 bound for Australia. When it took off from Heathrow, the No. 2 engine caught fire and the pilot made an emergency landing at the airport. Miss Harrison and the steward opened the rear galley door and inflated the escape chute. Because it was twisted, the steward climbed down it to straighten it and was unable to return. Miss Harrison was left alone to get the passengers out of the aircraft even as "flames and smoke were around her face". She was preparing to jump but turned back to rescue more passengers. There was another explosion and she was not seen alive again. In August 1969, Barbara Jane Harrison became the only woman to receive the George Cross in peacetime, and its youngest female recipient.

141   Twenty-three-year-old Neerja Bhanot was a flight attendant on a Pan American aircraft that was hijacked by terrorists at Karachi on September 5, 1986. As soon as the hijackers boarded the plane, she alerted the flight crew and they escaped through an overhead hatch in the cockpit. After

a tense 17-hour standoff, when the terrorists began firing and setting off explosives, Neerja sacrificed her own life saving passengers.

142   It took the crash of a Mohawk Airlines F-227 at Albany, NY, on March 3, 1972, for the FAA to issue an Airworthiness Directive prohibiting aft-facing stewardess' crew seats mounted against the lavatory wall. Found by rescue crews under a pile of suitcases from the rear luggage storage shelf, the stewardess Sandra Baker suffered a spinal fracture and head injuries.

143   Because the human body has less resistance to acceleration forces in the lateral than in the longitudinal direction, the stewardesses in sideways facing seats were more exposed to injury than occupants of forward or aft facing seats.

144   See the author's, B*race for Impact: Air Crashes and Aviation Safety.* Toronto: Dundurn, 2016

145   Bruce Handy. *Glamour with Altitude*, Forbes, October, 2002.

146   Playtex marketed their airline girdles with television ads that showed a stewardess demonstrating her girdle to be comfortable enough for passengers to fly in — and perfect for leisure and romance.

147   "Eskimo" a culturally ignorant term, wasn't considered offensive then to describe the Inuit people

148   To fly for the U.S. military, pilots previously had to be between 5 feet, 4 inches and 6 feet, 6 inches tall, with a sitting height of 34 to 40 inches. That physical requirement supposedly disqualified about 44 per cent of the U.S. female population between the ages of 20 to 29 years. Cockpits were made more inclusive in May 2019.

149   One of NASA's recruiters was actress Nichelle Nichols who played Lt. Ohura on the "Star Trek" series.

150   On *The Tonight Show,* Johnny Carson joked that the shuttle flight would be delayed because Dr Ride had to find a purse to match her shoes.

151   Some requirements for the perfect flight attendant do not change. "Virgin attendants tough to find, Chinese airline says." China Air has a recruitment problem. The national flag-carrier is having trouble finding virgins to train as flight attendants. Each year hundreds of young women - all under 19, bright and eager - apply for coveted places at Beijing's flight attendant training school. But not all pass the chastity test. "They must be virgins," explains school director Hao Yu-ping, who admitted that it was getting harder to find a chaste woman in China. *Toronto Star,* April 21, 1992

152   Albert J Mills, T*he Invasion of the Body Snatchers: The Jet Age and the Eroticization of the Female Employee.* Sex, Strategy, and the Stratosphere, 2006 p.137-172.

153   "Stewardess Barbie" debuted in 1961 but "Pilot Barbie" not until 1990.

154   Purported to be the "wacky, sizzling adventures" of stewardesses Trudy Baker and Rachel Jones, the book was ghostwritten by Donald Bain who first marketed it as nonfiction. It did so well that in 1969 it was followed by Bernard Glemser's "The Fly Girls" about stewardesses who "underneath their uniforms, they were simply girls, warm, soft yielding creatures who lived too fast and loved too recklessly..."

155   P.80, N. Jill Newby "The Sky's the Limit" Canadian Flight Attendants Association, 1987

156   Ward's grooming regulations led to bitter controversies with the flight attendants. He forbade a male flight attendant to wear an earring on duty because passengers would worry about contracting AIDS from him. He then enforced the ruling that all female flight attendants wear only skin tone or white bras. To their discomfort, the women discovered that passengers on every flight kept staring at their breasts to see if they were wearing the mandatory bras!

157   With deregulation and rising oil prices, Maytag was sharp enough to sell out to Pan American for $400 million in 1979, leaving the "girls" as they were called, to their own fates.

158   Mock's flight, typical of her gender's achievements,

has been overlooked in aviation history. She must have taken solace on receiving a telegram from Muriel Earhart Morrissey, Amelia's sister which simply said: "I rejoice with you."

159   Bjornson married Bill Pratt who later flew as her co-pilot. The airline did not know what to do about her two pregnancies- there were no maternity leaves, because there had been no female pilots.

160   My daughters insists that I add Scout Finch from Harper Lee's "To Kill a Mockingbird" to the list - she's good in a fight and sticks up for what she believes in- and also Disney's Mulan who does the same for her country and gender - and like them is Chinese. My granddaughter is adamant that Peppa Pig makes the list but I am somewhat dubious as to her logic.

161   How do you operate in a profession that wasn't made for you in mind? The military is attempting to make it easier for female fighter pilots to relieve themselves during long sorties. The bladder-relief gear was designed for men, and while the U.S. Air Force does have devices for women, female fighter pilots say they aren't really practical in a cramped fighter cockpit while wearing a G-suit, harness, and combat vest.

162   Accommodating lactating pilot and flight attendant mothers on the flight deck or cabin is an issue that makes male -dominated airline management and pilot unions squirm. For safety and security reasons, airlines are exempt from the provision which requires employers to provide private, non-bathroom spaces for nursing or pumping to accommodate new mothers. To pump in the cockpit or the toilet every three or four hours is hardly private or healthy.

ALSO BY PETER PIGOTT

The Golden Age of Flying Boats (2020)

Brace for Impact: Air Crashes and Aviation Safety (2016)

Air Canada: The History (2014)

From Far and Wide: A Complete History of Canada's Arctic Sovereignty (2011)

Sailing Seven Seas: A History of the Canadian Pacific Line (2010)

Canada in Sudan: War Without Borders (2009)

Canada in Afghanistan: The War So Far (2007)

Royal Transport: An Inside Look at the History of British Royal Travel (2005)

On Canadian Wings: A Century of Flight (2004)

Wingwalkers: The Rise and Fall of Canada's Other Airline (2003)

Taming the Skies: A Celebration of Canadian Flight (2003)

Wings Across Canada: An Illustrated History of Canadian Aviation (2002)

National Treasure: The History of Trans Canada Airlines (2001)

Flying Canucks III: Famous Canadian Aviators (2000)

Wingwalkers: The Story of Canadian Airlines International (1998)

Flying Canucks II: Pioneers of Canadian Aviation (1997)

Flying Colours: A History of Commercial Aviation in Canada (1997)

Gateways: Airports of Canada (1996)

Hong Kong Rising: The History of a Remarkable Place (1995)

Flying Canucks: Famous Canadian Aviators (1994)

Kai Tak: The History of Aviation in Hong Kong (1988)

BIBLIOGRAPHY

Arthur, Max, *There Shall Be Wings, Vivid Personal Accounts of the RAF from 1918 to Today*, London, Hodder & Stoughton, 1993.

Babington Smith, Constance, *Amy Johnson*, London, History Press Ltd, 2004.

Barry, Kathleen M, *Femininity in Flight, A History of Flight Attendants*, Durham and London, Duke University Press, 2007.

Brooks-Pazmany, Kathleen L, *United States Women in Aviation 1919-1929*, Smithsonian Studies in Air and Space –No 5.

Culick, Fred E C & Dunmore, Spencer, *On Great White Wings, The Wright Brothers and the Race for Flight*, Hyperion, New York 2001.

Dunmore, Spencer, *Wings For Victory: The Remarkable Story of the British Commonwealth Air Training Plan* Toronto, McClelland & Stewart, 1994.

Ellis, Mary, *A Spitfire Girl, One of the World's Greatest Female ATA Ferry Pilots Tells Her Story*, Frontline Books, 2017.

Gibson, Emily K, *Flying is Changing Women!, Women Popularizers of Commercial Aviation and the Renegotiation of Traditional Gender and Technological Boundaries in the 1920s–1930s,* Master's Thesis, February 2014, University of Massachusetts Amherst.

Gils, Bieke, *Pioneers of Flight, An Analysis of Gender Issues*

317

in United States Civilian (Sport) and Commercial Aviation 1920-1940, University of Windsor, 2009.

Gossage, Carolyn *Greatcoats and Glamour Boots, Canadian Women at War (1939-1945),* Toronto, Dundurn Press, 1991.

Gregor, Molly, *Stuntwomen, The Untold Hollywood Story,* University of Kentucky Press, 2015.

Jackson, Joe, *Atlantic Fever, Lindbergh, His Competitors, and the Race to Cross the Atlantic,* New York, Farrar, Strauss, and Giroux, 2012.

Klick, Brighid, *Straighten Up and Fly Right, The Dichotomy between British and American Women Auxiliary Pilots of World War II,* University of Michigan, 2014.

Lovegrove, Keith, *Airline, Style at 30,000 feet,* London, Laurence King Publishing, 2000.

Lovell, Mary S, *The Sound of Wings, The Life of Amelia Earhart,* St Martin's Griffin, Illustrated edition, 2009.

Lovell, Mary S, *Straight On Till Morning, The Biography of Beryl Markham,* Century Hutchinson Ltd, 1987.

Markham, Beryl, *West with the Night,* New York, North Point Press, 1942.

Muir, Elizabeth Gillian, *Canadian Women in the Sky 100 Years of Flight,* Toronto, Dundurn, 2015.

Mulley, Clare, *The Women Who Flew for Hitler,* Pan Macmillan, 2018.

O'Brien, Keith, *Fly Girls, How Five Daring Women Defied All Odds and made Aviation History,* New York, Houghton Mifflin, 2018.

Omelia, Johanna & Waldock, Michael, *Come Fly With Us,*

BIBLIOGRAPHY

A Global History of the Airline Hostess, Collectors Press Inc, 2006.

Peniston-Bird, Corinna, *Of hockey sticks and Sten guns, British auxiliaries and their weapons in the Second World War,* Lancaster University, Women's History Magazine, Autumn 2014.

Pigott, Peter, *Flying Canucks II,* Toronto, The Dundurn Group, 1997.

Pigott, Peter, *National Treasure, The History of Trans Canada Airlines,* Harbour Publishing, 2000.

Plantz, Connie *The Life of Bessie Coleman,* Enslow Publishers Inc, Berkley Heights, NJ, 2015.

Ryan, Jason, *Race to Hawaii, The 1927 Dole Air Derby and the Thrilling First Flights That Opened the Pacific,* Chicago Review Press, 2018.

Thaden, Louise, *High, Wide and Frightened,* University of Arkansas Press, Illustrated Edition, 2004.

Vance, Jonathan, *High Flight: Aviation and the Canadian Imagination,* Toronto, Penguin Canada, 2002.

Ware, Susan *Still Missing, Amelia Earhart and the Search for Modern Feminism,* New York, W W Norton & Company, 1993.

Wein, Elizabeth E, *A Thousand Sisters: The Heroic Airwomen of the Soviet Union in World War II,* Harper Collins, 2019.

Wright, Sharon, *Balloonomania Belles: Daredevil Divas Who First Took To The Sky,* Pen & Sword, 2018.

Index

INDEX

INDEX

Made in the USA
Monee, IL
09 June 2026

5c1881db-5d8e-4d2d-aad8-536eeb3d5778R01